SHARED AND INSTITUTIONAL AGENCY

SHARED AND INSTITUTIONAL AGENCY

Toward a Planning Theory of Human Practical Organization

Michael E. Bratman

OXFORD
UNIVERSITY PRESS

Oxford University Press is a department of the University of Oxford. It furthers
the University's objective of excellence in research, scholarship, and education
by publishing worldwide. Oxford is a registered trade mark of Oxford University
Press in the UK and certain other countries.

Published in the United States of America by Oxford University Press
198 Madison Avenue, New York, NY 10016, United States of America.

© Oxford University Press 2022

All rights reserved. No part of this publication may be reproduced, stored in
a retrieval system, or transmitted, in any form or by any means, without the
prior permission in writing of Oxford University Press, or as expressly permitted
by law, by license, or under terms agreed with the appropriate reproduction
rights organization. Inquiries concerning reproduction outside the scope of the
above should be sent to the Rights Department, Oxford University Press, at the
address above.

You must not circulate this work in any other form
and you must impose this same condition on any acquirer.

Library of Congress Control Number: 2021060587
ISBN 978–0–19–758090–5 (pbk.)
ISBN 978–0–19–758089–9 (hbk.)

DOI: 10.1093/oso/9780197580899.001.0001

9 8 7 6 5 4 3 2 1

Paperback printed by LSC Communications, United States of America
Hardback printed by Bridgeport National Bindery, Inc., United States of America

For Gregory, Kristin, Scott, and Emy

CONTENTS

Preface   xi

Overview: Intention, plans, and practical organization   xv

PART I: *Individual Agency, Shared Agency, Social Rules*

1. The planning theory of individual and shared intentional agency   3

    1.1 Individual temporally extended intentional agency   3
    1.2 Shared intentional activity   8
        1.2.1 Reflexivity, construction, rationality, sufficiency   11
        1.2.2 Too demanding?   20
        1.2.3 Scaling up, vagueness, interdependence, and interlocking   21
        1.2.4 Authority-according shared intentions   24
        1.2.5 The interplay of plan rationality and the interrelatedness of sharing   26

2. On the way to organized institutions: Social rules   33

    2.1 Modesty, modularity, and rule-guided infrastructure   33
    2.2 Hart on social rules, criticisms and demands, and rule content   34
    2.3 Dual design specifications   40

3. A shared policy model of social rules, part 1   42

    3.1 Together organizing how we live with each other   42
    3.2 Double reflexivity, vagueness, and non-agglomeration   44
    3.3 *Shared* policies?   48

3.4 Criticisms and demands? Rationality and reasons 50
3.5 "A wide range of 'normative' language" 56
3.6 The proposal so far 57

4. A shared policy model of social rules, part 2   59

    4.1 Eight problems in search of a theory 59
         4.1.1 Fragility, robustness, and conditions of persistence 59
         4.1.2 Weak interlocking and interdependence 61
         4.1.3 "Fundamentalist" participants and cognitively grounded dependence 62
         4.1.4 "Alienated" participants and kernel-penumbra structures 66
         4.1.5 A Lockean model of diachronic robustness 75
         4.1.6 Non-cotemporaneous kernels? 78
         4.1.7 Pretense all the way down? 80
         4.1.8 Social rule content 82
    4.2 Putting the pieces together 85
    4.3 "Massively shared agency" 89
    4.4 Where's the normativity? 92

PART II: *Rule-Guided Infrastructure of Organized Institutions*

5. On the way to organized institutions: Social rules of procedure   99

    5.1 Institutional procedural positivism 99
    5.2 Initial model of social rules of procedure 100
    5.3 Outputs: Two distinctions 103
    5.4 Acceptance-focused outputs 104
    5.5 Action-focused and rule outputs 105
    5.6 Authority-according social rules of procedure 106
    5.7 Further ideas 109
         5.7.1 Induced teleology 109
         5.7.2 Historical thickness 110
         5.7.3 Continuity, discontinuity, and core capacity 111
         5.7.4 Social rules of procedure and secondary rules 113

6. A procedural social rule model of organized institutions   115

    6.1 An organized institution's web of social procedural rules   115
    6.2 Institutional outputs   122
    6.3 The rule-guided infrastructure of an organized institution   127
    6.4 Searle on institutional roles   129

PART III: *Institutional Intent*

7. Institutional intention   135

8. A Davidsonian challenge   142

    8.1 Davidson on interpretation, content, and the holistic density of mind   142
    8.2 Frankfurt on "the structure of a person's will" and where "the person himself stands"   145
    8.3 Davidson meets pluralism   147
    8.4 Ludwig, List and Pettit, Rovane, and dense holism   150
    8.5 Rejecting the primacy of individual intention: Interpretation and construction   152

9. Institutional intention without a dense holistic subject   156

    9.1 Cross-temporal, mind-shaped, rational organization   156
    9.2 Giving "substance" to institutional intention   159
    9.3 Discursive dilemmas and incompleteness   161
    9.4 Social extendedness and content   166
    9.5 Further aspects of intention?   167

10. Institutional intentional agents   171

    10.1 Guidance by institutional intention, guidance by institutional intentional agent: Robustness   171
    10.2 Guidance by institutional intention, guidance by institutional intentional agent: Institutional standpoint   174
    10.3 Constructive reduction   178

10.4 Acting for a reason, rational guidance 181
10.5 Social rule model of institutional intentional agency 182
10.6 Institutional commonalities and social unity 185

PART IV: *Toward a Broader Philosophy of Human Agency*

11. Rethinking the Davidsonian synthesis   191

12. Conclusion: Our core capacity for planning agency   197

Notes   203

References   231

Index   245

PREFACE

From 1987 to 2018 I published a quintet of books in which I explore a planning theory of human agency. These books focused on the roles of our planning agency in the interrelated phenomena of human temporally extended agency (as in growing food in a garden) and human small-scale social agency (as in string quartets). The main question to which I turn in the present book is: to what extent can these planning models of temporally extended and small-scale social agency contribute to our understanding of the larger-scale organization involved in human, rule-guided organized institutions (such as a college or university)? Here my thinking has been shaped by a thought from Scott Shapiro that we can make progress by bringing these planning theories together with ideas from H. L. A. Hart concerning social rules and their role in the rule-guided institution of law. My conjecture is that this strategy leads to a theoretically illuminating approach to rule-guided human organized institutions. Further, if this is right, it supports the broader thesis that our planning capacities play a core role in a fundamental trio of interrelated forms of human practical organization: diachronic, small-scale social, and institutional. The conjecture, then, is that my development in this book of a plan-theoretic framework for understanding human organized institutions supports the overall conjecture that our planning capacities are core capacities within our human practical lives.

Philosophy is an experimental discipline. The experiments are sustained—and frequently shared—efforts systematically to think through where certain ideas take us. This book is a further stage of an experiment structured by the conjecture that it is a deep fact about us that we are planning agents.

I tried out early versions of some of these ideas about organized institutions in my essay "The Intentions of a Group" (in Eric W. Orts and N. Craig Smith, eds., *The Moral Responsibility of Firms* [Oxford University

Press], 36–52) and in my review of Kirk Ludwig's *From Plural to Institutional Agency: Collective Agency II* in *Notre Dame Philosophical Review* (2018). I also tried out some of these ideas in lectures at the 2018 Conference on Collective Intentionality, the Northern New England Philosophy Association, the University of Vienna, the University of Pennsylvania, the Society for Philosophy and Technology, and the 2019 New Orleans Workshop on Action and Responsibility, and in seminars at Stanford. While I was working on this book, I was also writing two related essays: Bratman 2021b and Bratman forthcoming b. Thanks to Oxford University Press and the *Journal of the American Philosophical Association* for permission to include overlap with these essays in this present book.

I am deeply grateful for the very many ways in which my thinking for this book has benefitted from collegial interaction. This includes early discussions with Shapiro when we were both Fellows at the Center for Advanced Study in the Behavioral Sciences in 2004, and a research year in 2018–19 at the Stanford Humanities Center, where I benefitted from multiple discussions with David Plunkett. I have significantly benefitted from many group discussions of all or part of earlier versions of this manuscript. These include the Action and Responsibility Reading Group (led by Thor Grünbaum), the Yale Moral Philosophy Reading Group, a Yale Law School Workshop (organized by Scott Shapiro), the Online Reading Group in Ethics (organized by David Velleman), a Latin America Free Will, Agency, and Responsibility seminar (led by Manuel Vargas and Santiago Amaya), a Dartmouth Seminar on Mind, Language, and Morality (led by Jonathan Phillips and David Plunkett), and Stanford University Graduate Seminars in 2019 and 2020. Very many thanks to the many participants on these occasions.

Facundo Alonso, Frank Hindriks, Barry Maguire, Tristram McPherson, Elijah Millgram, Grace Paterson, David Plunkett, Abraham Roth, and Leif Wenar have each provided extensive written comments, from which I have very much benefitted. In addition, many others have greatly contributed to my thinking by way of correspondence and/or discussion. Though I will not attempt a complete list here, I do try in many cases in the book to note specific ideas that arose in these contexts. I am deeply indebted to these multiple forms of cooperative, scholarly support. I also want to thank Daniel Friedman and Elise Sugarman for help in preparing an early version of this manuscript, Elise Sugarman for preparing the index, and Emy Kim for recommending the image used on the cover of this book.

I have been privileged to work with a wide range of wonderful students at Stanford, many of whom have in effect become my teachers. The transition from teacher-student relation to colleagueship in shared cooperative scholarly activities is one of the great joys of life in the academy and has been for me an important part of my continuing philosophical education. Thank you.

And, as always, Susan, Gregory, and Scott were each an anchor of love.

OVERVIEW: INTENTION, PLANS, AND PRACTICAL ORGANIZATION

Our human lives involve and depend on complex forms of mind-shaped practical organization. There is the diachronic organization of an individual's temporally extended activity. Think about growing food in a garden, or taking a trip with a complex itinerary, or writing a book. There is small-scale social organization, when several individuals act together in shared intentional/shared cooperative ways. Think about a string quartet, or painting a house together, or having a conversation together. And there are larger-scale organized institutions such as a neighborhood association, a club, a religious congregation, a small business, a professional association, a city council, a college or university, a non-profit organization, a limited liability corporation, a political party, a legal system, or a democratic state.

These remarkable forms of mind-shaped practical organization are a basic feature of our human agency and are at the bottom of much that is good in our human, social lives. A philosophically illuminating theory of human agency should provide disciplined, systematic, articulated resources that help us better understand these multiple forms of human practical organization and their interrelations.

I propose that we do this in part by appeal to our capacity for planning agency. As resource-limited agents, we achieve striking forms of cross-temporal organization in our individual intentional activity by settling in advance on partial, largely future-focused plans that pose problems of means and, in pursuit of coordination, filter options that are potential solutions to those problems. These forms of planning guide our thought and action over time. And my conjecture is that this capacity for planning agency also underlies small-scale social and institutional forms of human practical organization. In this sense our capacity for planning agency is, for us, a *core capacity*.[1]

In Bratman 1987 I explored ways in which planning underlies the cross-temporal organization of our individual intentional agency. This led to a theory that highlights the rational dynamics of somewhat stable partial plans in the mind-supported cross-temporal organization of our individual temporally extended activity. And it showed the theoretical fecundity of seeing intentions as states in this plan-infused system: intentions, so understood, are plan states.

In Bratman 2014a I then developed a planning model of small-scale shared intentional activities (SIAs) and underlying shared intentions. A basic idea is that the planning capacities central to the cross-temporal organization of our individual activities are also central to the interpersonal organization of SIA. There is a theoretical continuity between the conceptual, psychological, metaphysical, and normative resources at work in our planning theory of our individual temporally extended agency and our planning theory of shared intention and SIA.[2]

These efforts support the idea that the best explanation of these twin human capacities for temporally extended and interpersonally shared intentional activity will appeal to our human capacity for planning agency.[3] And a central question of this book is: does this foundational role of our capacity for planning agency extend to our organized social institutions? Does the capacity for planning agency that underlies our temporally extended and small-scale shared agency also thereby underlie our organized social institutions?[4] This book explores and defends an affirmative answer to this question.

A guiding thought is that, given that our planning capacities are central to the organization of our individual agency over time and of small-scale cases of our thinking and acting together, it is reasonable to explore the conjecture that the deep structure of human organized institutions also involves these plan-infused forms of human practical organization. Other elements will of course be involved, including forms of normative judgment.[5] But the conjecture to be explored is that plans and planning are central to the organizational structure of human institutions.

I aim to defend a version of this conjecture. I will propose a planning theory of organized institutions that builds on our prior understanding of the role of planning in individual temporally extended activity and, thereby, in shared intention and SIA. On this approach, our capacity for planning agency supports basic structures of our organized institutions in part by way of the support it provides for our capacity for SIA.

Let me contrast this approach with two other strategies for seeing planning as central to human organized institutions. First, we might highlight the personal plans and planning of multiple individuals, each of whose personal plans and planning are conditional on the personal plans and planning of others. Each intends personally to follow certain plans of action given their expectations about the plans and planning of others; and all this is public.[6] Insofar as we try to characterize institutional organization along these lines, we eschew appeal to the kind of interpersonally shared intention highlighted in Bratman 2014a. This would be a *strongly individualistic planning approach to organized institutions*.

A second way of appealing to plans and planning in understanding human organized institutions would be to attribute such planning attitudes and activities directly at the level of the institution itself, without constructing them out of interpersonal webs of individual and shared plans and planning. This is to seek an understanding of organized institutions that parallels our planning model of individual agents but does not try to construct the institutional elements out of the elements in that model of individuals or an associated model of shared intentionality. This is a *parallel planning approach to organized institutions*.[7]

In contrast with both these approaches, I aim to contribute to our understanding of organized institutions by *constructing* them (in a sense that I will explain), using as building blocks the interpersonally shared intentions highlighted in Bratman 2014a. This is a *sequential shared planning approach*.

In pursuing this approach, I will be highlighting the *modest and modular place* of shared intention in human organized institutions. On the one hand, the functioning of organized institutions will normally involve various interrelated shared intentions and shared intentional activities, sometimes on the part of subgroups and sometimes on the part of the overall group of institutional participants. Think of the interrelated functioning of various subcommittees in a university or the National Science Foundation; or think of shared activities of an admissions subcommittee in deciding whom the department should admit into its graduate program. Within our organized institutions we frequently think and act together in shared intentional ways. This is an aspect of the ubiquity of shared intentional agency in our human social lives. Our model of human organized institutions should do justice to this modest and modular role of shared intention.

On the other hand, organized institutions normally involve hierarchy and differentiated roles, offices, and subactivities; participation in an organized institution will frequently be localized; some participants may not buy into the overall ends of the institution; and there is normally change over time in individual participants. So, we can expect that the overall functioning of those organized institutions will not in general be shared intentional activity on the part of all participants. Some of those who participate in the projects of an institution will not be participants in an overall shared intention in favor of those projects; perhaps they are participants only in a subinstitutional shared intention, or perhaps they are just earning a living.

I seek, then, to understand human organized institutions in a way that highlights (but does not overstate) basic roles of our shared intentionality. This will be a *modest* sequential planning theory of human organized institutions.[8] I will explore such a modest, sequential approach to extending the foundational role of our capacity for planning agency and shared intention to basic structures of our organized institutions. This approach draws from the theoretical resources of the planning theory of shared intention. It sees organized institutions as broadly constructed out of interpersonal social phenomena that involve such shared intentions. It aims to articulate forms of sharing and cooperation that are involved in the deep structure of an organized institution. But it aims to do this without supposing that the activities of the institution are, quite generally, shared intentional activities of all participants.[9]

A key will be to draw on ideas from H. L. A. Hart's (2012) groundbreaking theory of law. A philosophical experiment at the heart of this book is to try to use ideas central to Hart's framework, adjusted appropriately, to develop an illuminating model of human organized institutions more generally. The experiment is to do this by bringing together aspects of Hart's framework with ideas from the planning theory of individual and shared intention.[10] Such a Hart-friendly sequential planning theory of human organized institutions promises to add further range to the planning theory of human practical organization to which I allude in the book's subtitle.

I will focus on two main questions. First:

(A) Can our planning theory of shared intention and SIA play a basic role in an illuminating model of the social functioning characteristic of such organized institutions?

Here I will take on board Hart's fundamental thought that law—and, I take it, organized institutions generally—is *rule-guided and rule-governed*. So, as Hart emphasized, we face the question "What *are* rules? What does it mean to say that a rule *exists*?" (8). Hart then turns to the question "What is the acceptance of a rule?" (55). He associates the relevant social acceptance of a rule with a "social rule," where a social rule is social not just in its content but also in its realization in the interpersonal causal order. And, given this phenomenon of a *socially realized* rule, Hart then goes on to ask how best to understand the step from a pre-legal world of social rules to an institution of law.

And that is, broadly speaking, the framework within which I will be responding to (A). In Chapters 2–4, I seek a model of Hart-friendly social rules that builds on the plan-theoretic model of shared intention presented in Chapter 1. A guiding idea is that in such social rules we are together organizing how we live with each other. Then, in Chapters 5 and 6, I seek to use this model of social rules to understand the rule-guided infrastructure of organized institutional functioning. Here a Hart-inspired thought is that the step from a world of social rules to human organized institutions involves distinctive kinds of social rules.

This will then put me in a position, in Chapters 7–10, to ask my second main question:

(B) Can we thereby explain in what sense, if any, such organized institutions can themselves have *intentions* and be *intentional agents*?

Suppose, for example, that Medic Supply is a non-profit medical supply organization that (in some sense) decides to send medical aid to a certain country[11] and then proceeds to do that. To what extent can we expect relevant functioning within that institution to involve shared intention and shared intentional agency as understood by the planning theory? And to what extent does our answer to this question shed light on whether Medic Supply is *itself* an intentional agent, one that intends to send the aid and intentionally sends the aid?

Aspects of our commonsense thought do seem to appeal to institutional intention and intentional agency. Consider a recent commentary in the *New York Times* by the philosopher Matthew Liao:

> Facebook would have crossed a red line if it had intentionally assisted in the dissemination of hate speech in Myanmar. But the evidence indicates that Facebook did not intend for those things to occur on its platform. (Liao 2018)[12]

I suspect that most readers of this newspaper did not find these comments mysterious and, given relevant evidence, would have been prepared to ascribe such intentions and intentional actions to Facebook. But can we really make sense of such ascriptions of intention and intentional agency to Facebook, in contrast with appeal simply to multiple forms of individual and smaller-scale shared intentional agency? Turning to other examples: can we make sense of the idea that Medic Supply intends to send the drugs to a certain city, or that the Stanford Philosophy Department intends to admit certain students, or that General Motors intends to phase out production of gasoline-powered cars? And if so, what is the philosophical backbone of such thought about institutional intent? Here my response will be that we can indeed make sense of and demystify such commonsense thoughts about institutional intention and intentional agency by way of a modest, sequential planning theory of human organized institutions.

In developing such a theory, my aim is not to chart in detail the many ways in which different kinds of organized institutions function. We can expect much variation in such details, variation that is the concern of social scientific investigation. My aim is rather to articulate an abstractly specified infrastructure that is common to and important for a broad range of human organized institutions, despite wide variability across those institutions. And my conjecture is that this infrastructure can be realized by the planning structures—both individual and shared—highlighted by the planning theory.

I do not assume that to pursue these theoretical ambitions we must ourselves be participants in the organized institutions under study. In *Law's Empire* Ronald Dworkin avers that "a social scientist must participate in a social practice if he hopes to understand it, as distinguished from understanding its members" (1986, 55). But the theoretical understanding I seek of organized institutions is not subject to this constraint, though it seeks to understand those institutions, not just their members.[13]

As indicated, one key here will be the relation of the planning theory of SIA to what Hart calls a *social rule*—where Hart saw such social rules as socially realized building blocks of a rule-guided and rule-governed legal system. A second key will be a distinctive kind of plan-constructed social rule that is characteristically at work in the rule-guided infrastructure of human, organized institutions.[14]

A complexity is that this move to organized institutions will draw on ideas about authority that go beyond what is needed in our basic model of SIA. This raises the question whether, given this discontinuity in the step from SIA to organized institutions, we should revisit our approach to SIA and at this earlier stage directly draw on those further theoretical resources. Olle Blomberg, for example, worries that such further "elements required for explaining the nature of social institutions, large organizations or social roles and practices might seep down and 'contaminate' cases of modest sociality."[15] My response will be to show how we can hold intact the planning theory of shared intention and SIA and then use it sequentially, together with further theoretical resources, in modeling human organized institutions. This latter step will draw on ideas of authority that are not needed for our basic model of SIA. But this discontinuity need not—to use Blomberg's metaphor—"contaminate" the basic model of SIA.

What will emerge is a strategy both for endorsing the reductive ambitions of the planning theory of SIA and for recognizing rule-guided organized institutions and institutional intentional agents, despite the tension between these perspectives. This strategy proceeds through a series of steps, each of which, after the first step, builds on the previous step:

(i) a planning theory of individual temporally extended agency (Section 1.1)
(ii) a planning theory of shared intentions and shared policies (Section 1.2)
(iii) a shared policy model of social rules (Chapters 2–4)
(iv) a model of social rules central to the rule-guided infrastructure of organized institutions—namely, authority-according social rules of procedure (Chapter 5)
(v) a model of a rule-guided organized institution and its institutional outputs (Chapter 6)
(vi) a model of institutional intention (Chapters 7–9)
(vii) a model of institutional intentional agency (Chapter 10)

This involves a significant continuity in the move from (i) to (ii); a continuity in the move to (iii) given the role of (ii)-type shared policies; and a discontinuity in the move to (iv), given the role of authority in the rule-guided infrastructure of organized institutions.

This stepwise strategy will lead us, in (iv) and (v), to an understanding of complex structures of pluralism-compatible, rule-guided institutional functioning. It will lead us in (vi) and (vii) to constructions of institutional intention and institutional intentional action. And it will lead us to highlight the cited trio of forms of human practical organization, the roles of plans and planning in realizing these forms of practical organization, and the implications of this shift in focus for our understanding of agency, time, and sociality. This will point to adjustments in the deeply influential Anscombe-and-Quine-influenced Davidsonian synthesis (Davidson 1980) of ideas about intention, reason, mind, and agency.

If successful, this would significantly extend the conjecture that our capacity for planning agency is a core capacity. We would have described how our capacity for planning agency can support our temporally extended agency, our small-scale shared sociality, and, thereby, our rule-guided organized institutions. This would support the conjecture that the best explanation of these multiple forms of practical organization in our human lives involves forms of plan-constituting, prospective practical thinking.[16] This would provide support for an overarching planning theory of human practical organization. And it would help provide a philosophical backbone for our thought and talk about institutional intentional agents. So, let's see.

INDIVIDUAL AGENCY, SHARED AGENCY, SOCIAL RULES

1 THE PLANNING THEORY OF INDIVIDUAL AND SHARED INTENTIONAL AGENCY

I begin with central ideas in my plan-theoretic approach to individual temporally extended intentional agency and, building on that, shared intentional agency.

1.1 Individual temporally extended intentional agency

A fundamental feature of our individual, human agency is its organization over time. Think again about growing food in a garden, or taking a trip, or writing a book. A central idea is that our capacity for planning agency is at the heart of this cross-temporal organization of our individual, human agency.[1] Appeal to this role of our capacity for planning agency both fits our commonsense self-understanding and, I conjecture, would be a part of an empirically informed psychological theory that begins with—but potentially adjusts—this commonsense self-understanding. The basic thought is that we are resource-limited agents who achieve cross-temporal organization in part by settling in advance on prior, partial plans. These somewhat stable partial plans help pose problems of means and preliminary steps, and in pursuit of needed coordination help filter potential options. They thereby provide a background framework for downstream thought and action.

These framework-providing roles of our prior, partial plans involve guidance by rationality norms of effectiveness-tracking means-end coherence, coordination-tracking consistency in what is intended and between intention and belief, agglomerativity of what is intended, and plan stability over time.[2] Intentions are states in this plan-shaped, temporally extended psychic economy, and these rationality norms are built into this psychic economy. Not all agents are such planning agents. So, it does not follow that these planning norms are essential to agency in general. But the conjecture is that we humans are a distinctive kind of agent, a planning agent. Our planning agency is partly constituted by a psychic economy that involves at least implicit guidance by these norms of plan rationality. And a human planning agent will normally have an "oh darn it!" reaction upon recognizing a violation on their part of these norms.

A central thought is that a key to the distinction between a merely causal system and intentional agency is rational guidance. A version of this idea is built into Donald Davidson's philosophy of action (1980). On Davidson's approach, a key to intentional agency is the rational guidance provided by "primary reasons" constituted by relevant pro-attitudes and beliefs that potentially make sense of—"rationalize"—certain activities. Though Davidson saw the explanatory role of primary reasons as involving causation, he saw the distinction between a merely causal system and intentional agency as also involving such rationalization.

When we turn specifically to planning agency, we need to understand the rational guidance characteristic of intentions and plans. Here it would be a mistake to see intentions as, quite generally, playing the same role in our practical thinking as Davidsonian primary reasons. Our intentions and plans are in the first instance responses to such reasons; to see them as quite generally providing yet further such reasons would be to risk an inappropriate form of double counting and/or bootstrapping (Bratman 1987, 24–27). The rational guidance provided in general by our intentions and plans involves instead the cited norms of plan rationality. For example, my intention in favor of an end brings to bear a rational norm of means-end coherence. Guidance by these norms of plan rationality helps distinguish agency from a merely causal system, where the kind of agency at issue is planning agency. We follow Davidson in seeing rational guidance as central to intentional agency, but we diverge from Davidson in highlighting distinctive forms of plan rationality.

Intentions are states in a planning system that settle matters about what to do, including especially what to do in the future. Such intentions involve a present practical commitment to future action. Even when they are not guiding present action, these commitments are poised to guide downstream thought and action in characteristic ways.[3] Such a practical commitment is not ordinary expectation: I might expect that I will later act in ways I do not currently intend. And these practical commitments to future action go beyond an ordinary desire in favor of future action: I might desire to A but still not be appropriately settled on A-ing. Intentions to act do not merely incline but *settle practically* what *to* do: in this sense they prescribe and direct.[4] Further, they are constrained to be compatible with one's relevant beliefs: they are not mere wishes, even wholehearted wishes. They involve a singular-first-personal reflexivity: my intention to A prescribes and directs *my* action. And when their contents are suitably general, intentions constitute *policies*. The planning theory aims to understand such cognitively constrained practical commitments by locating intentions in the rational dynamics of planning agency.

What is the relation between such planning agency and language? On the one hand, I do not assume that the central forms of functioning characteristic of planning agency strictly require language.[5] On the other hand, much of our human planning does involve linguistically articulated, complex scenarios. And it is these forms of language-infused planning agency that will be candidates for a core role in our organized institutions. So, given the aims of this book, I will focus on language-infused planning agency.

The larger plans within which future-directed intentions are embedded will normally have a hierarchical, end-means structure. Such plan-hierarchies will typically be partial and leave as so far unspecified some steps that will be needed in the pursuit of intended ends. This partiality of our plans is fundamental and, given our human limits (Simon 1955, 1983), pretty much unavoidable. We normally do not know enough, or have sufficient resources of time and attention, sensibly to fill in all the details of our plans prior to putting them in place as guides to thought and action. Given these limits, we settle in advance on partial plans and trust ourselves to fill them in as needed and as time goes by. Our prior partial plans then provide a more or less settled background framework within which further downstream, coordination-tracking, and instrumental reasoning takes place.

The normal stability of these frameworks is traceable in part to our resource limits. Given these limits, the activity of reconsidering one's prior intention has costs and risks. Further, such reconsideration normally is not the issue of explicit deliberation about whether to reconsider. Instead, what is normally at work are habits that serve coordination over time and socially. Yet further, even if one does reconsider one's prior intentions, there are pressures in favor of the stability of those intentions given the general benefits of such stability within our resource-limited human lives.[6]

Given the normal stability and partiality of our prior plans, this background framework poses problems of means for further deliberation and, given demands of consistency, filters potential solutions to those problems. In these ways our prior plans help answer the question "Where do decision problems come from?" (Bratman 1987, 33). And such prior, partial plans provide a background framework that structures weighing of reasons for and against various options. It is a mistake to think of our weighing of reasons as taking place in an unstructured context. A primary role of prior intentions is to frame such weighing of reasons rather than to provide new reasons to be weighed (though there are cases in which prior intentions—e.g., career decisions—do both). This is how our prior plans play basic roles as inputs into practical reasoning without being tied to the provision of new reasons in a way that raises worries about unacceptable bootstrapping of reasons.[7]

Our prior plans involve, then, a characteristic trio of dispositions. First, while they are subject to revision, these plans involve a disposition in favor of stability over time. Second, given their partiality, the effectiveness of these plans involves a disposition further to specify means and preliminary steps as time goes by. Third, the coordinating roles of these plans involve a disposition in favor of consistency of the different things one intends with each other and with one's beliefs. These dispositions help support the cross-temporal organizing roles of such plans. Further, these are not simply causal tendencies: they involve the (implicit) acceptance of and guidance by rationality norms of stability, coherence, and consistency. These rationality norms play a triple role: they are at the bottom of the explanatory structures provided by the planning system, they help shape and guide an agent's practical thinking about what to do, and they are a ground for third-personal assessment and criticism.

We do not only reason about means to an already-intended end; we also take our intention at t_1 to A at t_2 into account in our practical reasoning at t_1 about options yet further downstream at t_3. How does the intention at t_1 to A at t_2 rationally shape such reasoning at t_1 about options at t_3? How should we understand what Facundo Alonso (2020) calls "planning on a prior intention"?[8]

If one's intention at t_1 to A at t_2 strictly required one's belief at t_1 that one will A at t_2 we would have an answer: one plans on one's intention to A at t_2 by way of planning in light of one's belief that one will A at t_2. However, as I see it, it would be a mistake to build such a strong belief condition into our theory of intention (Bratman 1987, 37–40). But then: how should we understand planning on a prior intention?

There are three main things to say here concerning the role of one's intention at t_1 to A at t_2 in one's reasoning at t_1 concerning options at t_3. First, given the demand for intention-belief consistency, one is constrained at t_1 not to settle on an option at t_3 that would not, given one's beliefs, be compatible with one's A-ing at t_2. Second, one is frequently in a position to infer that, given that one intends at t_1 to A at t_2, and given the rest of one's beliefs about the world, one will indeed A at t_2. So, one is in position rationally to believe that one will A at t_2. Given this inferentially supported belief, one would normally be in a position to plan at t_1 for t_3 on the assumption that one will A at t_2 (Bratman 1987, 37). Third, even if one is not in a position strictly to believe that one will indeed A at t_2, there can be practical considerations—for example, considerations of efficiency in practical thinking, given one's intention at t_1—to take it for granted, in one's reasoning at t_1 about options at t_3, that one will A at t_2. This would be a matter of *accepting*, in the context of one's practical reasoning at t_1 about options at t_3, that one will A at t_2 even though one does not strictly speaking believe one will (Bratman 1999d; Alonso 2014; Núñez n.d.). (Though, given the demand for intention-belief consistency, one also does not believe that one will not A at t_2.) In this trio of ways, one's intention at t_1 to A at t_2 can constrain and support one's further "planning on a prior intention."

In saying that intentions are plan states, I am working within a broadly functionalist approach to mind. We can distinguish between two functionalist ideas here: (a) Intentions are higher-level functional states of being in some state or other that plays the cited roles. (b) Intentions are those lower-level states that play these functionally specified roles. While (a) is a version of so-called role functionalism, (b) is a version of so-called functional specification theory. Here I proceed along the lines of (b).[9] Plan states are states of the system, including dispositions of thought and action, that play the web of interrelated roles specified by our underlying theory of the functioning characteristic of human planning agency (functioning that involves relevant practical thinking). This underlying theory begins with a broadly commonsense understanding of these phenomena, but is potentially adjusted, modified, articulated, explicated, and systematized in the light of broader theoretical and empirical considerations concerning "the features of real-world agents."[10]

Intentions-as-plan-states are different from and have complex relations to ordinary desires and normative/evaluative judgments. I can intend X even while, in a familiar sense, not wanting or desiring X. I can on balance desire to X without yet intending to X—without yet practically settling on X. I can decide on an option in cases of normative underdetermination in which I judge that other, alternative options are no worse: my intention in such a case should not be identified with my normative or evaluative judgment (Bratman 1999b). And intentions are sometimes akratic and diverge from relevant normative/evaluative judgments.[11] We understand what such intentions are not by collapsing them into desires or normative/evaluative judgments[12] but by locating them within a plan-based, norm-guided, practical psychological economy, one whose rational dynamics is at the heart of fundamental forms of cross-temporal organization in our human, resource-limited lives.

This plan-based cross-temporal organization normally involves both future-looking and past-looking cross-temporal referential connections. My present plan to give a lecture next month at least implicitly refers to my later, then-present-directed intention to give the lecture; my later intention will normally at least implicitly refer back to my earlier intention to give the lecture. The diachronic stability of my intention helps support the cross-temporal coordination. And these cross-temporal constancies and referential interconnections induce a more or less settled background framework for further reasoning. My activity over time is thereby embedded within a temporally extended structure of interwoven, partial, referentially interlocking, hierarchical, and more or less stable plan states—plan states that provide a background framework for further thought and action.[13]

This appeal to cross-temporally stable and referentially interlocking attitudes is in the spirit of Lockean approaches to personal identity over time (Locke 1975, bk. 2, chap. 27; Parfit 1984; Yaffe 2000). The standard functioning of our planning agency involves such broadly Lockean cross-temporal ties, and so can be an aspect of the Lockean persistence of the agent over time.

The conjecture, then, is that our human cross-temporally organized intentional agency is normally grounded in such a planning psychology.[14] The next step is to turn to small-scale shared intentional action.

1.2 Shared intentional activity

There is a distinctive form of social organization in—to use Margaret Gilbert's example—our walking together as a shared intentional activity, in contrast with our merely walking alongside each other (Gilbert 1990).

Granted, merely walking alongside without bumping into each other involves coordination and responsiveness. The organization of our actions is strategic in the sense that you and I are each acting in pursuit of our own individual ends given our knowledge of what the other is doing, where we each know that what each is doing is shaped by her knowledge of what the other is doing. In contrast, walking together in a shared intentional way involves some further form of sharing between us—roughly, we act in the pursuit of a *shared* end of walking together. Or consider a string quartet. When it plays a Mozart quartet there is a great deal of responsiveness and accommodation of each to each. But there is also a further form of sharing that lies behind this mutual responsiveness and accommodation—something like guidance by a shared end in favor of the group's performance.

These forms of sharing are ubiquitous in our human lives. They matter to us intrinsically—think about our singing or dancing together. And they are how we get things done—think about our together building a house. While our human social lives are replete with strategic interactions, it would be a mistake for a theory of our social lives to fail to come to grips also with these forms of shared agency. And a central claim of this book is that a recognition of such shared agency also contributes to our understanding our human organized institutions.[15]

In Bratman 2014a I explain how our capacity for planning agency can lie behind the social organization characteristic of small-scale cases of acting together. There is an illuminating commonality underlying both the cross-temporal structure of our individual agency and the social structure of our acting together.[16] I proceed to sketch some central ideas.

In a basic case,[17] when we J together in a shared intentional way, our J-ing is guided by, and so in part explained by, our shared intention to J. And in a basic case our shared intention consists in a structure of interrelated attitudes of each. Each of us, publicly and interdependently, intends the following:

> We J by way of the intentions of each that we J, meshing subplans of those intentions, and J-tracking mutual responsiveness in thought and action.

Further, in a basic case the relevant conception of our J-ing is "neutral with respect to *shared* intentionality" (Bratman 2014a, 46). What we each intend in intending that we J is a web of interrelated intentional activities of each of us. For example, in a basic case of our sharing an intention to walk together we each intend that we each intentionally walk alongside each other at a similar pace and in ways that involve relevant adjustments.[18] This web can then be an element in our *shared* intentional activity in part because of the connection of our activity to our shared intention, a connection that involves intended mesh, mutual responsiveness, and interdependence.[19]

The intentions of each that are elements in the shared intention are individual practical commitments with a social content—they prescribe for *us*. These intentions of each have common contents. In their interpersonal cross-reference to the role of the intentions of each and their meshing subplans, they referentially interlock.[20] And they are interdependent in their persistence, other things equal: if you were to cease intending that we J, then, other things equal, I would as well.[21]

There are different forms of such persistence interdependence.[22] There may be this interdependence because we each know that the desirability of the participation of each in our J-ing depends on there being a joint activity of J-ing. There may be this interdependence because we each know that the realistic possibility of success depends on the participation of both. Or there may be this interdependence because there has been a kind of interaction between us (for example, mutual promises) that supports moral obligations to continue so long as the other does. While such obligations are not essential to shared intention, they can in certain cases support the relevant interdependence. And given interdependence in any of these forms (or perhaps others), I am in a position to some extent to trust that you will continue with our sharing if I do.

These structures provide a social glue that is analogous to the Lockean intrapersonal ties that are common in the temporally extended agency of a single planning agent.[23] And there can be such shared intentions even if different agents participate for different reasons: I might participate in our shared intention to paint the house because I dislike the color, whereas you participate because you dislike the mildew. Indeed, on the overall view in this book, such divergence of background reasons, and resulting partiality of convergence, is a common feature of our human sociality, both small-scale and institutional.[24]

What about the role of language? On the one hand, I do not assume that small-scale shared intentionality must involve language. On the other hand, shared intentionality among adult humans will frequently concern language-articulated possibilities and will frequently involve linguistic exchanges, as in "I will if you will." And it is these forms of language-infused shared intentionality that will be candidates for a basic role in human organized institutions. So, given the aims of this book, I will focus on language-infused shared intentionality.

I turn now to a series of further matters.

1.2.1 Reflexivity, construction, rationality, sufficiency

Ordinary intentions to act involve a *first-person singular reflexivity*: such intentions concern one's *own* action. The intentions to which we are now appealing—intentions that *we* J—also have a first-personal-singular reflexive aspect. As understood within our theory, my intention *that we* J involves my intention *to* act accordingly. This helps ensure the role of one's intention that we J in guiding one's own action.[25] In addition, such intentions-that-we also have a *plural* reflexive aspect, since they involve a specification of a targeted group as, from the intender's perspective, *us*. This is built into the use of "we" in the expression of the intention. So, these intentions of each that we J involve two interrelated forms of reflexivity: they are *doubly reflexive*.

This appeal to a web of interrelated attitudes of each is part of a *strategy of construction*: we aim to understand shared intention by building it out of elements drawn in large part from the planning theory of the intentions of individuals. This is in the spirit of, though not as strong as, Fred Dretske's thought that "if you can't make one, you don't know how it works" (1994). We seek to understand how shared intention "works" by articulating a construction that can be shown to work in that way. Our Dretske-inspired strategy is to *ground relevant functioning in an underlying construction*.

Further, in building these constructions we broadly follow H. P. Grice's (1974–75) *sequential* methodology of "creature construction." Grice highlighted the idea of a *series* of constructions that cumulatively build on each other. And appeal to such a series of constructions is central to my proposed *sequential* planning theory of organized institutions.[26]

We can distinguish two related but different ways of understanding this idea of a sequence of constructions. On the one hand, we can see different stages in such a sequence as stages in an envisioned historical process—a just-so story—of the emergence of increasingly complex structures.[27] On the other hand, we can see these sequences as articulating conceptual, psychological, metaphysical, and normative structures in phenomena that are part of our social world. In my strategy of construction, I am primarily interested in such conceptual, psychological, metaphysical, and normative structures—though associated, just-so etiological stories can help us in articulating these structures (Bratman 2007a, 50).

So, we seek a broadly individualistic model of shared intention, one that specifies a construction of shared intention whose building blocks include the plan-states of individuals, as they are understood within the planning theory of our individual temporally extended agency.[28] In specifying such a construction, our model helps to demystify phenomena of share intentionality in a way that emphasizes their ubiquity in our human lives, captures their characteristic and complex forms of social functioning, and systematically ties this functioning to that of individual participants.

Our *model* of shared intention is a theory that aims to understand important aspects of our actual social world. The *construction* specified by the model is seen as a complex feature of the actual social world being modeled. An overarching aim is to articulate a construction of shared intention such that when its interrelated attitudes of individuals function in accordance with the rational dynamics of individual planning agency, there is normally the social functioning (including relevant forms of practical thinking) characteristic of shared intention.

In articulating such a construction, our model can engage in idealization in which it abstracts away from other elements—for example, emotions or moods. But this is not quite Peter Godfrey-Smith's idea (2006, 2005) that our "model systems" are hypothetical systems that can be seen in some sense to resemble the real-world system in which we are interested, and which thereby only "indirectly" represent that real-world system. My proposed model of shared intention is a theory that aims directly to represent a real-world system, though various forms of idealization can be at work.[29]

The plan states of individuals to which we are appealing are characterized by appeal to relevant functional roles. And the aim is to see shared intentions as constructions of such plan states, constructions that play characteristic social roles. But what, more exactly, is that social functioning?

At the heart of the intentions of individuals are their roles in the rationally structured, cross-temporal organization of the individual's practical life. An individual's intentions coordinate and organize their planning and action in part by providing a partial background framework for further downstream practical thinking. This involves guidance by norms of individual plan rationality: norms of consistency, means-end coherence, and stability. And my proposal is that the characteristic roles of our *shared* intention to J are, analogously, the support of *inter*personal coordination and organization of action and planning in pursuit of J, in part by way of framing relevant thinking about how we are to J. And for a shared intention successfully to play these roles, the relevant plans of the participants will need—taken together—to satisfy (though perhaps not to be guided by) analogous norms of social consistency, social means-end coherence, and social stability.

Our aim, then, is to specify a structure of interconnected plan states of individuals that would, when functioning in the rational-norm-guided ways characteristic of individual planning agency, play these interpersonal social roles of shared intention and support the satisfaction of these associated social rationality norms. We aim to explain how relevant forms of social functioning and social rationality emerge from forms of individual plan functioning and plan rationality in which the intentions/plans of each involve relevant social contents and interrelations.

My proposed construction aims to satisfy this desideratum in part by way of the condition that each doubly reflexively intends "our" joint activity.[30] For example, if I intend that *we* (you and I) paint the house, effectiveness-tracking demands of means-end coherence on my intention will normally induce rational pressure on me in favor of helping you if you need it, given the need for your contribution to our joint activity. And coordination-tracking demands of intention consistency induce rational pressure against forming intentions to act in ways that would baffle our joint house painting. By putting *our* activity into the contents of my intention we begin to explain how standard forms of coordination-and-effectiveness-tracking plan-theoretic reasoning rationally support our shared intentional activity.

However, not just any case in which it is public that each of us intends that we J is a case of shared intention. Two mafia members might each publicly intend that they go with each other to New York, where each intends that this happens by way of throwing the other into the car trunk (Bratman 2014a, 49). Here our theory appeals to the condition that each intends that we J *by way of the corresponding intention of each*— the condition, not satisfied in the mafia case, that these intentions of each *referentially interlock*. A key is the difference between just knowing what someone intends and intending that her intention be successfully executed. In intending that we act in part by way of your analogous intention, I am rationally committed to supporting your intention-shaped role in our activity and to adjusting my own contributions accordingly. In this way, in going beyond a condition of public intentions of each that we go to New York, the interlocking condition supports important, characteristic functioning of shared intention.

Consider, further, a case in which each intends that we go to New York by way of a corresponding intention of the other, but neither intends that the activity go by way of the subplans of the other. Instead, each is fully prepared to use force or deception to thwart or bypass those subplans of the other. Perhaps each intends that the intention of the other that we go to New York leads him to get into the car, where he will then be captured. Or in a master-slave relation, the master intends that the job be done but is fully prepared to use force or deception to get it done in ways that do not accord with the subplans of the slave. Here, in contrast, our theory appeals to a further condition of each *intending that the activity proceeds by way of mesh in subplans*. And we thereby yet further support functioning characteristic of shared intention.

Can I really *intend* that *we* act in a certain way? Can I intend that *we* sing the duet? Well, my intention that we sing the duet can stably support relevant means-end reasoning on my part aimed at our singing. And it can filter relevant alternatives with an eye to consistency with our singing. In these ways it can *settle practically* for me whether we sing. Further, I can know that my intention supports your intention that we sing, and vice versa. In particular, I can know that if I intend that we sing, so will you, and so, as a result of our each so intending, we will indeed sing. And you can be in an analogous epistemic situation. In neither case need one of us be exercising an unusual form of control of or authority over the other. My expected influence over your intention may be like a case in which I know that if I ask you for the time, you will tell me. And analogously for you. This is the ordinary predictability of human agents, not an agency-undermining control (Bratman 1999c, 155). So, my intention that we sing can in this way for me also rationally lead to my belief that we will indeed sing, and thereby for me *settle cognitively* whether we sing; and analogously for you (Bratman 1999c; Bratman 2014a, 60–67). So, I can plan on my prior intention that we sing; and analogously for you. So, my intention that we sing can settle for me, both practically and cognitively, whether we sing. I conclude that my attitude in such a case is an intention that we sing the duet.[31]

This shows that there is not—as some have thought[32]— a fundamental objection to the very idea of my intending that *we* J, in cases of shared intention. Granted, these reflections involve a strong assumption that if I intend that we J, then so will you, and vice versa. But once we see the structure of this defense of intending that we J, we can extend it to cases in which there is a weaker connection between my intention and yours. I might know that my intention, though it does not ensure that you too intend, is consistent with my beliefs about you and tends to support, in this public context, an analogous intention of yours. My intention does not by itself fully settle cognitively for me the theoretical question whether you also so intend, and so whether we so act. But my intention can nevertheless both filter relevant options, given constraints of consistency, and provide prima facie support for a belief that you will so intend. If that belief is thereby in place, it can normally support practical reasoning on the assumption that we will so act. And even if my epistemic situation does not support such a belief, strictly speaking, I might still go on to accept in the context that you will so intend, and so that we will so act. So, my intention can play one or the other of the cognitive roles in my planning concerning the yet further future that can be played by ordinary intentions to act, as discussed in Section 1.1.

Consider Hume's famous example: "Two men who pull at the oars of a boat, do it by an agreement or convention, tho' they have never given promises to each other" (Hume 1896, bk. III, pt. II, sec. II). One way to see these rowers is to see the first rower as strategically responding to what the second rower is doing, where the second is strategically responding to what the first rower is doing. The content of the intentions of each is something like: row this way, given that the other is rowing that way in response to my intention and action. This sees the rowers as like people walking alongside each other. But a second way to see the rowers is that they each intend the (shared intention neutral) joint activity of rowing together. This does not require promises. But it goes beyond simply supposing that the intentions of each in favor of her own actions respond to the intentions of the other concerning her own actions. The content of the intentions of each involves the joint action of rowing together. These intentions of each are not merely intentions to act in a certain way given that others do. After all, in an intention to A *given that p*, the condition p is *believed* but need not be *intended*. Indeed, one might intend to A given that p while trying to prevent p, even while expecting not to succeed in preventing p. In these ways, intending to A given that there are the other elements of the joint activity contrasts with intending that joint activity.

The planning theory of shared intention and SIA involves the conjecture that such intentions in favor of the joint activity are at the heart of an important form of human sociality. This allows that there are forms of solely strategic interaction, and it allows for interrelations between these two forms of sociality. The claim is that, in addition to strategic interaction, the highlighted form of shared sociality is also vitally important to our human lives, and it would be a failure if our theory did not come to terms with it or simply failed to see the difference between it and strategic interaction. We need to take seriously within our overall theory of human agency the ways in which we together organize how we act with each other.

A central pair of conditions in our construction of shared intention is that the intentions of each that we J are appropriately interdependent in their persistence and interlock in the sense that the contents of each involve reference to the effectiveness of those intentions of others.[33] These conditions are poised to interact: given interdependence, the constancy of my intention supports the constancy of yours (and vice versa); and given interlocking, I intend that that stabilized intention of yours play its role in our activity (and vice versa).

Such interdependence and interlocking are supported by the condition that these elements are out in the open.[34] This out-in-the-open condition need not concern deep features of the minds of each, features that are not easily knowable by others. Nor is this a condition that the minds of each are accessible to the minds of the others in a non-evidence-based way. The idea is only that evidence concerning relevant aspects of minds of the others is publicly available and each is in a position to reason from that evidence to true conclusions about the minds of others. There are limits of such knowledge in our messy lives. This can later become apparent, as when one says, "I thought we were J-ing, but it turns out that you thought we were doing something else." But we can suppose that in a wide range of cases there is, frequently with the help of language, convergence in the understanding of each of relevant non-depth-psychological aspects of the minds of each.

The construction then draws on the distinctive contents of and interrelations between these intentions of the individuals to explain central forms of social functioning associated with shared intentional activity. As noted, these are forms of social functioning that are analogues of the characteristic forms of individual, cross-temporal organization induced by individual planning agency. In this way we extend our broadly functionalist approach from individual to shared intentionality. But we do not rest content simply with appeal to the functional roles that are characteristic of shared intention. Instead, we seek a plan-theoretic construction that systematically grounds the functioning characteristic of shared intention.

These analogous forms of social functioning include interpersonal coordination of action and planning, and related forms of bargaining and shared deliberation about how to fill in relevant plans and thereby to proceed with the shared activity. These social roles of shared intentions are associated with corresponding norms of social rationality, including norms of social consistency and social means-end coherence. There is relevant social consistency with respect to a shared intention to J when the various intentions of the participants that constitute their subplans concerning how they are to J are co-realizable given views about the world that are held in common.[35] There is relevant social means-end coherence when there is a sufficient web of intentions and subplans for the effective pursuit of what is favored by the shared intention. What is favored by the shared intention is, when fully spelled out, the group's J-ing by way of relevant intentions of each. So, social means-end coherence will involve a sufficient web of intentions for the effective pursuit not just of the group's J-ing but also of the group's J-ing by way of relevant intentions of each.

A key idea is that given the special contents of relevant, interrelated intentions of individuals, conformity to these social norms is normally induced by the rational, individualistic plan dynamics as applied to these distinctive intentions of the individuals. Returning to our example: if we intend to paint the house together and you fall, my intention that we paint in part by way of your intention will normally support, by way of the demand for means-end coherence on my own intentions, an intention on my part to help you get up. So, in responding to an individualistic norm of means-end coherence on my own plans concerning our painting, I support the social means-end coherence of our painting together by way of each of our intentions in favor of that. And this involves my intending the successful execution of your intention, not just knowing that you so intend.

The idea, then, is that the basic step from temporally extended planning agency to shared intention and SIA involves distinctive social contents of relevant plans of each (they favor the joint activity by way of intentions of each, mesh in subplans, and mutual responsiveness) and interdependence between these plans of each, all of which is more or less out in the open. Given these distinctive contents, interrelations, and contexts, the forms of normative guidance that are fundamental to SIA remain, in the basic case, the forms of normative guidance that are fundamental to planned individual temporally extended activity: forms of individual plan-rationality-shaped guidance that track coordination, effectiveness, and stability. We then show that, given these special plan contents and interrelations and contexts, the rational plan dynamics characteristic of SIA—a dynamics induced by norms of individual plan rationality as applied to distinctive social contents—will normally induce satisfaction of norms of *social* consistency and means-end coherence.

We are, so far, seeing satisfaction of these norms of social rationality as *emerging* from the guidance by norms of individual plan rationality of individual participants in a shared intention. We are not yet supposing that these individuals are directly *guided* by these norms of social rationality. However, when those individuals see this normative emergence, they may come to accept these norms of social rationality and to appeal directly to these norms of social rationality in their practical reasoning. This would add further support to their conformity to the demands of the shared intention.[36]

As noted, different agents can participate in a shared intention for different reasons. Many important forms of SIA in a pluralistic social world like ours will involve some such divergence in underlying reasons for participating in the sharing.[37] This partiality of convergence, and pluralism of our social world, will be an important theme in the discussion to follow.[38]

This possibility of diverging reasons for participating in a shared intention induces a further complexity: your overall, fully specified intention might be that we paint as a way of reducing the mildew, whereas my overall, fully specified intention might be that we paint as a way of changing the color. To get at the joint-act-type with respect to which we share an intention we need to find a relevant intersection of these different overall contents, one that is itself the content of an intention of each. For example, in this case the content of our shared intention is the more generic activity of our painting, which is something we each intend. This is a strategy of abstraction.[39]

The proposal is that the cited structure of intentions constitutes the *basic case* of shared intention. I express my proposal in this way because my main strategy is to argue that the proper functioning of this social-psychological structure is *sufficient* for relevant forms of shared thought and action. This *strategy of sufficiency* seeks to provide, within relevant constraints, broadly reductive, theoretically illuminating sufficient conditions for the target phenomenon. This strategy allows for the possibility of other broadly reductive conditions that are also sufficient for the phenomenon—it allows for multiple realizability of shared intention. I assume, however, that any plausible sufficient condition of the sort we seek for shared intention will involve a condition that the individual participants each in some appropriate way buy into the shared thought or action.[40]

Let me say more about this strategy of sufficiency. Our central questions concern a trio of forms of human practical organization: (1) temporally organized individual intentional agency, (2) socially organized shared intentional agency, and (3) large-scale organized social institutions. We seek models of each of these fundamental phenomena and of their interrelations, models that provide a systematic framework for further study. The part of our strategy for doing this that is currently on the table is a construction of (2) whose main elements come primarily from (1). Later we will seek a construction of (3) —in part by way of a construction of social rules—whose main elements come primarily from (2), as well as from (1). In each case, we need to show how such constructions would realize the target phenomena. In doing this we demystify and make philosophically defensible room, within our world of interrelated individual agents, for these important social phenomena. In each case we show how—drawing on an image from Kripke (1972, 153)—once God created all the elements of the proffered construction, there would be no more work to do for there to be the target phenomenon (Bratman 2014a, 8). In none of these cases do we need to show that our proposed construction is the unique such possible construction.[41]

In each case, a question in the background is: sufficiency for what? In following this strategy of sufficiency, we seek to model an appropriately broad version of the target phenomenon—as it may be, shared intention or social rules or organized institutions. Assessments of appropriate broadness of target phenomenon will be anchored in part in judgments of explanatory fecundity. Sufficient conditions for what is plausibly seen as an overly limited and narrow version of the target phenomenon would not provide the theoretical illumination we seek.

Given a model of sufficient conditions for an appropriately broad version of the target phenomenon, we will then need to keep an eye out for the possibility of alternative constructions of that phenomenon. If faced with some such alternative construction, we can, in some cases, simply allow for multiple realizability of that target phenomenon. In some cases, however, we can ask whether one such realization is more explanatorily fecund than the others. In some such cases, an affirmative answer will take the form of an inference to the best explanation that supports a conclusion that privileges one such sufficient construction. Indeed, I will return at the end of this book to such a defeasible inference concerning the roles of our planning capacities. For present purposes, however, we can focus primarily on the effort to provide relevant sufficient conditions for sufficiently broad target phenomena.

Returning in particular to shared intention, we have a plan-theoretic construction that moves from structures of cross-temporal organization to structures of shared intention. We then provide constructive, sufficient conditions for the condition that a group's shared intention appropriately guides their activity and so they act together in a shared intentional way. Finally, we can extend this model to shared *policies* concerning potentially recurring situations—for example, a shared policy of meeting weekly, or of following a certain voting procedure. Such shared policies involve interlocking and interdependent intentions of each in favor of the group's acting in a certain way in a certain kind of circumstance. Such shared policies will loom large when we turn to social rules.

1.2.2 Too demanding?

Does this appeal to doubly reflexive, interlocking intentions in favor of the joint activity by way of meshing subplans impose overly demanding pressures on the minds of participants? The first thing to say is that in many cases a complex content can be tacit or implicit. Perhaps a participant has an intention that she would express simply as "we are to J." Nevertheless, she is also disposed to support the highlighted roles of attitudes of each in their J-ing. And she is disposed toward a relevant "oh darn it!" reaction if she were to fail to support these roles of the others. These dispositions can support the attribution of the more complex contents cited within the theory—implicit or tacit contents that involve interlocking and support of mesh.

Further, these (perhaps implicit) contents of the intentions of each need not specify details all the way down. I can intend that we tango by way of each of our intentions and meshing subplans without intending each of the subtle and interpersonally responsive movements in which our intentions issue. These adjustments of each to each can be framed by our shared intention but be the issue of relevant subpersonal mechanisms "without the details of those adjustments appearing in the contents of our intentions" (Bratman 2014a, 105).

Yet further: "Less demanding social psychological phenomena might in certain cases to some extent functionally substitute for these more demanding attitudes of each" (Bratman 2014a, 105). In some cases, such functional substitutes will be framed by a background shared intention, as in our tango dancing. But there may also be cases—the shared activities of four-year-old children, perhaps—in which such less demanding subpersonal structures on their own support relevant mutual responsiveness and interdependence in support of the joint activity. About such cases, we can follow Philip Pettit (2018, 51) when he notes that the "intentional planning" of the sort highlighted by my model "can be mimicked by other sub-intentional processes."

We need, however, to remember that we are seeking a model of shared intentions that will be involved in social rules that play a central role in organized institutions. Such rule-guided organized institutions are the targeted phenomenon for which we seek apt sufficient conditions. So, given the more or less public functioning at this institutional level it will be appropriate for us here to focus on cases of shared intention that involve at least a basic framework of intentions with relevant, perhaps-implicit contents—where this may still involve important subpersonal mechanisms.

So, in response to the worry that my account of shared intention is overly demanding we can say: (i) it allows for tacit/implicit contents; (ii) it allows that shared intentions, so understood, can frame the operation of relevant subpersonal processes, detailed specifications of which need not enter into contents of relevant intentions; (iii) it allows for cases in which less demanding mechanisms, as Pettit says, mimic the operation of the sort of shared intention I have modelled even though these mechanisms are not framed by such shared intentions; but (iv) with an eye on the targeted phenomena of our larger theoretical enterprise, it highlights shared intentions that involve at least a basic framework of intentions with relevant, perhaps-implicit contents.

1.2.3 Scaling up, vagueness, interdependence, and interlocking

I have been focusing on cases of our shared intention to J in which what each intends requires that each of us plays their role in J—for example, each plays their part in the quartet. But in larger-scale cases of a shared intention to J, what each of us intends might—while it continues to involve first-person singular reflexivity—only require broad but not universal participation on the part of others.

Suppose I am part of a large group of people who share an intention to participate in a protest march. Each of us realizes that the march does not strictly depend on everyone's intentions and actions. What it depends on is that enough of those in this group appropriately intend and act. And suppose that each of us is not fully confident that there will not be some dropouts. In light of this, what each of us intends is that a (vaguely specified) sufficient number of us participate. In each case, this intention is consistent with the intender's beliefs. In each case the intention that enough of us participate in the march involves that person's intention to participate—it involves first-personally-singular reflexivity. But what is intended also involves vagueness about the extent of conformity of others, and so vagueness in its plural reflexive aspect.

Nevertheless, it might be that all of us do in fact share an intention to participate in the march. In such a case there can be a shared intention among all of us to march together even if what each intends is only that enough of us participate. Each participant's intention does not strictly depend on the intention of each of the others but only on the condition that enough of the others appropriately intend. The dependence on the intentions of others need only be indirect, by way of a belief that enough of the others appropriately intend.

When we turn to larger-scale cases of shared intention to J, then, we will want to make two adjustments. First, we will want to understand the relevant intentions that we J as—while continuing to involve first-person singular reflexivity—in some cases prescribing only that enough of us play our roles. And second, we will want to weaken the interdependence condition and allow that there can be a shared intention to J even if the dependence between the intentions of each is only an indirect dependence that goes by way of the dependence of the intention of each on the condition that enough others appropriately intend.

What about the idea that in shared intention the intentions of each interlock? Well, with respect to each of those who do intend that enough of us participate in the march, I intend that our marching go in part by way of that person's intention—though (in contrast with small-scale cases that involve direct reference to others) I may need certain general concepts (e.g., "those in this political group") to refer to them. So, insofar as there are these intentions of each, my intention interlocks with them, though perhaps by way of such general concepts. So, we can continue to see the relevant intentions that we J as interlocking even in such larger-scale cases of shared intention to J.

But is my commitment to the condition that enough of us march an *intention* that we (vaguely specified) march?[42] Well, my commitment can support my relevant means-end reasoning in response to pressures of means-end coherence with respect to both my participation and the sufficiently general conformity; and it can help filter relevant alternatives in light of pressures for intention-belief consistency. So, it can, for me, settle the practical question of whether enough of us march. Further, I can know that my commitment, though it does not ensure that there be sufficient participation among us, tends to support, in this public context, analogous commitments on the part of the others. My commitment does not by itself settle cognitively for me the theoretical question of whether enough of us will march. But my commitment can nevertheless provide prima facie support for a belief that enough of us will march. And if that belief is in place, it can then help support practical reasoning and planning concerning the yet-further future—planning on my prior intention. Further, even if my epistemic situation does not fully support such a belief, I might still go on, for relevant practical reasons, to accept in the context that enough of us will march. So, my commitment in favor of a sufficient number of us marching can play one or the other of the cognitive roles in my planning concerning the yet further future that can be played by ordinary intentions to act, as discussed in section 1.1.

In these ways my doubly reflexive commitment that enough of us march can support the functional roles characteristic of intending—roles in framing ongoing planning, practical reasoning, and action—in the direction of our marching and further downstream planning. This includes framing relevant further planning with an eye to adequately filing in further means and preliminary steps in ways consistent both with other such commitments and with relevant beliefs about how our activity is in fact playing out. And this includes the way in which my commitment, though it may not itself ensure that there will be sufficient participation among us, can nevertheless help support my belief or acceptance about our marching, a belief or acceptance that can then help shape my planning concerning the yet-further future. These considerations support the conclusion that my doubly reflexive commitment that enough of us march can indeed be an *intention* that *we* (vaguely specified) march even though my commitment by itself may not fully settle for me the theoretical question of whether enough of us march. So, the weaker, indirect interdependence that we are allowing within our account of *shared* intention is compatible with continuing to see the individualistic building blocks of those shared intentions as *intentions* of each that we (vaguely specified) J.

So far, then, our account of the interdependence and interlocking involved in shared intention, with the cited adjustments, survives extension to larger-scale cases of shared intention. The next step concerns authority.

1.2.4 Authority-according shared intentions

In some cases, a shared intention will involve intentions that favor patterns of *according and accepting authority*.[43] I might not just intend that we play the quartet in part by way of your corresponding intention; I might intend that we play the quartet *in part by way of my accepting your authority* to set the tempo, and in that sense *according you this authority*. And you might intend that we play the quartet in part by way of *my deferring to your authority* by acting in accord with and because of the tempo you set. Or, again, in our shared intention to build a house together my intention that we build might accord you authority to draw up the plans, plans which I intend to follow. I might intend that we build the house together in part by way of *my accepting and so deferring to your authority* to prepare the plans.[44]

I have emphasized that the shared intentions normally involved in SIA involve intentions that the joint activity proceed in part by way of the intentions of each. So, it is part of the intentions of each to adjust to and respond to the intentions of others. Nevertheless, it is one thing to intend that we act in part by way of your analogous intention, another to intend, more specifically, that we act in part by way of acceptance by each of us of your authority to settle certain aspects of our acting together. The interlocking of our intentions that is central to our basic model of shared intention need not involve intentions that involve according and accepting authority. However, in certain cases shared intentions do involve interlocking in which what is intended is that the intentions of each work their way through in part by way of practical thinking that involves such authority acceptance and deference.

We do not need to appeal to such authority acceptance within our general model of shared intention and SIA: the interlocking of intentions, and associated intentions in favor of mesh in subplans, need not involve according of authority. But there are special cases in which the contents of the relevant intentions do involve according authority. These intentions interlock in part by way of favoring a distinctive form of practical thinking on the part of each. What practical thinking is that?

In accepting your authority with respect to certain aspects of our shared activity I am set, at least implicitly, to treat you as having an associated *right*—defeasibly and within our shared activity—to settle practically certain matters. Further, I am set, at least implicitly, to see myself as having a *duty*—defeasibly, and within our shared activity—to defer to your authority-accorded decisions about relevant matters. Perhaps in our quartet I am set to treat the first violinist as having a right to create a duty on my part to follow a certain tempo, and I am set to conform to that induced duty. My practical thinking thereby goes beyond instrumental concerns with our joint performance and at least implicitly involves, as well, this web of according rights and duties within our shared activity. Certain cases of shared intention involve such authority-according interlocking: each intends that the joint activity go in part by way of such accorded-and-accepted-authority-shaped practical thinking on the part of each.

In our basic step from individual planning agency to SIA we highlighted coordination-tracking and broadly instrumental reasoning with respect to social ends such as our playing the quartet together by way of interlocking intentions and meshing subplans. Such reasoning is shaped by plan-rationality norms of consistency, coherence, and stability. But now we are introducing a further structure of practical thinking, one that in addition involves according rights and associated duties within a shared activity. We have the beginnings of structures of deontic practical thinking broadly along the lines classically analyzed by Wesley Hohfeld.[45]

The existence of this further structure of practical thinking would not, however, directly entail that there are *normatively substantive* rights and duties and associated substantive normative reasons. After all, there can be such accorded-authority-structured practical thinking within a morally awful gang, or a group engaged in torture or ethnic cleansing, or a group constituted by severe forms of coercion, or a morally awful practice of slavery. And it is at least not clear that in such cases there are not only—as we can say, broadly following Stephen Darwall—*de facto* but also *de jure* rights and duties.[46] In their shared activity of torture, the group may accord authority to a leader to determine who, when, and where, and thereby accord that leader a kind of *de facto* authority within that shared activity. But that leader may well not have a normatively substantive right to determine that a given prisoner be tortured, and the other participants may not have a normatively substantive duty to act in accordance with the leader's directives. When we look at this social web, we can ask whether a participant has any good normative reason to proceed with the torture; and we may conclude that he does not. Again, we may recognize that the social web in Shirley Jackson's frightening story "The Lottery" (1948) accords some a *de facto* right and duty, within the social practice, to kill by throwing stones, and yet reject the claim of a good normative reason to do that.

Darwall contrasts merely "conventional authority relations" with the existence of *de jure* authority. His central example of the former is the sort of conventional authority relation studied in J. L. Austin's theory of speech acts (Darwall 2006, 3–4, 52–54; Austin 1975). Such Austin-type authority relations are relativized to certain conventions. I am here appealing to a related idea of, as we might say, *merely shared-intentional authority relations*: authority relations that are relativized to a specific authority-according shared intention. There are such relativized shared-intentional authority relations when the involved interlocking intentions favor the joint activity by way of relevant forms of accorded-and-accepted-authority-shaped practical thinking on the part of each. Each intends that the joint activity go by way of the relevant intentions of the other in a way that involves, *inter alia*, practical thinking that is shaped not only by norms of plan rationality but also by accorded, shared-activity-relativized authority, rights, and duties. But one might recognize that such relativized shared-intentional authority relations are in place and still think there is no good normative reason—either a good moral reason or a reason grounded in some other defensible value (e.g., religious, or aesthetic, or epistemic values)—to conform to the decisions of the authority.

1.2.5 The interplay of plan rationality and the interrelatedness of sharing

Our proposed plan-theoretic construction of shared intention draws on the roles of norms of plan rationality—norms of coherence, consistency, and stability—in individual planning agency. These rationality norms have a constitutive role within individual planning agency, though they can on occasion be violated. Our basic model of planning, one within which we say what it is to intend, essentially involves a rational dynamic that tracks conformity to these norms. These norms play a role in the explanation of action, in a planning agent's practical thinking, and in criticism of breakdowns. And (perhaps only implicit) guidance by these rationality norms is a basic element in the distinction between, on the one hand, a merely causal system and, on the other hand, a planning agent.

Two philosophical traditions converge here. There is the functionalist idea—extended to include implicit guidance by rationality norms—that we say what it is to plan/intend by appeal to an overarching theory of functioning that involves a characteristic rational dynamics.[47] And there is the idea, traceable (with adjustments) to Donald Davidson, that in interpreting a system as an intending/planning system we need to understand it as satisfying such rationality norms, plus or minus a bit.[48] Both ideas support the thought that these norms of individual rationality are *non-separable* from these forms of practical organization and temporally extended agency. Further, a central result of our construction of shared intentionality using the building blocks of individual planning agency is that, given conformity within the construction to norms of individual plan rationality, there will tend to be conformity, within such shared intentionality, to analogous norms of *social* rationality—in particular, norms of social consistency and coherence.

This is not yet fully to explain why these norms of individual plan rationality are normatively significant and are not simply common (and perhaps even regrettable) patterns of thought. Why does conformity to these norms matter? I address this question in Bratman 2018a.[49] Here I will take it as given that we can answer it.

Suppose that you and I share an intention to paint the house together. On the plan-theoretic model, we have public, interlocking, and interdependent intentions that we paint by way of each of our intentions that we paint, meshing subplans, and associated mutual responsiveness. This is the characteristic interpersonal interrelatedness in shared intention, an interrelatedness that is missing in our case of two mafia members going to New York. Further, we are each subject to wide-scope rationality constraints (Broome 2013) in support of either opting out of the shared intention or adjusting in response to considerations of painting-related social consistency and social means-end coherence.

There is here an *interplay* of these norms of plan rationality and the interrelatedness involved in sharing: the application of these rationality constraints to each is sensitive to the interlocking, interdependence, and intended mesh involved in sharing an intention.[50] Since what each intends is in part the effectiveness of intentions of the other, by way of mesh in subplans with the other, what rationality demands of the thought and action of each is sensitive to the thought and action of the other.[51] Further, given public interdependence, the constancy of my intention supports the constancy of yours, and vice versa. Since for each of us our reasons for so intending normally involve the presence of the intention of the other, as does the reference within the interlocking intentions of each to the associated intention of the other, this public mutual support can contribute to the rationality of the stability of intentions of each (Alonso 2008, sec. 7.3). And this interplay can also involve responsiveness to authority that is accorded within shared intentions, if such there be.

Suppose that neither of us opts out and our shared intention persists. If, even so, one of us were not appropriately to conform to pressures of social consistency and social means-end coherence, she would thereby be failing to respond to pressures of individual plan rationality. What these pressures on her support will be sensitive to relevant thought and action of others. This does not entail that she has thereby violated an obligation to those others. But we can ask whether it is nevertheless true that some such obligation will in general be present. Would a breakdown on the part of one of us in responding to these rational pressures also be a violation of an obligation to the other?

We noted earlier that in special cases the interdependence built into shared intention is grounded in interactions—such as an exchange of promises or assurances—that induce familiar forms of moral obligation. But our question now is whether there is a quite general connection between shared intention and mutual obligation.[52]

There are two potential claims here. One is that certain mutual obligations suffice for shared intention. The second is that shared intention quite generally involves mutual obligations. Here I focus on the second idea.[53]

The idea of obligation that is relevant here is that of an obligation that has substantive normative force.[54] To support a necessary connection between shared intention and such a normatively substantive obligation we would need to go beyond norms of plan rationality and appeal to a further, normatively substantive premise, one that would support the cited substantive obligations of each to each. And this further normative premise would itself need to be defended in substantive normative theorizing.

What normative premise? Any answer would need to confront hard cases (Bratman 2014a, 110–13). An initial point is that there can be shared activity that is trivial and short-lived, as when we spontaneously walk together briefly. Sarah Paul (2021, 150) provides another example: "In a nightclub, perhaps, one person might dance up to another and dance together with them for a period of time, and then dance away again without fanfare." It seems at best strained to suppose that obligations distinctive of shared intention are incurred in such cases.

In other cases, there are rich threads of shared intention, but other conditions potentially defeat supposed obligations. Perhaps the shared activity is morally awful, as when we together engage in torture. Or consider the shared stone throwing in "The Lottery," or the shared activity of "particicution" in Margaret Atwood's *The Handmaid's Tale* (1986). What if the participation of some in the shared intention is coerced by others in that activity (think about the shared building of the bridge on the river Kwai) (Bratman, 2014, 102, 111)? What if the participation of some in a shared intention arises from significant deception or manipulation (Gorin 2014) by other participants? What if each has been reading Ayn Rand and, though all participate in the sort of shared intention I have described, each insists: "But, no obligations." In such cases there is shared intention and associated rational pressure on each participant with respect to relevant conditions of social rationality. But in each case, it is unclear whether each has a normatively substantive obligation—either a moral obligation or some other form of normatively substantive obligation grounded in a defensible value—to the other to act in accordance with the shared intention. In each case other aspects of the sharing seem potentially to block supposed obligations. So, we cannot quite generally simply reason directly from the existence of shared intention to associated mutual obligations. Instead, in each case we need, further, a relevant, defensible, substantive norm; and in certain cases, such a defensible norm may not be available.

This issue remains even for the special cases of authority-according shared intention. After all, there might be such authority-according shared intentions among torturers, or participants in the shared activity of stoning someone to death in "The Lottery." Such authority-according shared intentions do induce wide-scope rational pressure on participants either to defer to accorded authority or to withdraw from the shared intention. But the applicability of these norms of plan rationality to authority-according shared intention does not yet ensure a web of normatively significant, substantive obligations, of each to the others, to defer. Here again, to get to such obligations we need a relevant, defensible, substantive norm; and such a norm may not be in the offing.

The next point is that in many cases of SIA what does the core explanatory work are the cited interconnected, rationally guided planning structures. In the case of our string quartet, for example, these interconnected planning structures include each intending the joint activity of quartet playing, interlocking and interdependence of these intentions, and intentions in favor of mesh in subplans and associated mutual responsiveness, all of which is more or less out in the open. And in many cases the proper functioning of these public plan-theoretic structures, taken together with great skill, suffices for the coordination and responsiveness and accommodation that are characteristic of playing the quartet together in a shared intentional way. I sync my viola part with your playing of your cello part because I intend that there be mesh in our joint activity (as do you), relevant matters are out in the open, and I am implicitly guided by norms of plan rationality. Given the explanatory role of our public shared intention in favor of this end—where this involves interdependent and interlocking intentions of each, intended mesh in subplans and associated mutual responsiveness—we are not using each other as a mere tool[55] (though each does see the activity of the other as a means to the shared end). We are acting together in ways that involve intelligent mutual responsiveness in the service of our shared end.

When I listen to a good string quartet playing Mozart I am struck with the extraordinary interpersonal coordination and responsiveness. And it seems that in many cases the cited structures of interconnected intentions and plans, taken together with extraordinary skills, suffice to explain this (at the relevant level of explanation). The sufficiency of these explanatory conditions for these forms of organization does not depend on the presence of the cited obligations, even if such there be. Nor need it depend on beliefs about such obligations. Fans of Ayn Rand can play together in a quartet even while eschewing obligations to each other. They need to be mutually responsive in the pursuit of their shared end; but such interpersonal mutual responsiveness need not involve judgments about obligations of each to each, though it may.

So, on the one hand, the explanatory social mechanisms directly underlying such cases of acting together involve structures of interconnected intentions and plans but need not in general involve structures of (supposed) interpersonal obligation even if such there be. On the other hand, when we try to say what interpersonal obligations sometimes enter into our acting together, we need to appeal to further normative premises that are themselves in need of normative defense; and so, we need to sort out hard questions in normative philosophy. And my proposal is that in pursuit of a model of shared agency that can support wide-ranging research in philosophy and the social sciences, we draw directly on our planning model as basic, while leaving room for further research on various ways in which these interrelated planning structures, and their common concomitants, can engage, or be thought to engage, potentially defensible norms of obligation—where those obligations, when present, may further support the functioning characteristic of shared intention.

Granted, such mutual obligations are common within our human shared activity and in many cases support the ongoing shared activity, including the involved interdependence. There are broadly moral pressures to be helpful and courteous. Further, in many cases, there will be moral obligations grounded in specific forms of interaction. In many cases the etiology of a shared intention will involve forms of assurance, intentionally induced reliance, and the like that normally engage associated moral obligations (Alonso 2009). This is one way (though it is not Gilbert's way) of understanding Gilbert's appeals to "expressions of readiness" to participate in the shared activity (Gilbert 2008, 11; 2009, 180). And in many cases the formation of a shared intention will lead to downstream forms of associated obligation-inducing assurance or intentionally induced reliance. Further, other norms of moral obligation may be engaged in specific cases. Laura Valentini, for example, proposes "a pro tanto obligation to respect people's genuine commitments . . . provided those commitments are morally permissible" (Valentini 2021, sec. 4). Again, in some cases a shared intention may engage specific obligations of, for example, friendship or collegiality. And other kinds of moral elements may be engaged in certain cases—for example, a moral permission to favor one's partners in an SIA (Stroud 2010).

This is a rich stew of common forms of substantive obligation and the like. In each case, however, we do not simply and directly infer from the existence of shared agency that there are these obligations. Instead, to support an inference to such obligations we appeal to further, substantive norms, norms that in turn require defense in normative reflection. Such substantive norms play major roles in our shared agency. But to defend relevant claims about obligation we need to appeal to and to defend some such further norms. We should not suppose that we can simply and directly infer from the existence of shared agency that there are these obligations.

So, within our theory there is a contrast between the status of norms of plan rationality and the status of norms of interpersonal obligation.[56] Norms of plan rationality are an essential element within our model of our individual planning agency, and thereby within our model of shared agency. And in cases of shared intention, what is rationally demanded of each is sensitive to the interlocking, interdependence, and intended mesh involved in sharing an intention. But this interplay of plan rationality and the interpersonal interrelations involved in shared intention does not by itself entail interpersonal obligation. The ground for such interpersonal obligations, when such there be, will involve norms of interpersonal obligation that, while central to our social lives and to the successful functioning of much shared activity, are separable from the basic structure of our shared intentionality and need further defense.

We have, then, our planning theory of shared intention and SIA. And our question is whether we can bring these resources to bear within a construction of human organized institutions.[57]

2 ON THE WAY TO ORGANIZED INSTITUTIONS: SOCIAL RULES

2.1 Modesty, modularity, and rule-guided infrastructure

Return to our first question about shared intention and human organized institutions:

(A) Can our planning theory of shared intention and SIA play a basic role in an illuminating model of the social functioning characteristic of such organized institutions?

Will the structures of thought and action highlighted by the planning theory of shared intention play a basic role in a theoretically fruitful model of our organized-institutional functioning?

Here we need to keep track of the modest and modular place of shared intention in human organized institutions. Within our organized institutions we are to some extent thinking and acting together. But the functioning of those organized institutions will not in general be a form of shared intentional activity on the part of all participants. I seek to understand human organized institutions in a way that does justice to both these ideas.

And, as indicated, I think we can make progress by bringing our plan-theoretic framework together with Hart's insights concerning the roles of social rules in the rule-guided infrastructure of, in particular, law.[1] I think we can see Hart's theory of law as having something like the modest and modular structure for which we are looking—namely, implicit appeal to a form of shared intentionality in its model of relevant social rules; a broadly individualistic construction of such shared intentionality; and a modest and modular role of that social-rule-constituting shared intentionality in the rule-guided infrastructure of the institution. So, let's turn first to Hart.

2.2 Hart on social rules, criticisms and demands, and rule content

Hart asks, "What *are* rules?" (2012, 8). This leads him to reflect on the social realization of rules, and thereby on *social rules*. Hart then goes on to ask how to understand the transition from a pre-legal world of social rules to the existence of a legal system. Here his strategy is to appeal to social rules with distinctive contents. So, he needs an understanding of social rules prior to legality such that when we give such social rules appropriate contents, we are on our way to legality. This strategy can allow that there are multiple phenomena that might aptly be labeled social rules; what it needs is to articulate a kind of social rule that will fit into its strategy for understanding the transition from pre-legal to legal.

Hart's strategy for understanding this transition involves his distinction between primary and secondary rules—especially a secondary rule of recognition (2012, chap. V). A primary rule specifies what to do in a given circumstance. Secondary rules "confer powers" (81) to ascertain or to shape what the valid primary rules are or how they bear on given cases—they "specify the ways in which the primary rules may be conclusively ascertained, introduced, eliminated, varied, and the fact of their violation conclusively determined" (94). The appeal is to a system of rules within which certain secondary rules, taken together with other conditions, can shape what other rules are (or are "ascertained" to be) elements in this rule-system and are, in this sense, *valid* rules.[2]

I'll return in Part II to the neighborhood of such secondary rules. But first we need to focus on primary social rules. What are they?

In one sense, rules are abstract objects.[3] But, Hart's distinctive focus is on social rules that are actual social phenomena: social rules that are social not just in their content but also in their realization in the interpersonal causal order. This is indicated by his transition from his initial questions "What *are* rules? What does it mean to say that a rule *exists*?" (8)—questions that might be seen as targeting abstract object rules—to the question "What is the acceptance of a rule?" (55)—a question about social psychology. The idea, I take it, is to look at actual social regularities, some of which, given certain further features, help constitute a socially realized rule with an abstract object rule as, as I will say, their *rule content*.[4]

To take an example from Hart (9): a complex web of social phenomena might have the rule content (roughly): *remove your hat when in church.* A challenge for a theory of social rules is to explain both what these further features of a social regularity are such that there is indeed a social rule and, further, what it is about this social phenomenon that gives it a certain rule content. This latter is the *problem of social rule content.*

The content of a social rule specifies both a mode of thought and action and a *range* of those to whom it applies. A rule enjoining taking off your hat in church has as its range: whoever enters a church. A rule enjoining wearing a yarmulke in a synagogue has as its range: those who enter a synagogue. A rule enjoining a majority vote procedure for settling certain issues for a group has as its range: those in the group facing these issues. The content of the rule favors certain modes of acting and thinking by those in its range. A solution to the problem of social rule content needs to explain why its content specifies a given mode of thought or action, and why it specifies a given range.

Now, some social regularities are mere regularities rather than elements in a social rule, as when, in Hart's example, most have tea at breakfast (2012, 9). But some social regularities are explained by a distinctive kind of social guidance, as when graduate students ask the first questions at colloquia, or the winning team stays on the court in a series of pickup basketball games at a gym, or most stop at red lights, or most wear masks in public during the pandemic or a yarmulke in synagogue or a tie at a business meeting. Hart's thought is that in these cases the social regularity is in part explained by the "internal aspect of rules" for which

> what is necessary is that there should be a critical reflective attitude to certain patterns of behavior as a common standard, and that this should display itself in criticism (including self-criticism), demands for conformity, and in acknowledgements that such criticism and demands are justified.[5]

A key to such social rules is the role of this distinctive form of practical thinking on the part of individuals. This practical thinking involves a "critical reflective attitude" that sees the regularity as a common standard that is to be followed by each, and so is set to criticize violations of this standard and demand conformity to this standard. Individuals take an "internal" point of view toward the standard, in contrast with an "external" point of view that might be taken by a detached observer of the behavioral regularities (88–89). Such an internal point of view involves

> the standing disposition of individuals to take such patterns of conduct both as guides to their own future conduct and as standards of criticism which may legitimate demands and various forms of pressure for conformity. (255)

So, an understanding of such Hart-type social rules will involve an understanding of these modes of criticism and demand.[6]

Further, Hart's thought is that this stance of many toward this general standard (where these stances of each are interrelated in ways to be articulated) partly constitutes the fact that the relevant rule *content* of this complex social phenomenon is given by that standard. This is, in outline, Hart's implicit solution to the problem of social rule content.[7]

Such a stance toward a general standard specifies modes of acting and thinking—but how does it specify the range of the social rule? Hart's appeal to "a general standard to be followed by the group as a whole" (2012, 56) suggests that a specification of this "group as a whole" is at least implicit in the relevant attitudes of relevant individuals, and that this specifies the range of the "common standard." I return to this issue about range in Section 4.1.8.

An implication of this approach to social rule content is that our understanding of that content is grounded in our understanding of the relevant attitudes of individuals, attitudes whose roles help make it true that there is indeed a social rule. In this respect, Hart's implicit solution to the problem of social rule content is broadly individualistic. And a virtue of this solution is that it makes manifest the explanatory significance of social rule content: it is tied to content-possessing attitudes of participants that help explain relevant social activity.[8]

This allows, as it should, that the contents of the individuals' relevant attitudes are normally shaped by broad social influences, including various forms of communication, teaching, and education (Dewey 1916; Tomasello 2014, 80–81). And these contents may draw on broad ideas from the person's culture—for example, ideas about race or gender (Haslanger 2018). Nevertheless, the content of the social rule is grounded in the contents of attitudes of relevant individuals, and the existence of the social rule with that content depends on relevant individual attitudes with relevant contents. Further, though this is to go beyond Hart's reflections, we can allow for impacts, on contents of attitudes of individuals, of the causal context of the use of certain names or natural kind terms (Putnam 1975) and of relevant linguistic practices of the linguistic community (Burge 1979).[9] Finally, this Hart-inspired solution to the problem of social rule content can allow that the contents of relevant attitudes of individuals can themselves be partly constrained by relevant facts about actual social regularities of action. Indeed, I will be highlighting such constraints in Section 4.1.3. Nevertheless, a key to the determination of social rule content lies in the contents of interrelated attitudes of relevant individuals.

Hart begins with social behavioral regularities and asks what else is involved in a social rule. So, the kind of social rule he is tracking involves, in part, the behavioral regularity. This is why he calls his theory a "practice theory" (255). Granted, there are related phenomena that might be described as social norms or social rules even though there is widespread non-conformity (Brennan et al. 2013, 20–21). But this need not be an objection to Hart. His concern is to characterize a kind of social rule that will work for his strategy of moving from the pre-legal to the legal. The thought is that this involves secondary social rules for which such a practice theory of social rules is apt.

The social regularities of action involved in Hart-type social rules need not involve strict, universal conformity: they may only involve a (vaguely specified) sufficiently general conformity to a pattern, R. But the *content* of the relevant social rule will abstract from this complexity and be simply: *those in this "group as a whole" are to conform to R*. The content of the social rule is, for example, those in this group are to wear masks, while the relevant social regularity is one in which there is sufficiently general conformity to this content.

In a Hart-type social rule, the relevant regularity is supported by a common standard. This idea of a common standard involves three subideas. First, the standard is *accepted by most or all* the relevant participants.[10] Second, the standard that is accepted by each *prescribes* not merely for the one who accepts it but also for each of those in the relevant *group*: it is a "standard to be followed by the group as a whole" (56). And third, the fact that most accept the standard is *out in the open*: it is a "public, common standard" (116). This leaves it open whether the commonness of the standard involves yet further interrelations between the acceptances by individuals of the standard. So, I will say that the relevant commonness of a standard involves a kind of *interpersonal web* that includes, but may go beyond, such an out-in-the-open condition.

A fourth point emerges in Hart's addition, in his response to Dworkin in the "Postscript" to *The Concept of Law*, of the idea that "rules are conventional social practices [of the sort central to law] if the general conformity of a group to them is part of the reason which its individual members have for acceptance." As Hart highlights, this is a way in which social rules of the relevant sort are not merely a matter of "a consensus of independent *conviction*."[11]

A worry here is that if the social practice is extremely bad then that general conformity may not be part of a *normative* reason for acceptance. General conformity to the stone-throwing practice in "The Lottery" may not provide a normative reason that pro tanto justifies the acceptance of that practice.[12]

I take it that Hart's response would be that he is talking about *motivating* reasons that may or may not correspond to *normative* reasons. But I take it, further, that Hart wants to point not just to some sort of causal-psychological backing of the acceptance of the practice but also to some sort of normative relation between the general conformity and the acceptance of the practice. So, I propose to take the liberty of interpreting Hart as saying that there is a *rational dependence* of the acceptance of the standard on the general conformity—where we leave room for the possibility of such rational dependence whether or not the conformity provides substantive normative reason for the acceptance, and we leave it as an issue for our theory how exactly to understand this rational dependence.[13]

In developing Hart's view in this way, I am drawing on a distinction between norms of *rationality* and substantive *normative reasons*. In a version of Bernard Williams's example (1981), one's intention to drink gin and belief that what is in the glass is gin rationally cohere with intending to drink what is in the glass. But if one's belief is false and what is in the glass is petrol, one may have no good, normative reason to drink what is in the glass.[14] I will here assume that some version of this distinction survives scrutiny, and I will draw on it in exploring central issues about human practical organization.

This appeal to a dependency of the acceptances of each on the general behavioral conformity is not yet an appeal to a dependency relation between the acceptances themselves. So, there are here two potential kinds of dependency. There is Hart's appeal, as I am understanding it, to a rational dependency of the acceptances of the standard on the general behavioral conformity. And there is a potential dependency of each participant's acceptance of the standard on others' acceptances of the standard, as a possible further aspect of the social web of acceptances involved in a social rule.

Drawing these threads together, I propose to interpret Hart as pointing to four interrelated conditions that will be satisfied by social rules of the relevant sort:

(a) a *public social pattern* of action, the full explanation of which involves
(b) *endorsement* by participants of that pattern as a *common standard* that prescribes for the group as a whole, where those endorsements are embedded in a public social web, and where
(c) these embedded endorsements of the pattern support characteristic interpersonal *criticisms, demands, and guidance* of action; and
(d) there is a *rational dependence* of the endorsements in (b) on the general conformity in (a).[15]

Further, Hart's proposal is that the standard in (b) that is endorsed by participants helps provide the *rule content* of the social rule. I will call (a)–(d), so understood, *Hart's social rule schema*.

In what sense do the embedded endorsements in (b) support the interpersonal criticisms and demands in (c)? There are two ideas here. We can get at the first idea by drawing on what Nicholas Southwood calls "minimal normativity": "[a] phenomenon is minimally normative inasmuch as it involves *rules* or *requirements* that permit, forbid, and require certain actions and attitudes" (2019, 35). And one idea within this Hart-inspired schema is that the relevant support of criticisms and demands goes by way of an endorsed common standard that can be expressed as "*rules* or *requirements* that permit, forbid, and require certain actions and attitudes." A second idea is that the criticisms and demands in which these rules or requirements issue are seen by participants as (at least prima facie) justified. As Hart says, "Not only is such criticism in fact made but deviation from the standard is generally accepted as a *good reason* for making it" (55), and there are "acknowledgements that such criticism and demands are justified" (57).

Now, Hart would acknowledge that there can be social rules that favor bad things and for that reason are such that criticism of divergence from the rules would not be on balance justified. After all, a group of torturers might have a social rule that specifies who and how. But we can ask whether, nevertheless, the existence of a social rule that realizes Hart's schema ensures some sort of minimal grounds for relevant criticisms. I return to this question in Section 3.4.

2.3 Dual design specifications

The conjecture is that Hart's schema points to a kind of social rule that is central to a wide range of rule-guided institutional infrastructures. Since the social rules at the heart of the rule-guided infrastructure of an actual, up-and-running organized institution will normally involve actual, sufficiently general behavioral regularities, it is reasonable to include condition (a) in this schema. But how should we understand conditions (b)–(d)?

We might see these conditions as directly postulating a basic attitude of acceptance of a pattern as a common standard. Indeed, Hart talks of "a distinctive normative attitude to such patterns of conduct which I have called 'acceptance'" (255). But a second way to see Hart's social rule schema is as articulating a *design specification* that an attitude needs to realize if it is to help constitute a social rule. We then ask what attitude does that: what social psychological phenomenon realizes this design specification?

I will proceed in this second way. I seek to articulate, by way of an underlying model of the social psychology of human agents, a social psychological phenomenon that realizes this design specification. I seek thereby to embed Hart-type social rules organically within a theory of human action whose main elements are theoretically motivated by our prior efforts to understand human temporally extended agency—namely, the planning theory. I aim to construct a realization of such a design specification that uses as its basic building blocks the elements already at work in our human temporally extended planning agency.

Proceeding in this way, we have in effect two interrelated design specifications. There is, first, the idea of a social psychological structure that guides action, and helps explain the regularity in (a), in part by favoring a common standard for the group as a whole and thereby supporting relevant demands and criticisms, where that social psychological structure is itself rationally dependent on the regularity in (a). Call this the *basic social rule design specification*. Second, there is the idea of a social psychological structure that underlies the rule-guidance characteristic of a wide range of human organized institutions. Call this the *institutional-role design specification*.

A guiding thought is that the social functioning that realizes the basic social rule design specification will continue to be involved in the functioning at issue in the institutional-role design specification. And the idea is that the step to the rule-guided infrastructure of an organized institution involves distinctive versions of such social rules.

The basic social rule design specification involves both an underlying social psychology and an associated pattern of behavior. The pattern of behavior is to some extent explained by the social psychology in (b) and (c), and that social psychology is to some extent dependent on that pattern of behavior. Further, we can see conditions (b) and (c), understood in a way that does not itself entail (a),[16] as together articulating what Hart would call the "internal aspect" (56) of this basic social rule design specification.

A Hart-inspired conjecture is that there is a social psychological structure that, in our human lives, realizes the first design specification in a way that plays a major role in realizing the second design specification. Our question is, what social psychological structure is that? And our answer seeks a model of the realization of the basic social rule design specification that enables us to develop an associated model of the realization of the institutional role design specification.

This allows that there may be other kinds of social rules that do not play the most basic roles in the rule-guided infrastructure of organized institutions. Further, our aim is to provide, within relevant constraints, appropriate *sufficient* conditions for the functioning specified in these dual design specifications; and in doing this we can allow for the possibility of multiple realizability of this pair of design specifications. The question before us is whether, given these qualifications, we can articulate coordinated realizations of these two design specifications. And my conjecture will be that we can do this by appeal to structures of shared policies.

3 A SHARED POLICY MODEL OF SOCIAL RULES, PART 1

3.1 Together organizing how we live with each other

Hart's idea is that in a social rule of the relevant sort, many accept a common standard that prescribes for "the group as a whole" (2012, 56). And this acceptance of a standard for "the group as a whole" supports relevant criticisms and demands. Each does not simply personally intend to act in certain ways given expectations about the activity of others, activity of others that each might even want to thwart if they could. Instead, each has attitudes that prescribe what those in the group, including oneself, are to do. And this accepted standard supports interpersonal criticisms and demands.

This contrasts with cases of strategic equilibrium in which it is public that each personally intends to act in a certain way given her expectations concerning others. Perhaps it is public that each intends to stop at red lights given her belief that others will. Each expects the others so to act but does not prescribe that they so act. So, while such strategic equilibria are important, we do not yet have the kind of prescription for "the group as a whole" that Hart highlights.[1]

What is involved in a Hart-type social rule that goes beyond such a strategic equilibrium and involves acceptance of a standard for "the group as a whole"? An initial thought is that there is an illuminating parallel between, on the one hand, Hart's distinction between a mere social regularity and a social rule and, on the other hand, the contrast we have studied between simply walking alongside each other and walking together as a shared intentional activity. When we walk together on the basis of our shared intention, we each are set to reason, and to reason together, with an eye on our shared end rather than merely strategically in pursuit of personal ends given what the other is doing. And the thought is that the contrast between mere social behavioral regularities and social rules involves a somewhat analogous idea: social rules of the sort of interest involve a kind of sharing that is like that involved in shared intention.[2] And this points to the project of constructing coordinated realizations of our Hart-inspired dual design specifications for social rules by appeal to structures of shared intention.[3]

If you and I are just walking alongside each other, each of us just intends to walk in a certain way given that the other is walking in a certain way. But we might shift gears and begin to walk *together*, where this involves a shared intention within which we together organize our walking with each other. Analogously, we might add to our public pattern of personal intentions (e.g., in favor of mask-wearing) the condition that we *together* organize this aspect of our sociality. And the thought is that we would thereby move in the direction of a Hart-type social rule.

The idea would be to appeal to shared intentions/policies that we conform to the relevant regularity.[4] We see Hart-type social rules as involving forms of shared intention that are roughly continuous with those that are characteristic of small-scale cases of acting together. And this potentially supports our overall strategy of sequential plan-theoretical construction of the rule-guided infrastructure of organized institutions.

That said, the idea that an X-favoring social rule within a given population involves a shared policy in the population in favor of X—where that sharing is among all and involves the highlighted forms of interlocking, interdependence, and intended mesh—seems too strong to apply to many cases of more or less disparate, disconnected, and fractured populations. So, if we are to be guided by this idea, there will be a lot of work to do. But that will be my philosophical experiment.

Begin with two preliminary issues. First, we can ask whether the highlighted phenomena of criticizing/demanding—in contrast with mere adverse reaction—essentially involve modes of thought that go beyond those involved in shared intention. And my answer is no. On our theory, shared intentions are plan-theoretic constructions; planning involves guidance by rationality norms; guidance by such norms potentially involves thoughts along the lines of "that was a mistake"; and such thoughts are incipient forms of criticism and, perhaps, demand. So, structures of shared intention are poised to play roles in criticisms and demands characteristic of social rules.[5]

A second concern is that the demands and criticisms to which Hart appeals normally involve, for adult human agents like us, language-infused speech acts. As Hart says: "For the expression of such criticisms, demands, and acknowledgements a wide range of 'normative' language is used" (2012, 57). Granted, there are in our human lives forms of non-linguistic demand and criticism. As Barry Maguire has emphasized, we sometimes signal demands and criticisms in our manner of acting rather than linguistically. Perhaps I stare at your face in a way that is understood by both of us as signaling a criticism for not wearing a mask in the pandemic. Nevertheless, Hart seems right in thinking that in our human world as we know it, social-rule-based criticisms and demands characteristically involve language-infused speech acts. Since planning and shared intentionality need not involve language, it may seem that appeal to structures of shared intention will not suffice to realize our design specifications for social rules.

My response is that, while I have allowed that planning and shared intentionality need not involve language, I have also emphasized that the forms of human planning and shared intentionality that will be front and center for our investigation of human organized institutions will be language infused. What we have just noted is that this will be especially apt for our efforts to understand Hart-type social rules by appeal to shared intention.[6]

So, our question is whether, given these observations about criticism/demand and about language, we can articulate shared-intention-infused social psychological phenomena that realize, in a coordinated and illuminating way, the dual design specifications for social rules. In this chapter I sketch an initial effort to do this—an initial shared policy model of social rules. I then turn in Chapter 4 to a series of adjustments.

3.2 Double reflexivity, vagueness, and non-agglomeration

We begin with the initial conjecture that the internal aspect of our social rule in favor of our conformity to social pattern R is realized by our shared policy in favor of our R-type social pattern of action—for example, in favor of our stopping at red lights, or our wearing masks in public or a yarmulke in a synagogue, or our forming a queue at a bus stop, or our using a specific voting procedure. Such a shared policy consists in public, interdependent, and interlocking policies of each in favor of our conformity to this R-type social pattern by way of subplans that mesh.

The initial understanding of our conforming to R that is at work here is that of a distributed pattern of relevant, individual intentional activity of each. It is not that of a shared intentional activity of conformity to R (though there are cases in which there is such shared intentional activity). So, a preliminary statement of the content of the relevant policies is that we distributively conform to R. But we need to reflect further on these policies.

Our shared policy in favor of our conforming to R involves my policy/general intention in favor of our conformity to R. This intention is *doubly reflexive*: it involves my intention *to* conform, and it involves my intention that *we* (where that includes *me*) conform. However, as noted in Section 1.2.3, in larger groups the intentions of each that we conform to R may involve vagueness about the extent of conformity of others. In contrast, there is not an analogous vagueness about the singular, first-personal reflexive aspect: in intending that we conform to R each intends *her own* conformity.

The cited vagueness about the extent of conformity of others allows that each can, without intention-belief inconsistency, have a relevant policy in favor of conformity to the R-type pattern of action even while believing that (as will normally be the case) there will not be universal conformity to R. So, we can say that my relevant intention that we conform to R is doubly reflexive but involves potential vagueness with respect to the extent of sufficiently general conformity by others, though not with respect to myself. And this sufficiently general conformity by others is itself intended, not just an expected condition given which I intend to conform.

My doubly reflexive intention/policy in favor of our sufficiently general conformity to R is, as noted, consistent with my belief that there will not in fact be universal conformity. It would be inconsistent with a belief that there will not even be sufficiently general conformity. But we are supposing that if there is a social rule there is in fact a relevant, public social pattern of action. So, in the context of such a social rule, participants will not believe there is not sufficiently general conformity, though they may believe that there is not universal conformity.

Suppose that I doubly reflexively intend our sufficiently general conformity to R. I intend to conform. But it does not follow that I intend the conformity *of each* of the others. So, it is not clear that my intention prescribes for each of the folks in the targeted group in the way in which a social rule would. My intention prescribes that enough of us conform; but that could happen without your conformity. So, it is not clear that the prescriptive force of my intention reaches directly to you.[7]

My response is to add that I intend not only the sufficiently general conformity but also that *each* conforms—where my reference to each can go by way of relevant general concepts (e.g., is a club member). We say that I *doubly reflexively intend the conformity of each, as elements in our (perhaps vaguely specified) sufficiently general conformity*. Rationally so to intend, I do not need to believe of each that she will conform; though I do need, with respect to each of those included within the scope of what I intend, not to believe that she will not conform.[8]

This involves rejecting a strict rational demand for agglomeration of intention, since we are supposing that I might rationally intend the conformity of each, and yet not intend universal conformity. In this respect the situation is analogous to that of a large lottery in which I believe of each ticket that it will lose and yet do not believe that every ticket will lose.

There are different views about such lottery beliefs, and I will not try to sort this out here. What we have seen is that analogous issues arise concerning intention in large-scale cases of shared intention. Indeed, these issues arise even before we turn to shared intention. It seems that I might rationally intend each element in my large, extended, complex plan but not, strictly speaking, intend the overall conjunction.[9] So, in allowing a breakdown in agglomeration in such large-scale cases with respect to our intentions that each of us conform to the relevant regularity, we are not introducing a basic discontinuity with intentions that are at the heart of our individual temporally extended planning agency. Having noted these issues, I propose to work with the idea that the normal rational pressure of agglomeration on intention is potentially weakened in certain kinds of large-scale cases and to proceed with a model that rejects a strict rational demand for intention agglomeration in certain large-scale multipersonal cases.

What about my attitude to someone about whom I am fully confident that she will not conform, even given my intention? About her, I am not in a position, without violating the norm of intention-belief consistency, to intend that she conform. So, my rational, doubly reflexive intention that each conform as an element in our sufficiently general conformity will not extend to her. I can nevertheless *aim* at her conformity;[10] and I can think that—perhaps because of the sufficiently general conformity (as in our stopping at red lights)—she *ought* to conform. Indeed, it may also be possible for me—perhaps together with others who also intend the sufficiently general conformity—to take steps (e.g., putting certain incentives in place) that increase the chances that she will conform. Such steps would thereby potentially increase the scope of what I can rationally intend. I return to this idea in Section 4.1.4.

I propose, then, that in participating in the shared policy that is central to our social rule in favor of R, I *doubly reflexively intend the conformity of each as elements in our (perhaps vaguely specified) sufficiently general conformity to social pattern R*. This is the core of my relevant attitude of intending our conformity to R—the intention-attitude of mine that helps constitute my participation in the shared policy that, on the theory to be developed, is central to the social rule in favor of R.[11] Since my intention in favor of our conformity is doubly reflexive, I intend to conform. Since it prescribes that each conform, it can help constitute a social rule that is addressed to each. But since (given that we have eschewed a strict agglomeration demand) it need not involve an intention in favor of universal conformity, it is not rationally threatened, given a norm of intention-belief consistency, by a belief that there will not be such universal conformity. So, it is poised to function as a policy on the part of each that helps constitute a social rule in favor of R.

Our plan-theoretic construction will, then, draw on such doubly reflexive intentions/policies of each in favor of the conformity of each as elements in the sufficiently general social conformity. These policies of each, when appropriately public, interdependent, interlocking, and mesh-supporting, will help constitute an associated *shared policy* in favor of the conformity of each as elements in the sufficiently general conformity to social pattern R. Since this shared policy would be constituted in part by such doubly reflexive intentions/policies of each, we can say that this shared policy is itself, in this derivative sense, doubly reflexive.[12]

Such doubly reflexive shared policies ensure out-in-the-open endorsement of, and prescription in favor of, both sufficiently general conformity and conformity on the part of each. They involve interlocking of the relevant policies of each, intended mesh in subplans, and (perhaps indirect) persistence interdependence, other things equal, between those policies of each.[13] These public interrelations constitute a social web. In these ways such doubly reflexive shared policies promise to realize the design specification in (b) in Hart's social rule schema—public-web-embedded endorsement by participants of a common standard that prescribes for the group as a whole. And given that the underlying policies of each involve both singular and plural reflexivity, they promise to realize the role of (b) in explaining (a).

Is this appeal to doubly reflexive shared policies too demanding on the minds of participants? This returns us to our discussion in Section 1.2.2 of the analogous issue concerning shared intention. I there noted that my model of shared intention (i) allows for tacit/implicit contents; (ii) allows that shared intentions can frame the operation of relevant subpersonal processes, specifications of which need not enter into contents of relevant intentions; (iii) allows that less demanding mechanisms might mimic the operation of shared intention; but (iv) given the overall theoretical target of rule-guided organized institutions, nevertheless highlights shared intentions that involve a framework of intentions with relevant, perhaps-implicit contents. And we can extend these points in defense of our initial shared policy model social rules. In particular, the public nature of the social rules central to organized institutions provides support for an analogue of (iv) concerning the role of shared policies in social rules.

We need now to turn to two interrelated issues. First, why should we appeal in our model of social rules to *shared* policies? Why go beyond appeal to public policies of each in favor of the general conformity and appeal to further conditions of sharing—conditions of interlocking, intended mesh, and interdependence? Second, how does this approach understand the elements of criticism and demand, and associated roles of "'normative' language"? I begin with the first issue.

3.3 *Shared* policies?

I have justified an appeal to policies that *we* conform—in contrast simply with policies personally to conform given that others do—by appeal to the idea that the internal aspect of a social rule prescribes for *us*. But, even taking this point on board, why should our model of social rules go on to appeal to the interdependence and interlocking and intended mesh that are characteristically involved in *shared* policies?

Well, in the absence of at least some form of interdependence across the attitudes of each it would not be clear that these attitudes are, strictly speaking, *intentions* in favor of our conformity. It would not be clear that each can see her attitude as impacting downstream action in a way needed for her to see it as an intention (Bratman 1999c). But this does not explain why such interdependence—and, further, interlocking and intended mesh—is needed for social rules; it only explains why in the absence of these interrelations the relevant attitudes of each may not be, strictly speaking, intentions. So, we need directly to ask: why should our plan-theoretic model of social rules appeal to these interrelations?

My answer highlights two aspects of the interplay between plan rationality and the interrelatedness of shared intention. I'll consider the first of these in this section, and the second in Section 3.4.

The first point is that properly functioning social rules that are central to rule-governed organized institutions will normally involve a kind of social rationality. And our appeal to *shared* policies in our model of social rules helps explain this.

To see this, return first to our construction of small-scale shared intention. Recall that the individually rational functioning of the relevant attitudes of each in the shared intention, given their distinctive contents and interrelations, normally induces satisfaction of corresponding forms of social rationality—in particular, forms of social consistency and social means-end coherence. This social rationality emerges from relevant individual rationality given appropriate individual attitudes, contents, and interrelations. This is in part because the intentions of each are—given their interlocking, intended mesh, and interdependence—coordinated with, supportive of, responsive to, and supported by the overall web of intentions of each. So, for example, my intention that we paint in part by way of your intention that we paint induces, by way of a norm of means-end coherence on my intention, rational pressure on me to support the role of your intention in our painting, and thereby to support social means-end coherence with respect to our shared intention. This pressure on me to support you comes in part from the interlocking of my intention with yours, since what I intend includes the role of your intention in our painting. (As noted, this contrasts with a mafia case in which neither intends that the joint activity go by way of the intention of the other.) And this interlocking interacts with the interdependence: given interdependence, the constancy of my intention tends to support the constancy of yours; and given interlocking, I intend that that intention of yours play its role in our activity.

And now the point is that in appealing, within our model of social rules, to shared policies in favor of our conforming to R we provide a basis for an analogous connection between individual and social rationality. Our shared policy of conforming to R involves not just publicness but also interlocking, intended mesh, and interdependence. This is not, so to speak, a policy-level mafia case: the policies of each favor, and are at least indirectly dependent on, the proper functioning of the policies of each.

So, the rational functioning of the policies of each involves supporting the interpersonal web of policies of each. A breakdown in the role of the policy of someone will tend also to be a breakdown in the role of relevant policies of others since the latter policies interlock with the former policy. As a result, given the sharing, what will tend to emerge from the *individual rationality* of the functioning of the policies of *each* will be a *social rationality* of the overall web of intentions, where that will involve forms of social consistency and means-end coherence. This *emergence of social rationality* is supported in part by the cited interconnections and dependencies across the policies of each: these interconnections and dependencies support relevant, rationally induced cross-policy responsiveness in a way that would not be ensured just by a condition that policies of each, in favor of our conforming to R, are out in the open. This is a manifestation, at the level of social rules, of the interplay of plan rationality with the interrelations involved in sharing.

So, these shared policies, together with the satisfaction of norms of individual plan rationality as they apply to the involved policies of each, induce a characteristic social rationality. That social rationality will emerge from individual plan rationality as it applies to these interrelated policies of each. So, in appealing to *shared* policies in our model of social rules, we help explain why properly functioning social rules characteristically involve such social rationality. Since such social rationality is, I take it, characteristic of properly functioning social rules of a sort that are central to rule-governed organized institutions, we thereby arrive at our first argument for appealing to *shared* policies in a model of social rules that aims to realize our dual design specifications.

I turn next, as promised, to a second aspect of the interplay between plan rationality and the interrelatedness of shared intention, and thereby to a second reason for appealing to *shared* policies in our model of social rules.

3.4 Criticisms and demands? Rationality and reasons

Our Hart-inspired social rule schema appeals to endorsement of a pattern as a common standard that prescribes for the group as a whole and that supports interpersonal criticisms of non-conformity and demands for conformity, where this involves "acknowledgements that such criticism and demands are justified" (Hart 2012, 57). The next point is that our appeal to *shared* policies helps explain the relation between social rules and such criticism and demands, given the interplay between plan rationality and the interrelations of sharing.

How? Such shared policies apply to and prescribe for the group as a whole. This is built into the way in which intentions prescribe, and into the "we" content of the involved intentions/policies. But how is this connected to "acknowledgements that" associated "criticism and demands are justified"? And what are these justifications?

If shared intentions/shared policies constitutively involved normatively substantive obligations—along lines developed by Gilbert (1999)—then we would have an answer to these questions. However, while I agree with Gilbert that shared intentions involve distinctive interpersonal interrelations, and that these interrelations help explain the basis for criticisms and demands associated with social rules, I have argued against an appeal here to constitutively involved normatively substantive obligations. So, we need a different approach.

Here I emphasize two ideas. First, the sharing of intentions and policies, while it does not ensure associated, substantive obligations, does engage norms of plan rationality whose application is shaped by the interlocking, intended mesh, and interdependence characteristic of the sharing. The initial normative impact of the interpersonal interrelations characteristic of shared intention is not a Gilbert-type constitutive, mutual obligation. Instead, it goes by way of the interplay of plan rationality and the interrelatedness in sharing. And this role of norms of plan rationality with respect to shared intention then extends to social rules: this is a continuity between the basis in shared intention for criticisms and an analogous basis in social rules. Second, there are also in many cases substantive normative reasons, and substantive obligations, to perform in accord with the shared policy.

I will develop these ideas in five stages.

Stage 1. Suppose we all participate in the shared policy that is central to a social rule in favor of R. So, for each of us a failure to intend to conform to R in a given case would be a breakdown in plan rationality. In this way, norms of plan rationality underlie a basic form of criticism of self or others for non-conformity to R.[14]

Further, the impact of these norms of plan rationality is extended by their interplay with the interrelatedness of sharing: the application of these norms to each is sensitive to the public interlocking, mesh-intending, and interdependence characteristic of a shared policy. Given public interdependence, the constancy of my intention supports the constancy of yours (and vice versa); and this can help support the rational stability of intentions of each. Given that what each intends includes the effectiveness of intentions of the others, in part by way of mesh in subplans, what rationality demands of the intentions of each will be sensitive to and tend to support relevant intentions of the others. In these ways the impact of these demands of plan rationality on each is shaped in part by a social context that involves interrelated intentions of others.

This potential rational criticism of non-conformity to a social rule in favor of R does not depend on substantive normative reasons in favor of conforming to R. A shared policy of, say, torturing certain people in a certain group would be awful, and there may be no substantive normative reasons (neither moral reasons nor reasons grounded in other substantive values) in favor of conformity. Nevertheless, such a shared policy engages rationality norms of plan consistency and coherence, norms whose impact is extended by their interplay with the social relatedness of sharing. If you participate in that shared policy and yet you intend not to conform, then you violate these norms of plan rationality, though that would be better than were you to conform.

Stage 2. The appeal so far is to rationality norms of plan consistency and coherence. But these are wide-scope norms. So, even if we so far have a shared policy in favor of R, each can escape criticism for non-conformity that is grounded in those norms of consistency and coherence by abandoning participation in that shared policy.

However, abandoning participation in that shared policy will itself sometimes be rationally criticizable. As noted, the public interdependence between our intentions can help support the rational stability of intentions of each. This is in part because each person's reasons for so intending may involve the presence of the intention of the other. In sticking with my policy, I support the persistence of yours, where that persistence of yours enters into my reasons for my policy and thereby helps support its stability. Further, given our resource limits the very activity of reconsidering one's prior intention may itself be rationally criticizable. Yet further, even if one does reconsider one's prior intentions, there are rational pressures in favor of the stability of those intentions. These rational pressures involve both the general benefits of such stability within our resource-limited human lives and the way in which sticking with one's intentions over time can be an element in one's self-governance over time (Bratman 2018b).

Stage 3. Stages 1 and 2 help explain why participants in a shared policy involved in a social rule are subject to rational pressures for stability and rational criticism for non-conformity. What about *demands*? Well, my noting to you that you are being irrational is itself a kind of demand on you. But there may also be the basis for a different kind of demand—an authoritative demand. In a shared policy the underlying policies of each interlock in the sense that they favor the relevant pattern of action by way of the relevant intentions/policies of each. As discussed in Section 1.2.4, there can be special cases in which what is intended is that this goes in part by way of accorded and accepted authority. In a version of this, the shared policy has the content that we conform to regularity R in part by way of each according certain participants authority to settle what others are to do within the shared activity, and to demand that they so act. This may involve a specification of roles such that agents in those roles have, according to the shared policy, authority in this sense to settle and to demand. Shared intentions/policies do not always have this authority-according content, but they can. And such authority-according shared policies would induce rational pressure on participants either to act in accordance with relevant authoritative demands or to drop out of the shared policy. In the background of such authoritative demands will then be this application of norms of plan rationality. In this way our shared policy model of social rules can in certain cases realize a condition of rationality-supported authoritative demands on participants.

Stages 1–3 explain how our shared policy model can realize conditions for criticizing participants in the shared policy involved in a social rule for their non-conformity, and for demanding their conformity. These criticisms and demands are grounded in norms of plan rationality and their interplay with the interrelations characteristic of sharing. Given the role in these explanations of the interrelations characteristic of sharing, this provides, as anticipated, our second argument for appealing to *shared* policies in our model of social rules.

I turn next, in stage 4, to a quartet of potential stability-supporting and criticism/demand-supporting substantive reasons.

Stage 4. First, once one is a participant in the public shared policy there will normally be reputational effects of publicly opting out. In publicly opting out one would give others evidence of one's unreliability as a partner in mutually beneficial shared activities, and one would thereby diminish the chances of benefiting from such activities. This "reputational mechanism"—to draw from Philip Pettit (2019)—would induce prudential reasons for not opting out of the shared policy.

Second, in many cases these shared policies will be good solutions to important social problems, and there will be substantive normative reasons—reasons of specification (Richardson 1997; Bratman 2011)—in favor of these specific solutions. In such cases those reasons will defeasibly transmit to reasons in favor of continued participation in and follow-through with those shared policies.

Third, in participating in a shared policy one normally knowingly induces reliance on the part of others that one will continue to participate (Alonso 2009). Such knowingly induced reliance is not only associated with potential reputational effects; it also defeasibly induces relevant moral obligations, including obligations to continue to participate. And there will be analogous normative impacts of related phenomena of assurance that are also commonly involved in such shared policies.

Fourth, authority-according shared policies do not in general ensure that participants have normative-reason-involving duties. After all, there might be an authority-according shared policy among stone throwers in Jackson's short story, or perhaps the participation of some is coerced in ways that block a substantive obligation. Nevertheless, in many cases there will be, in the background, defensible norms that see an authority-according shared policy as, in the particular case, grounding normatively substantive duties to act as demanded by an accorded authority.

In these ways, then, our shared policy model can in many cases realize a condition of normative-reason-supported stability of shared policy and criticism of/demands on participants in the shared policy.[15]

Stages 1–4 concern those who are participants in the shared policies that help constitute the social rule. What about non-participants?

Stage 5. The normative reasons at work in stage 4 include reasons that favor conformity to social rules that solve important social problems. These reasons may well apply even to those who are not participants in the shared policy. Further, once the shared policy is up and running it can induce new reasons for individual conformity, reasons that apply not only to participants in the shared policy but also to those who do not participate in the shared policy. For example, once a shared policy of stopping at red lights is up and running it can induce strategic reasons to stop at red lights whether or not one participates in that shared policy. And there can be cases in which the shared policy induces forms of legitimate authority to demand. So, our shared policy model of a social rule can in some cases realize a condition of normative-reason-supported criticisms of/demands on those who are not participants in the shared policy.

In summary: Our shared policy model of social rules provides quite generally (stages 1–2) for rationality-based criticism, of participants in the shared policy, for non-conformity or instability. In relevant authority-according cases, our model provides for rationality-based authoritative demands on participants (stage 3). And stages 1–3 complete our argument for the appeal to *shared* policies in our model of social rules. Further, in many cases our model provides for normative-reason-based support of criticism of/demands on participants in the shared policy concerning stable participation in and conformity to the shared policy (stage 4). And it can in many cases provide for normative-reason-based support of criticism of/demands on some who are not participants in the shared policy (stage 5). We thereby have, associated with a social rule, a multidimensional structure of rationality and potential substantive normative reasons in support of the criticisms and demands in which social rules characteristically issue.

Granted, and as Tristram McPherson has emphasized (in correspondence), in many cases we will be especially concerned with reasons-based support of criticism, if such there be. But it is also important to note the cited forms of rationality-based support, support that is sensitive to the interplay of plan rationality and the interrelatedness of shared intention. And "acknowledgements that . . . criticism [of non-conformity] and demands [for conformity] are justified" can involve acknowledgments of such rationality-based and/or reason-based considerations.[16]

We can now return to our question: given that there can be social rules that favor awful activities, does the existence of a Hart-type social rule nevertheless ensure some minimal ground for criticisms and demands? Well, on the one hand, there is no guarantee that if there is a social rule then individuals who participate in the background shared policy have normative reason to continue to do so or to conform to the social rule. This contrasts with a Gilbert-type view that, quite generally, the "joint commitments" involved in such social rules constitutively involve normatively substantive obligations. But, on the other hand, there is a guarantee that those who do continue to be participants in the shared policies that help constitute the social rule will be under wide-scope rational pressure to conform in the particular case; and so, their non-conformity can to some extent be subject to criticism and demands grounded in norms of plan rationality. Nevertheless, there are cases in which a participant who judges that such criticisms/demands are on balance justified is making a mistake, since there are conclusive reasons to drop out of the background shared policy.

3.5 "A wide range of 'normative' language"

Return now to the roles in social rules of speech acts of criticizing and demanding. We have noted Hart's thought that "for the expression of . . . criticisms, demands, and acknowledgements" involved in a social rule "a wide range of 'normative' language is used" (2012, 57). We now note how our initial shared policy model can help make sense of this role of broadly normative language.

Suppose we have the kind of shared policy that is central to a social rule in favor of R. We do not want simply to say that each participant's policy in favor of our conforming to R is, quite generally, a judgment that we ought to conform to R. Intentions are not to be identified, in general, with ought judgments. Nevertheless, we have seen how our shared policy in favor of R engages norms of plan rationality. And we have seen how in many cases there will also be in the background support by relevant normative reasons. Thus there will be a basis for expressing in normative language these rational and, in many cases, reason-based considerations associated with our shared policy, and so our social rule. This points to support for multiple, prima facie or pro tanto oughts or rational requirements that may be expressed/implicit in relevant criticisms, demands, and acknowledgments. These include requirements of plan rationality—where the relevant, interconnected plans sometimes involve accorded authority—and, in many cases, oughts of substantive normative reasons. And these further substantive reasons can in certain cases apply even to some who do not participate in the background shared policy.

So, the framework of shared policies, together with the forms of rationality and, in many cases, substantive reasons in the background of these shared policies, provides support for speech acts of criticism and demand and acknowledgment in which—to return to Hart—"a wide range of 'normative' language is used." And we have seen how these uses of normative language in the expression of criticisms and demands do not require that the basic form of participation in the social rule—namely, a doubly reflexive policy in favor of "our" conformity—is itself an ought judgment and/or a judgment of substantive normative reasons.

3.6 The proposal so far

Return to a community's social rule of wearing masks in public during a pandemic. On the present proposal this involves a general practice of mask-wearing that is in part explained by their doubly reflexive shared policy in favor of that general practice. This shared policy consists in appropriately interrelated, public, doubly reflexive policies on the part of each in favor of mask-wearing of each as elements in their sufficiently general conformity to that social pattern.

Another example: a social rule that the winning team stays on the court in a series of pickup basketball games at a gym. On the present proposal this involves a general practice within a roughly specified group of basketball players that is in part explained by their doubly reflexive shared policy in favor of their conformity to this practice.

Another example: a social rule, within a musical community, that in string quartets the first violinist sets the tempo. On the present proposal, this involves a general pattern of tempo-setting that is in part explained by a doubly reflexive shared policy in favor of conformity to this pattern. This shared policy consists in appropriately interrelated, public, doubly reflexive policies of each in favor of the conformity of each as elements in their sufficiently general conformity to that social pattern. And this shared policy may be authority-according.

Such social rules involve shared policies and thereby a kind of shared intentionality continuous with that of small-scale cases of shared intention. In such social rules, the consciously explicit content of relevant policies of each might be simple, as in "we wear masks." But these policies might support complex dispositions of tracking, responsiveness, and tendencies toward relevant "oh darn it!" reactions, dispositions that support the attribution of more complex, implicit or tacit contents.[17] And these shared policies can support relevant criticisms and demands. If members of the losing team attempt to stay on the court for the next game, they can be subject to rationality and, normally, reason-based criticisms for violating a policy that the players in the basketball community share.

These shared policies will be cognitively dependent on the cited patterns of behavior. It may be that these patterns of behavior precede and help explain the emergence of these shared policies, but this need not be true. Ours is a theory of the constructive structure of social rules, not a theory of their etiology.

This initial shared policy model of social rules will, however, need to be developed and qualified by way of reflection on a series of problems.

4 A SHARED POLICY MODEL OF SOCIAL RULES, PART 2

4.1 Eight problems in search of a theory

4.1.1 Fragility, robustness, and conditions of persistence

Suppose that at a given time you and I share an intention to paint the house. Our shared intention consists in a synchronic network of interrelated, public attitudes of each of us. As time goes by, certain changes in those attitudes are compatible with the continued persistence of our shared intention. I might, for example, fill in my subplans concerning my part of our painting in ways that mesh with your subplans. In contrast, if at some later time I drop out and Jones takes my place, our shared intention ceases to exist. Given this change in participant, it is no longer true that you and I share an intention to paint, though it is newly true that you and Jones share an intention to paint. In this sense, our shared intention is *diachronically fragile* with respect to changes in participants.

We are understanding shared intentions as a construction of public, interrelated intentions of participants. I have emphasized that this construction

  (i) plays relevant functional roles.

We are now noting that a proper understanding of this construction also involves

  (ii) relevant conditions of persistence.

We build a specification of these persistence conditions into our model of this construction. And one of these persistence conditions is *sameness of participants*.

But social rules differ from shared intentions with respect to (ii). There is not a new social rule about stopping at red lights when someone gets a new driver's license. The existence of a social rule depends on the existence of relevant attitudes of individuals, but the social rule normally persists despite changes in who those individuals are. Social rules, in contrast with shared intentions/policies, are *diachronically robust* with respect to certain changes in individuals whose attitudes help constitute the social rule. Shared intentions and social rules involve different conditions of persistence.

This poses a question: given that shared intentions/policies are diachronically fragile with respect to changes in participants, whereas social rules are diachronically robust with respect to certain changes in participants, how can we understand the internal aspect of social rules as in part constituted by shared policies?

Indeed, a version of this problem is in the background of Hart's criticism of Austin's (1995) theory of law as unable to account for the "continuity of legislative authority which characterizes most legal systems" (Hart 2012, 59). Hart aims to explain what that continuity consists in by appeal to the continuity of social rules—in contrast with a potential discontinuity of Austinian sovereign. This is an important objection to Austin's theory. But Hart's approach to social rules is itself broadly individualistic. So, there is a question of what constitutes and what explains the persistence of the same social rule over time despite changes in individual participants over time.

This gives us our first problem: Though shared intentions and shared policies are characterized in part by forms of temporally downstream functioning, they are themselves more or less time-slice phenomena and are fragile with respect to changes in participants. In contrast, social rules are temporally extended phenomena that can accommodate certain changes in participants over time. But then how can we understand social rules as constitutively involving shared policies?

My solution will involve two stages. We consider, first, the *time-slice projection* of a social rule. Such a (perhaps somewhat temporally thick) time-slice projection at t_1 consists in facts at t_1 that underlie the existence of that social rule at t_1. And the proposal on the table is to model the time-slice projection of the internal aspect of a social rule as a kind of shared-policy-shaped synchronic network—though we will need to do more work to spell this out. Second, we then understand the internal aspect of a temporally persisting social rule as a *diachronic network of such shared-policy-shaped synchronic networks*. In this way we see this internal aspect of a social rule as a temporally extended construction of the suitably related synchronic constructions that constitute relevant shared-policy-shaped synchronic networks.

A key question will then be how to understand what "glues together" over time these different synchronic networks. We seek an understanding of the glue characteristic of such a diachronic network that explains how it can accommodate changes in participants over time. We then say that for a social rule to persist from t_1 through to t_2 is in part for its time-slice projections at t_1 and t_2 to be suitably glued together. We aim in this way to explain how social rules can involve diachronically fragile shared policies but still themselves be diachronically robust.[1]

Following this two-step strategy, I will focus first (in 4.1.2–4.1.4) on the relevant shared-policy-shaped synchronic networks. I will then turn (in 4.1.5) to the interconnections across these networks that are characteristic of social rules.

4.1.2 Weak interlocking and interdependence

In cases of small-scale shared intention, the interdependence and interlocking are pairwise: for each two participants in a shared intention, the intention of each in favor of the joint activity is interdependent with and interlocks with that of the other. But as the size of the group grows, some may not be directly in touch with each member of the group. And as the size of the group grows, the intention of each in favor of the group pattern may be dependent only on the condition of a sufficient number of others having a corresponding intention. So, if we are to see shared policies as basic elements in the internal aspect of social rules, we will want to appeal to kinds of sharing-constituting interlocking and interdependence that are weaker than what is characteristic of small-scale cases.

Begin with interlocking. When you and I share an intention to walk together I will normally be in a position to intend, *of* your intention that we walk, that it plays a relevant role: my intention that we walk will semantically interlock with your corresponding intention in this *de re* way. In contrast, in larger groups each will normally be in such *de re* contact with at most only some others. Nevertheless, the content of a relevant intention of each can still specify that the relevant pattern of action go by way of relevant intentions of each of "us," where what counts as "us" is specified in general terms—for example, those in this protest march. So, there can still be a kind of *de dicto* interlocking within the larger group.[2]

What about interdependence? In many larger-scale cases of our shared intention in favor of R, my intention in favor of our sufficiently general conformity to social pattern R does not depend on my belief that every one of us will conform. Nevertheless, my intention is constrained by a rational demand for consistency with my beliefs. So, given that relevant matters are out in the open, my intention would be rationally threatened by a condition that enough others do not so intend. So, the persistence of the relevant intention of each will depend on the existence, in this public context, of a (vaguely specified) sufficient number of others who so intend. In this sense, the intentions of each are indirectly interdependent. This dependence can sometimes be because the larger social pattern is part of a participant's *reason* for intending it. But in any case, given an out-in-the-open condition and pressures of intention-belief consistency, the intention of each will *cognitively* depend on this sufficiently large pattern, a pattern to which the intentions of each will contribute.[3]

My proposal, then, is that when we extend our theory of shared policies to larger-scale cases, we understand the interlocking and interdependence conditions of sharing along these weaker lines. The policies need only be indirectly interdependent.[4] And these policies of each can interlock in only a *de dicto* fashion. So, within our shared policy model of social rules, we should understand those social ties as in these ways potentially weaker than in small-scale cases. Our model of social rules nevertheless retains its appeal to shared policies so understood.

4.1.3 "Fundamentalist" participants and cognitively grounded dependence

Return now to the Hart-inspired condition that there is a rational dependence, of the endorsements of the common standard, on the relevant general conformity in action. This will frequently be because each supposes that the pattern provides a reason for conformity to it—for example, the pattern of stopping at red lights provides a reason of safety for stopping at red lights—and that is in part why they endorse the pattern. But can there be participants in a social rule whose reason for endorsing the pattern of action does not involve the actual general conformity to the pattern? Suppose someone intends that we treat each other in certain ways because she thinks that is what respect for persons calls for whether or not others conform. Following Scott Shapiro, call this person a "fundamentalist."[5] Should we allow that such a fundamentalist might be a participant in a social rule of treating people this way?

We seek a social psychology that can help realize the rule-guidance characteristic of a wide range of organized institutions. And human, organized institutions may well involve some such fundamentalists. So, there is reason to make room for some such fundamentalists in our model of the relevant kind of social rules. But how is that compatible with Hart's dependence condition? As we have developed Hart's social rule schema, it sees a participant in the social rule as intending general conformity to the rule, *where this intention is rationally dependent on that general conformity*. But a fundamentalist who so intends will not so intend *for the reason* that there is that conformity. So how can we make room for the possibility that such a fundamentalist is a participant in the social rule?

My answer returns to the distinction between reasons and rationality. The *cognitive* constraints on *rational* intentions can induce a rational dependence on the general conformity of an intention in favor of that general conformity. There can be this rational dependence even if the agent's *reason* for her intention does not involve that general conformity.

One is (pro tanto) rationally required not both to intend X and to believe that, even given one's intention, not-X. So, a rational fundamentalist who intends sufficiently general conformity to R will need *not* to believe there is *not* sufficiently general conformity. But if there is not in fact sufficiently general conformity, and these matters are out in the open, then she will believe there is not this general conformity; and that will be in rational tension with her intending that sufficiently general conformity. So, given this cognitive condition on rational intention, her intention in favor of the sufficiently general conformity will depend on the sufficiently general conforming behavior of others. So, our fundamentalist can satisfy a cognitive version of the Hart-inspired dependence condition—even given that condition, one can be a fundamentalist participant in a corresponding social rule.[6]

Given that a certain behavioral regularity is out in the open, the cognitive conditions on rational intention will block a rational intention in favor of what is incompatible with that regularity. In this way, the contents of certain intentions are constrained by social facts. The Hart-inspired solution to the problem of social rule content can still maintain that this social rule content is grounded in the content of the attitudes of relevant individuals, but it needs to acknowledge such social constraints on that content.

Return now to the fundamentalist who intends that we treat each other in certain ways because she thinks that is what respect for persons calls for whether or not others conform. It is important not to identify the fundamentalist's moral judgment that you should treat people in these ways with the policy by virtue of which she participates in a corresponding social rule. That moral judgment may well not depend on the general conformity, but it can nevertheless help support a policy in favor of that conformity, a policy that does rationally depend on that conformity.

An objection is that there seem to be social rules in favor of patterns of action that are publicly known not to be the actual patterns. Examples might include a social rule in favor of giving 10 percent of one's income to charity even though it is public that the actual pattern is 8 percent, or a social rule in favor of driving at 65 mph even though it is public that the actual pattern is 70 mph.

Consider the first example. A shared policy *strictly* in favor of 10 percent would indeed be baffled by a public 8 percent pattern. But a shared policy to give *roughly* 10 percent would remain possible even given the actual, public pattern of 8 percent so long as the participants understood that 8 percent is in the ballpark of roughly 10 percent. So, even if the actual pattern is 8 percent, our shared policy model of a social rule, taken together with cognitive conditions on rational intending, allows for a social rule *to give roughly 10 percent*.[7] The content of the social rule is shaped by the content of the relevant doubly reflexive shared policies; the content of those policies is constrained by resulting sufficiently general, public patterns of action; but there is room for the cited flexibility in content. We thereby retain the Hart-inspired idea that it is the content of the relevant shared policies, not the actual behavioral pattern, that directly fixes social rule content. But we identify a way in which that behavioral pattern rationally helps shape the content of the shared policies, and thereby the social rule content.

This allows that there can be cases in which there is widespread normative belief that folks should conform to R even though it is out in the open that most do not conform to R. Perhaps there is a widespread belief that one ought not to engage in sexual relations outside of marriage even though it is public that there is a widespread pattern of sexual relations outside of marriage. In such a case it will not be rationally open for each to have a policy in favor of sufficiently general conformity to R. So, there will not be a social rule of the sort modeled here. Nevertheless, we can still use the words "social rule" or "social norm" and say that in a sense there is a social rule/social norm in such a case in favor of R, though a social rule commonly, publicly breached (Brennan et al. 2013, 20–21) As noted, there is room for multiple kinds of social rules/social norms. What we are interested in, however, are constructions that satisfy our *dual* design specifications—both basic and institutional role. I have supposed that to satisfy the institutional role design specification a construction needs to involve an actual pattern of (sufficiently general) conformity. But we can allow that in the cited kind of case of general, public non-conformity there can be, in a different sense, a social rule/norm consisting of a web of normative beliefs.

We have been focusing so far on the way in which the general policy of a fundamentalist can cognitively depend on the general behavioral conformity. We need now to turn to the inter-intention interrelations involved in a shared policy. Consider a fundamentalist who has a policy in favor of general conformity that depends cognitively on that general conformity, though that conformity is not her reason for her policy. For this fundamentalist to participate in a *shared* policy in favor of that conformity, her intention in favor of general conformity needs to interlock with and to be at least weakly dependent on the intentions of the others in favor of that general conformity.[8] But given that she is a fundamentalist, what would explain those inter-intention interrelations?

Well, in many cases it will be public that the explanation of the conformity of most goes by way of their each intending the general conformity. Other things equal, there would not be the general behavioral conformity if there were not this general pattern of intentions in favor of that general conformity. So, since the fundamentalist's intention in favor of the behavioral conformity cognitively depends on that actual behavioral conformity, her intention will depend, other things equal, on that general pattern of intentions in favor of that general conformity. So, in such cases there will be the kind of inter-intention interdependence characteristic of shared intention.

Will the fundamentalist's intention in favor of the behavioral conformity *interlock with* the intentions of others in favor of that behavioral conformity? Well, it is possible rationally (a) to intend E, know that E will come about by way of M, and yet (b) to *not* intend M (though also not intend not-M). So, for all that we have said, it is possible that our fundamentalist's intention in favor of the behavioral conformity (as in (a)) will not interlock with the intentions of others in favor of that behavioral conformity (as in (b)). Nevertheless, it is normally sensible to make the transition from

(a) to intending M. If our fundamentalist does make such a transition, she will intend that the general conformity go in part by way of the intentions of each. In such cases her doubly reflexive intention in favor of the sufficiently general conformity will include in its content the condition that the corresponding intentions of enough of the others play their roles in the general conformity. So, her intention that we conform will satisfy a relevant interlock condition even though she does not see those intentions of others as her reason for intending that general conformity.

So, once we take seriously cognitive conditions on rational intention, we can see why a fundamentalist's doubly reflexive intention in favor of the general conformity may satisfy the weak interdependence and interlocking conditions for being a participant in a relevant shared policy. It will satisfy these conditions even though her *reason* for her intention in favor of the general conformity does not depend on these intentions and/or actions of others. So, our shared policy model of the time-slice projection of the internal aspect of a social rule can make room for certain fundamentalist participants in that social rule. And that is what we wanted.

4.1.4 "Alienated" participants and kernel-penumbra structures

On our theory so far, the time-slice projection of the internal aspect of a social rule involves a doubly reflexive shared policy in favor of the group's conformity. The participants in that doubly reflexive shared policy intend the group's sufficiently general conformity. But there may be others who do *not* intend the *group's* general conformity but still intend personally to conform—they intend to conform in a way that meshes with the conforming activities of those who do participate in the underlying shared policy, and at least in part in response to reasons that trace to that shared policy.

One case involves strategic interaction. Perhaps some personally conform as a strategically sensible response to the shared-policy-induced conformity of others, but they do not themselves intend the general pattern itself. It is just that their own personal ends (e.g., personal safety) are best promoted, given that others conform to this pattern, by conforming to this pattern (e.g., stopping at red lights). Or perhaps the shared-policy-induced conformity leads to a pattern of negative social reactions to those who do not conform, and some respond to that without themselves intending that the group conform. Perhaps some share a policy that all wear masks in public in the pandemic, whereas others do not intend that all wear masks but do personally intend to wear a mask to avoid annoyed reactions of others.

Those who intend personally to conform without intending the general conformity are, we can say (following Shapiro 2014, 270 and Kutz 2000, 26), *alienated* from the end of *the group's* conformity.[9] Such an alienated person does not intend the group's conformity, but she personally intends to conform, and this intention is a response to reasons induced by the background shared policy, perhaps by way of its induced conformity by others.[10]

The cases of such alienation that have been noted so far are ones of informal, pre-institutional social rules. What about analogous organized-institutional cases? Well, Hart rules out the possibility of an alienated judge in a legal system. He writes:

> This merely personal concern with the rules, which is all the ordinary citizen *may* have in obeying them, cannot characterize the attitude of the courts to the rules with which they operate as courts. (Hart 2012, 115–16)

Hart's thought, I take it, is that judges need to be set to demand that other judges conform to the relevant rules and criticize those who do not. And he supposes that in simply intending personally to conform one is not in a position to demand and criticize in these ways. In contrast, Shapiro notes that it might be that "most judges accept their appointment to the bench simply in order to collect their paychecks" (Shapiro 2011, 108). Yet they remain judges who apply relevant secondary rules. So, should our model of institutional social rules accommodate such alienated participants?

We seek a social psychology of the social rules that help provide the rule-guidance that is characteristic of a wide range of human organized institutions. This is our institutional-role design specification. And it seems that human, organized institutions may well involve such alienated participants in their rule-guided functioning, where this alienation takes place against a backdrop of others who buy into that rule as a general standard for the group as a whole. So, given a background of the acceptance by some of the general rule, there is reason to make room for such alienated participants in our model of the relevant kind of social rules.[11] But how is that compatible with our appeal, in our construction of social rules, to shared policies in favor of the group's conformity?[12]

An analogous problem concerns what John Searle calls "collective acceptance" of a rule[13]—where we can see appeal to such collective acceptance as a way of understanding the internal aspect of social rules. Ludwig 2017 points to a view that understands such collective acceptance of a rule as involving relevant "we-intentions"—understood as intentions in favor of the group functioning—on the part of all who participate in this collective acceptance.[14] It follows from such a view that persons who are alienated in not endorsing the group functioning by way of relevant we-intentions will not be participants in the collective acceptance of relevant rules.[15] An alternative—one to which Searle turned in later work—would be to say that collective acceptance of a rule is primarily a matter of mutual belief that there is broad conformity to that rule (Searle, 2010, 57–58).[16] But this alternative would not capture the sense in which the participants in a social rule treat it as a standard that is to guide action and whose violation is criticizable.[17] However, if this thought were to lead us back to a tight connection between social rules and we-intentions on the part of all, we would again be faced with the problem that is posed by the possibility of alienated participants.

I propose here to draw on an extension and repurposing of Hart's distinction between legal officials and ordinary citizens.[18] The idea is that the time-slice projection of a social rule in favor of regularity R can involve a *kernel-penumbra* structure along the lines of:

1. A *kernel* of participants in the social rule who share a policy in favor of the group's conformity to R.
2. A *penumbra* of participants in the social rule who are not in the kernel but do intend generally to conform to R in ways that mesh with the R-conforming behavior of those in the kernel and for reasons that are induced by the kernel.

We understand the kernel shared policy in 1. along the lines we have developed: each doubly reflexively intends the conformity to R of each in the kernel group as elements in sufficient general conformity to R; and these doubly reflexive intentions of each are public and interrelated in relevant ways. Alienated participants are in the penumbra of the social rule: they do not intend the overall group conformity but do personally intend their part in R for reasons that are appropriately traceable to the kernel. As I will say: the kernel-traceable reasons for which they personally intend to conform to R are kernel-induced *extending reasons*.

Recall our example in which some share a policy in favor of sufficiently general conformity to mask-wearing, while others do not intend that general conformity but do personally intend to wear a mask to avoid annoyed reactions from those who participate in the shared policy. The former group constitute a kernel, and the latter an associated penumbra.

And my proposal is that we think of those in the penumbra as participants in the social rule, albeit alienated ones. This allows us to extend our model of a social rule to a wide range of cases that involve such forms of alienation. While penumbral participants are not in the kernel, they personally intend to conform, for reasons that have their origin in that kernel. In contrast with those in the kernel, the intentions of penumbral participants need not interlock or be interdependent with each other. The relevant dependency of these penumbral intentions is on the kernel, by way of extending reasons. (Though this might indirectly induce a kind of interdependency within the penumbra.) And my conjecture is that this *kernel-penumbra structure* is a key to developing our shared policy approach to social rules in a way that accommodates alienated participants.

Those in the penumbra intend to do what is in fact their part in R. This personal intention is general (though defeasible)—it is not just a one-time intention so to act. And those in the penumbra so intend at least in part for reasons that have their origin in the kernel. These reasons for which they intend to conform will at the least be motivating reasons; but they will also frequently correspond to normative reasons. Further, I will suppose that in intending to play what is in fact their role in R those in the penumbra know of their intended action that it conforms to R: they do not just intend some way of acting that, unbeknownst to them, conforms to R.[19]

Extending reasons can include cases of a strategic response to the general conformity that is induced within the kernel. Further, in some cases the general conformity on the part of many can induce moral pressures on others to conform by way, for example, of a duty to support just arrangements, or a duty of fair play given the overall benefits of the general conformity. There can also be extending moral reasons that are grounded in ways in which those in the penumbra are induced to assure others (including those in the kernel) that they will play their role in the actions supported by the shared policies in the kernel. These assurances, and related forms of intentionally induced reliance, will normally result in associated moral obligations to perform. Following through with such obligations may then lead to yet further interpersonal reliance. And this can induce a *snowball of obligation-inducing reliance*: This snowball can begin with reliance by others on such conformity; this further reliance can then induce further obligations to conform, which then keeps the snowball rolling.[20]

In many cases of informal social rules (concerning, for example, wearing certain kinds of clothing in certain kinds of circumstances) relevant extending reasons are not intentionally induced by those in the kernel—or, anyway, such efforts at intentionally inducing conformity by others are a minimal part of the underlying social dynamic. This will include cases in which the extending reasons are ones of informally induced social sanctions, or of strategic interaction, or of assurance- or reliance-based obligation, or of moral reasons of fair play. But there are also cases in which those in the kernel do intentionally set up extending reasons for individual conformity.

Consider those who participate in an underlying shared policy in favor of their general conformity to R. Each may have good reason to aim not just at the conformity to R by those—including herself—who participate in this shared policy but also by others. Conformity to R by some such broader group may be conducive to the aims that lie behind participation in the shared policy—for example, safety in a pandemic, or simply a valued form of social commonality. So, the participants in the kernel shared policy may also intend or, anyway, have it as an end[21] that there be conformity to R by some such broader group, one that includes but goes beyond those who participate in the underlying shared policy. They might intend, for example, that there be sufficiently general mask-wearing among those in this city, though it is known that some in this city do not participate in the shared policy in favor of mask-wearing. And this can support their intentional introduction of reasons for conformity that apply to those in that larger group.

Such kernel participants will have doubly reflexive intentions or ends that involve two different "we's": we_1 consists of those who share the underlying policy in favor of their conformity to R; we_2 consists of those who are either in we_1 or, while not in we_1, are in the targeted broader group. And the involved intentions or ends that we_2 conform to R may lead to the intentional introduction of reasons in support of that broader conformity. Kernel participants may, for example, intentionally set up a system of sanctions or incentives. Or perhaps they intentionally set up a system of authority that induces reasons in support of conformity to R, or a system that, because of its benefits, engages a duty of fair play to conform to R. In each case these impacts on the reasons that apply to those in the broader group are aimed at supporting the conformity to R by the larger group. This is *intentional* reason-grounded extension.[22] And this reason-grounded extension can help support beliefs that those in this larger group will indeed conform, beliefs that can in turn help satisfy cognitive constraints on intentions that we$_2$ conform.

The kernel of a social rule in favor of R is constituted by a shared policy in favor of conformity to R. We have seen that this kernel may be augmented by intentions/ends of some or all its participants, intentions/ends in favor of conformity to R by some yet larger group—where these further intentions/ends are grounded in the supposed contribution of such broader-based conformity to the aims that lie behind the shared policy. Such augmenting intentions/ends may be elements in a yet further shared policy that the larger group conform. But they may simply be intentions/ends of some of the kernel participants. In either case they may lead to the intentional introduction of extending reasons that favor further penumbral participation.

Suppose we have a structure of shared-policy-involving kernel together with a group of penumbral participants who are responding to kernel-linked, and perhaps intentionally induced, extending reasons. If all goes well there will be among those in the kernel a sufficiently general conformity to R grounded in the kernel shared policy. There will be extended conformity among penumbral participants. There will be forms of dependence both across attitudes of the involved individuals and between relevant individual attitudes and group conformity. The kernel attitudes will support relevant criticisms of divergence from R by those in the kernel as well as relevant demands. Extending reasons may provide grounds for criticisms of, and demands on, certain non-kernel non-conformers. So, both those in the kernel and those in the penumbra are subject to distinctive (though different) potential normative pressures in favor of conformity and are potentially targets of associated criticisms and demands. These different forms of endorsement, criticism, demand, and dependence are more complex than those that are built into the simple case of a shared policy in favor of R. But this is not a mere pattern of personally motivated behavior of each (as in Hart's case of a pattern of tea drinking). And it is not merely strategic interaction. Shared intentionality is at the center of this phenomenon even though some who are involved do not participate in this sharing.

Return to our Hart-inspired conditions for a social rule:

(a) a *public social pattern* of action, the full explanation of which involves
(b) *endorsement* by participants of that pattern as a *common standard* that prescribes for the group as a whole, where those endorsements are embedded in a public social web, and where
(c) these embedded endorsements of the pattern support characteristic interpersonal *criticisms, demands, and guidance* of action; and
(d) there is a *rational dependence* of the endorsements in (b) on the general conformity in (a).

An effective, public kernel-penumbra structure in support of R will involve the behavioral pattern in (a), one that includes both kernel and penumbral participants. Those in the kernel will satisfy (b) in a straightforward way, one that involves interdependence and interlocking and supports interpersonal criticisms, demands, and guidance of action. Participants in the penumbra will contribute to (a) in ways that respond to kernel-grounded extending reasons, and they will be potentially subject to criticisms and demands associated with those extending reasons. And there will be a complex, rational dependence of both kernel and penumbral attitudes on the actual behavior conformity, along the lines of (d).

I propose that we see such a public kernel-penumbra structure as, potentially, a time-slice projection of an important kind of social rule. To do this, however, we need to adjust (b) along the lines of:

(b*) (i) *endorsement* by some participants of that pattern as a *common standard* that prescribes for the group as a whole, where those endorsements are embedded in a public social web, in some cases together with (ii) personal commitments of others to conform to the pattern, where those personal commitments are grounded at least in part in (i), by way of extending reasons.

We thereby arrive at an *adjusted version of Hart's social rule schema*:

(a) a *public social pattern* of action, the full explanation of which involves
(b*) (i) *endorsement* by some participants of that pattern as a *common standard* that prescribes for the group as a whole, where those

endorsements are embedded in a public social web, in some cases together with (ii) personal commitments of others to conform to the pattern where those personal commitments are grounded at least in part in (i), by way of extending reasons,

and where

(c*) these embedded endorsements, in (b*)(i), and the extending reasons in (b*)(ii), support characteristic interpersonal *criticisms, demands, and guidance* of action;
and
(d*) there is a *rational dependence* of the endorsements in (b*)(i), and the commitments in (b*)(ii), on the general conformity in (a).

An effective, public kernel-penumbra structure in support of R will realize such an adjusted version of Hart's social rule schema—one that allows for a hybrid realization of (b). Such a public kernel-penumbra structure is, potentially, a time-slice projection of what I will call a *hybrid* social rule.

The social rules that tie together a core group of officials may be hybrid, a possibility illustrated by Shapiro's judge. And the social rules that tie together a larger group that includes but goes beyond a core group of officials may also be hybrid. This may be what is happening when there is large-scale personal conformity that is the issue of reasons induced by social rules within a core group of officials. We thereby articulate ways in which these cases are not merely ones of strategic interaction but involve explanatorily relevant hybrid social rules and involved shared policies, even though there can be alienated participants. We retain, but qualify, the centrality of shared intentionality to social rules.[23]

Consider now the role of education in bringing younger members of a society within its social rules. Younger members may be disposed personally to conform to a social rule—say, a rule about forming a queue at a bus stop—in response to social pressures from adult members. But they may not participate in the shared policy, among those adults, that "we" stay in line. Such younger folks would count as alienated participants, though they would be different from Shapiro's judge. And one role of education would be to bring these young folks into the fold of the shared policy—to support this transition from penumbra to kernel.[24]

Turn now to a challenge from Leif Wenar (in correspondence): the case of chattel slavery. A kernel of slave owners intend that the slaves conform to the rule that slaves pick cotton and owners sell cotton. They set up a structure of severe punishments that supports the conformity of the slaves to this rule. If the slaves do conform for these reasons, they will count as penumbral participants in a social rule that says that slaves pick cotton and owners sell cotton. But both groups might balk at this description. The owners might see their relation to the slaves not as one of co-participants in a social rule but simply as one in which they, the owners, control the slaves. And the slaves might well resist seeing themselves as co-participants with the owners.

Of course, the owners and slaves are not co-participants in a *cooperative* social rule, since extreme coercion is incompatible with cooperation.[25] But the overall pattern of behavior is not just a convergence of independent motivations of each. The overall rule-conforming pattern is grounded in a complex social psychology with a rule-guided structure, though one that involves morally repugnant coercion. In saying this we are not endorsing that rule; we are pointing to a rule-guided structure that both plays a social role and is morally awful.

Return to Shapiro's alienated judge. She intends personally to conform to relevant rules of adjudication. However, she does not intend the general conformity on the part of the overall group of judges. How can she engage in the criticisms and demands associated with a social rule?

While her situation is precarious, she can note that other judges do participate in a shared policy of conformity to the adjudicative rule. So, she can note that their failure to conform would be a rational breakdown on their part. She can note that failures to conform on the part of those in either the kernel or the penumbra may be in tension with extending normative reasons. There may, for example, be in place a system of sanctions for non-conformity. She can note any forms of obligation that have been created by relevant, induced assurances. Even though she herself does not intend the general conformity, she can note whatever normative reasons there are in favor of that general conformity, and she can note how those reasons transmit to reasons for conformity in a particular case. So, while she is alienated, there is available a web of rational demands and normative reasons to which she can appeal in support of criticisms of non-conformity on the part of other judges.

There is also here a potential for pretense. The alienated judge may find it useful to engage, in her judicial exchanges, in a pretense of endorsement of the general conformity: she may find it useful in certain contexts to act as if she herself intended the general conformity, though she does not. Such pretense may trigger a snowball of reliance, and thereby—given a background norm of reliance-based obligation—of associated obligations. This snowball can begin with reliance by others on her conformity to the relevant social rule, and related reasonable assumptions by others that she has assured them of her conformity. Such induced reliance and induced reasonable presumption of assurance can then induce obligations on her to conform. These obligations on her can then further support reasonable reliance by others on her performance. This then can induce our alienated judge herself to rely on their performance; and that can lead to obligations of the others to conform. In these ways what begins as pretense issues in actual obligations to which an alienated judge can then appeal in her criticisms and demands of others as well as of herself.[26]

So, in these multiple ways an alienated judge can be in a position not just personally to conform to the relevant social rules of adjudication but also to play roles of critic and demander with respect to those social rules. And this point generalizes. It shows us how we can make room for alienated participants in the social rules involved in an organized institution.

But there now emerges a possible concern about the need for the shared policy kernel itself. I have appealed to alienated, penumbral participants who do not intend the general conformity but do pretend so to intend. Their reasons for this pretense, and for their personal intentions to conform, to some extent derive from the actual shared policy kernel and associated extending reasons. But might everyone be pretending? Might there be a social rule in which there is pretense throughout in the absence of any shared policy kernel at all? Might this world of social rules be a stage on which all is pretense? This possibility would be in tension with Hart's implicit solution to the problem of social rule content.[27] Do we need to adjust that solution?

This challenge is due to Stephen Darwall (in conversation), so I will call it *Darwall's challenge*.[28] I address it in Section 4.1.7. But first let's return to the diachronic dimension of a social rule.

4.1.5 A Lockean model of diachronic robustness

The view so far is that the internal aspect of a social rule is a diachronic network of synchronic networks that consist in part in doubly reflexive shared policies, perhaps as elements in kernel-penumbra structures.[29] A relevant diachronic network will involve appropriate cross-temporal interrelations between such synchronic networks. What cross-temporal interrelations?

Begin with a temporal succession of non-hybrid synchronic networks within a given population. When does it constitute a diachronic network of a sort characteristic of a social rule? Well, there needs to be rough constancy over time in the contents of the involved policies in favor of the group's conformity, though there is room for some change in the target population over time. But it cannot just be a coincidence that there are synchronic networks at different times that exhibit this rough constancy of content. Persistence of the same social rule over time seems to involve some sort of supporting interdependence across these synchronic networks. Roughly, that there is a relevant synchronic network at a certain time needs to be to some extent explained by the synchronic networks at earlier times and needs to be set to help explain related synchronic networks at later times. This might be in part by way of teaching and learning (Tomasello 2014, 80–81). Further, there will normally be some sort of cross-reference: to some extent, doubly reflexive intentions at a certain time that "we" R at least implicitly include, within their target, participants in later synchronic networks, and there are overlapping strands of such cross-temporal reference. Further, there will normally be, at least implicitly, associated beliefs that involve cross-temporal cross-reference in both directions. There will, then, be overlapping strands of interdependence and interlocking across these synchronic networks. And we can expect such cross-temporal interdependence and interlocking to be normal given the functional natures of the underlying attitudes in the synchronic networks and (to draw from Sydney Shoemaker) their normal "playing out over time" (1984, 95), where that will involve characteristic forms of diachronic stability of these attitudes.

So, when there is a temporally extended social rule, the web of individual attitudes at earlier times will normally lead to a similar web by way of common forms of stability over time of individual attitudes together with common forms of social teaching and learning. There will normally be interlocking across these webs. And such cross-temporal interdependence and interlocking will help explain the normal social functioning of such social rules.

The shared policies that help constitute the synchronic networks associated with social rules involve weak, indirect forms of synchronic interdependence and interlocking across the individual policies that help constitute those shared policies. We now arrive at the idea that the explanatory diachronic "glue" associated with social rules involves forms of diachronic dependence and interlocking. In contrast with the weak interdependence at work in many larger-scale shared policies, however, this diachronic dependence seems normally to involve each of the relevant, synchronic networks along the way: we do not need here to retreat to a weak, indirect dependence.[30] We thereby arrive at an initial version of the idea that the relevant diachronic interconnections across synchronic networks are broadly similar to (though less thick than) the interconnections highlighted in Lockean theories of personal identity (Locke 1975, bk. 2, chap. 27; Parfit 1984; Yaffe 2000). This points to a broadly *Lockean construction* of the diachronic network of synchronic, shared-policy-infused networks that is associated with the internal aspect of a temporally persisting social rule.

Turn now to a hybrid social rule whose time-slice projections involve not only shared policy kernels but also associated penumbras. To construct the diachronically robust hybrid social rule we look first at the relevant kernels at each time. In articulating the relevant cross-temporal interrelations we appeal both to relevant constancy of content over time and to relevant interconnections across time. To this we add analogous cross-temporal Lockean conditions on the penumbras at each time along the way. These will include conditions of a kind of constancy of content: relevant personal intentions need to favor doing what is one's part in the general pattern articulated in the associated kernel (where there is diachronic constancy in that kernel-endorsed pattern). And these conditions will include relevant cross-temporal interconnections between those penumbras.[31]

In both cases, then, the diachronic networks are partly constituted by synchronic networks that involve policies with more or less constant contents in favor of the general pattern and also, in hybrid cases, associated personal, penumbral intentions. And these diachronic networks will involve Lockean cross-temporal interdependence and interlocking across those synchronic networks.[32]

This appeal to Lockean cross-temporal ties involves an analogy with a Lockean view of sameness of person over time. On such a view, a person can persist over time, despite various changes along the way, if there are the needed Lockean interrelations—where these will involve certain constancies of content (as in memory and intention) and cross-temporal connections. And the present idea is that a social rule can persist over time despite various changes in participants at times along the way. This can happen if, despite changes in individual participants, there are the needed

Lockean ties across synchronic networks that involve intentions with relevantly constant contents. (Though such broadly Lockean interconnections will not in general ensure the thickness of interconnections characteristic of a single person over time.)

Our model of a social rule thereby incorporates a condition of persistence that allows for diachronic robustness. So, we have, as anticipated, a contrast between shared intentions and policies, on the one hand, and social rules, on the other, even within our shared policy model of social rules. Change over time in participants in a shared intention or policy blocks persistence of that shared intention or policy, but certain changes over time in underlying participants are compatible with the persistence of a social rule even though a social rule is partly constituted by relevant shared policies.

4.1.6 Non-cotemporaneous kernels?

We have so far been assuming that the kernel and the penumbra in the time-slice projections of a hybrid social rule are cotemporaneous. Can there also be social rules in which there is a shared policy kernel at t_1 that induces a penumbra at t_2 by way of extending reasons that apply at t_2, even though at t_2 there is no longer a shared policy kernel that bears quasi-Lockean relations to the kernel at t_1?[33]

Suppose that an R-focused shared policy kernel at t_1 induces extending reasons that support a penumbral web of dispositions at t_1 both to conform to R and, in related ways, to criticize or demand. Suppose that there continues to be a broadly corresponding penumbral web at t_2 despite the demise at t_2 of the shared policy kernel; and suppose this is due in part to the impact of kernel-induced extending reasons at t_2. In many cases this downstream penumbral web will be attenuated, and the case will be one of the *non*-persistence of the social rule from t_1 to t_2. But if this kernel-induced penumbral web is sufficiently rich and stable in relevant ways, and sufficiently connected to the t_1 kernel, we can perhaps see such a case as one of a temporally persisting social rule even though the kernel itself does not persist. Such a temporally persisting social rule has a time-slice projection at t_2 that does not include relevant shared policies *at t_2*, though it does include a sufficiently rich penumbra at t_2 that is shaped by earlier kernel-shared-policies at t_1 and extending reasons in which they have issued. As we might say, borrowing from Friedrich Engels, in such a case the withering away of the kernel does not induce the withering away of the social rule.

What might this be like? Here we can draw from our earlier remarks about Shapiro's alienated judge. The participants at t_2 might be set to note that a failure to conform to R would be in tension with normative reasons associated with extending reasons traceable to the t_1-kernel. There may, for example, be a continuing system of formal or informal social sanctions for non-conformity, sanctions traceable to the t_1-kernel. The participants at t_2 might be set to note forms of obligation that have been created by induced assurances from those in either the penumbra or the t_1-kernel, and by related forms of intentionally induced reliance. Here again a snowball of assurance and reliance-based obligation may be in play. Further, even though the participants at t_2 do not themselves intend the general conformity to R, they can note whatever normative reasons there are in favor of that general conformity (which may include but also go beyond reasons intentionally induced by those in the t_1-kernel). Yet further, given a persisting system of social pressures, these participants at t_2 may find it personally useful to engage in a kind of pretense of endorsement of the general conformity endorsed by the t_1-kernel. And such pretense can have its own normative consequences by way of a snowball of reliance. In these ways the participants at t_2, while alienated, may nevertheless be in a position not just personally to conform to the R-focused social rule but also to play roles of critic and demander with respect to that social rule. And the thought is that if this penumbral structure at t_2 both has its origin in the t_1-kernel and is sufficiently rich and stable, we can have a case of a social rule that persists from t_1 through t_2 even though its kernel does not.

As noted, one way this can happen involves a snowball of assurance and reliance-based obligation. Another way this can happen, perhaps in parallel with a snowball of reliance, involves symbolic traces from the t_1-kernel—for example, written documents that spell out an R-type rule content (Epstein 2015). Such documents might function as institutional memory traces. And they might provide focus for a continuing system of reliance-based reasons to conform to R even though there is no longer a shared policy kernel in favor of R.

This involves yet a further divergence from Hart. In introducing the idea of hybrid social rules, I agreed with Shapiro in making room for alienated participants in our model of social rules. But I initially did not consider the possibility that at a given time all participants are alienated. I understood the time-slice projections of hybrid social rules as involving cotemporaneous kernels. And those cotemporaneous kernels continued to provide a Hart-inspired solution to the problem of rule content. But we are now allowing that in special cases the relevant kernels need not be cotemporaneous with the relevant penumbras: a kernel might precede that penumbra, though there remain demanding conditions for this to be a case of persistence of, rather than the withering away of, that social rule.

In this way we are yet further adjusting the Hart-inspired condition that it is essential to a social rule that there are those who regard the general pattern "from the internal point of view as a public, common standard" (2012, 116). We retain the condition of kernel shared policies as elements of the social rule, ones that help fix the content of that social rule. But we allow that this kernel may not be cotemporaneous with a relevant penumbra. Such cases may to a certain extent functionally mimic (Pettit 2018, 251) the central cases of cotemporaneous kernels.

Nevertheless, given our strategy of sufficiency and our theoretical aims, it seems reasonable to continue to focus primarily on central cases involving cotemporaneous kernels. But now we need to return to pretense.

4.1.7 Pretense all the way down?

Recall Darwall's challenge: Could there be a social rule that involves no actual shared policy kernel at all, but is instead pretense all the way down?

In talking of social rules, we are supposing that the relevant bevy of sociality has a *rule content*. And our Hart-inspired idea is that it is the general standard that is endorsed by relevant individuals from the internal point of view that fixes this rule content. This Hart-inspired way of fixing rule content requires, at least at some point in the construction, a web of actual shared attitudes that provides that content. We have allowed that that web can in certain peripheral cases be provided by an earlier but no longer present kernel, though one whose sufficiently extended impact continues to be present. But we have so far retained the Hart-inspired thought that we need at least that earlier shared policy kernel to provide for rule content. And now we face the question of whether this web of actual shared acceptance might be replaced by a web of, as Darwall puts it, "collective pretense."

Now, a kernel of shared policies need not be a kernel of deeply shared values. What is needed for our Hart-inspired approach to social rule content is not deep agreement about the right and the good. What is needed is only a kernel of policies in favor of general social patterns, where different folks may have different reasons for their commitment to such policies, and one can even have such a policy in favor of pattern R without thinking R itself is valuable. Even if one does not think the general pattern is especially a good thing, and one does not see oneself as agreeing on a range of relevant evaluative/normative judgments with relevant others, one still can intend the general pattern (as one's part of a shared policy in favor of that pattern) rather than merely pretend one so intends. Nevertheless, Darwall's challenge envisages cases in which there is at no time relevant shared intentions/policies even given that such shared intentions/policies can be in these ways evaluatively superficial.

A complexity is that when pretense is systematic it may to a large extent play the functional roles of intention. But in appealing to pretense, we are supposing that there remain functional differences between pretending to intend the general pattern and intending the general pattern. And let's suppose that there can be cases of such pretense all the way down. Such pretense can set into play snowballs of assurance and reliance-based obligations, and thereby induce extending reasons for conformity. But the ground of these extending reasons is not an actual kernel of shared policies.

Here we need to return to our strategy of sufficiency. This allows us to say that what we have uncovered is a kind of multiple realizability of social rules: so-far salient cases involve a shared policy kernel, but there remain, perhaps, possible cases that are pretense all the way down. Our Hart-inspired approach, if successful, would articulate sufficient conditions for a social rule, conditions that involve a shared policy kernel that helps fix social rule content. But now we consider the possibility of a different though related web of sufficient conditions.[34]

Is one of these constructions theoretically more basic, or should we simply allow for multiple constructions? My thought here is that in understanding the dynamics of such a system of pretense we see it as a *simulation* of a system grounded in actual shared policies, a simulation whose dynamics emulates the rational plan dynamics we have been describing. In this way, our understanding of such a system of pretense is like our understanding in Section 4.1.6 of cases of solely non-cotemporaneous kernels. In each case we recognize cases that diverge from a central case but sufficiently simulate or, as Pettit would say, mimic the social functioning of the central case to be a potential candidate for a kind of social rule. In particular, pretense that one intends the general conformity to a social rule is a sufficiently rich pretense that can help constitute the social rule only if it functions pretty much like a policy in favor of that general conformity. So even if we grant this alternative of pretense all the way down as a possible realization of a social rule, the primary case for our theoretical understanding of social rules will remain one that involves shared policies whose rational functioning may then be simulated. At the bottom of our theory of social rules will be a model of the rational functioning characteristic of this primary case.[35]

4.1.8 Social rule content

My proposal, then, is to see the internal aspect of a social rule as, in central cases, a Lockean diachronic network of shared-policy-shaped synchronic networks that involve shared policy kernels and, in hybrid cases, related penumbra. Focusing on such central cases, how should we understand social rule *content*? I first proceed in an informal way, and then turn to a more articulated framework.

We begin with a kernel shared policy in favor of "our" conformity to R. We ask whether this kernel is augmented by intentions/ends in favor of conformity by those in a larger group H, where H includes but goes beyond those in the kernel, and where these further intentions/ends are grounded in the supposed contribution of this broader-based conformity to aims that support the shared policy. And we ask whether the kernel induces—perhaps intentionally, perhaps not—extending reasons for personal conformity to R.

Penumbral participants are not in the kernel but nevertheless intend to conform to R in part because of extending reasons. In some but not all cases these extending reasons are intentionally induced.

Augmenting intentions/ends might be intentions/ends of only a small subgroup of a kernel. But let's focus on augmenting intentions/ends of a sufficiently extended subgroup within the kernel. (This will involve some vagueness.) We can then say that the social rule associated with a given kernel in favor of R *applies* to all those who are either in that kernel or in a group, H, that is the target of augmenting intentions/ends of a sufficiently extended subgroup within the kernel. Some non-kernel folks in H to whom the social rule applies may not be penumbral participants, since they do not personally intend to conform. And some conforming penumbral participants may not be in the group H to which the social rule applies but are responding only to extending reasons that are not intentionally induced by way of relevant augmenting intentions/ends.

We can highlight two kinds of potential criticism of divergence from R:

(i) If you are in the kernel, such divergence would be a rational failure to conform to the kernel shared policy in which you participate.
(ii) Even if you are not in the kernel, such divergence may be a failure to be responsive to normative extending reasons induced by the kernel (in some cases, intentionally).

And a social rule can in some cases apply to someone even though their non-conformity would be subject to neither form of criticism.

Given these ideas, we can describe the relevant web of possibilities as follows: We begin with

(K) a kernel shared policy in favor of "our" conformity to R.

We then ask whether

(1) that kernel is augmented by intentions/ends, on the part of a sufficiently extended subgroup of the kernel, that a larger group H conform, or
(2) it is not augmented in this way.

And we ask whether

(A) the kernel shared policy induces extending reasons for personal conformity, or
(B) it does not induce extending reasons for personal conformity.

In the case of (A), we ask whether

(A_1) the extending reasons are intentionally induced by way of (1), or
(A_2) the extending reasons are not in this way intentionally induced.

Case (2) can involve (A_2) but not (A_1). The social rule associated with (K) *applies* to all those in this kernel and, in case (1), to those in H. In both (A) and (B) we can ask whether certain non-kernel folks intend to conform to R. Those in case (A)—where this can include (A_1) and/or (A_2)—who do intend to conform for those extending reasons are *penumbral participants* in the social rule associated with (K).

So, the set of those to whom a social rule applies is not the same as the set of kernel-cum-penumbral participants; neither of these sets is contained within the other, but these sets intersect. We thereby pry apart interrelated conditions for being someone to whom a social rule *applies* and for being a kernel or penumbral *participant* in the social rule.

What account of the *content* of a social rule best fits the contours of this web of possibilities? The canonical content of a social rule is that *those in G are to conform to R*. On our theory, the specification of R is induced by the underlying, doubly reflexive kernel shared policy that "we" conform to R. What about the range, G? This will include those in the "we" built into the kernel shared policy. Can it also include others?

Well, the kernel may be augmented by intentions/ends, on the part of a sufficiently large subgroup of the kernel, in favor of some larger group's conformity to R. Perhaps those who share a policy in favor of mask-wearing in a pandemic have ends/intentions that favor mask-wearing on the part of all those in the city, both themselves and those who do not share their policy. I have said that in such a case the social rule associated with this augmented kernel *applies* to those in this overall group. And one way of understanding this is that the *content* of the social rule associated with this augmented kernel has a *range* that includes this overall group. This range is determined by attitudes of those in the kernel, but these attitudes can include augmenting ends/intentions. In this way, the rule content can involve a range that goes beyond those in the kernel of the social rule but nevertheless continues to be grounded in the underlying social psychology of the kernel.

Penumbral participants who are responding to extending reasons intentionally induced by a sufficiently large subgroup of the kernel will be in the range of the social rule. This will, I take it, include Shapiro's judge with respect to the social rules of adjudication. This range can also include some who do not intend to conform to R and so are not penumbral participants. But this range will not include non-kernel, penumbral participants who are responding to extending reasons but are not in the target of relevant augmenting intentions/ends. We thereby pry apart being in the range built into the content of a social rule and being a (perhaps penumbral) participant in the social rule.

A social rule can be directed at some who do not participate in that rule. And some who do participate, and whose participation is an element in the complex social embedding of the rule, may not be targeted by that social rule. A theory of social rules needs a theory of those it targets; it needs a theory of the modes of thought and action it prescribes; and it needs a theory of its social embedding. And these three aspects of social rules are related in complex ways.

So, while the specification of "R" in the social rule content is given by the doubly reflexive kernel shared policy that "we" conform to R, the range, G, in the social rule content can extend beyond those in the kernel. This extension will include those penumbral participants for whom operative extending reasons are intentionally induced by those in a sufficiently large subset of the kernel. But we retain the idea that the range of a social rule, as well as the mode of thinking and acting it enjoins, is grounded in the social psychology of the kernel. This is broadly in the spirit of Hart's idea that the content of a social rule is grounded in attitudes of those who take an internal point of view toward the behavioral pattern. But to make this work we have gone beyond the shared policies at the heart of that internal point of view and looked also at range-extending, augmenting ends/intentions.

The application of a social rule to those who are in its range but are not in its kernel may be accompanied by extending normative reasons—perhaps intentionally induced—for conformity to the rule. But such normative reasons are not ensured for all those in the range. Suppose, for example, that those in the kernel share a policy in favor of their mask-wearing, and also have the end that all in their city wear masks. Suppose that Jones lives in this city but does not intend to wear a mask and is neither a kernel nor a penumbral participant in this social rule. There may be normative reasons—perhaps intentionally induced—for Jones to conform. But whether or not there are these normative reasons, Jones is in the relevant range within the content of the social rule. The social rule applies to him. He does not block this just by failing to conform to the social rule.[36]

4.2 Putting the pieces together

We began with the Hart-inspired idea that social rules go beyond a strategic equilibrium of public personal intentions to act, and satisfy four interrelated conditions:

(a) a *public social pattern* of action, the full explanation of which involves
(b) *endorsement* by participants of that pattern as a *common standard* that prescribes for the group as a whole, where those endorsements are embedded in a public social web, and where

(c) these embedded endorsements of the pattern support characteristic interpersonal *criticisms, demands, and guidance* of action;

and

(d) there is a *rational dependence* of the endorsements in (b) on the general conformity in (a).[37]

We then proposed that a basic realizer of (b) and (c) is a shared-policy-shaped structure within which we together organize aspects of how we live with each other. To develop our account of this structure we turned to doubly reflexive policies in favor of the conformity of each as an element in the sufficiently general conformity to the social pattern. We appealed, further, to doubly reflexive *shared* policies in favor of our conformity, where this sharing involved publicness and conditions of interdependence, interlocking, and intended mesh. This gave us rationality-based and, in many cases, normative-reason-based support both for the stability of the shared-policy-shaped structure and for associated criticisms, demands, and acknowledgments. We then highlighted the diachronic robustness of social rules; a weak form of interpersonal interdependence; the way in which relevant dependence of attitudes on actual social patterns can involve cognitive conditions on rational intention; alienation, kernel-penumbra structures, and potentially augmented kernels; Lockean cross-temporal glue; and an account of the content of a social rule and its potentially extended range.

We were thereby led to a model of temporally persisting social rules as involving a relevant pattern of action that is appropriately explained by a robust Lockean diachronic network of shared-policy-shaped synchronic networks. The involved synchronic networks are shaped by (normally cotemporaneous) kernels of doubly reflexive shared policies and, in hybrid cases, also include penumbras induced by extending reasons. These extending reasons can be strategic and/or assurance- or reliance-based and/or intentionally induced by those in the kernel. This led us to adjust our Hart-inspired schema to make room for appropriate roles of alienated participants in a penumbra of a hybrid social rule. We thereby arrived at an *adjusted version of Hart's social rule schema*:

(a) a *public social pattern* of action, the full explanation of which involves
(b*) (i) *endorsement* by some participants of that pattern as a *common standard* that prescribes for the group as a whole, where those endorsements are embedded in a public social web, in some cases

together with (ii) personal commitments of others to conform to the pattern where those personal commitments are grounded at least in part in (i), by way of extending reasons,

and where

(c*) these embedded endorsements, in (b*)(i), and the extending reasons in (b*)(ii), support characteristic interpersonal *criticisms, demands, and guidance* of action;
and
(d*) there is a *rational dependence* of the endorsements in (b*)(i), and the commitments in (b*)(ii), on the general conformity in (a).

We have articulated shared-policy-grounded conditions that realize this adjusted social rule schema. We see temporally persisting social rules as involving a pattern of action that is explained by a Lockean diachronic network of shared-policy-shaped synchronic networks. These conditions specify a construction whose building blocks include, but go beyond, constructions of shared policies. This is a construction of constructions. We have seen how this higher-level construction will play relevant roles: we ground characteristic functioning in construction. And, drawing on an analogy with a Lockean view of the persistence of a person over time, we have specified within our model that the persistence conditions for these constructed social rules—in contrast with shared intention—allow for certain changes in participants over time.

The content of a social rule is fixed both by the content of kernel shared policies and by the potential extension of range induced by relevant augmenting intentions/ends (if such there be) in the kernel. This is a Hart-inspired, broadly individualistic account of the determinants of social rule content. But it is a sophisticated individualism that highlights several features: (i) The content of relevant policies of individuals can be constrained by the actual, public pattern of action. (ii) The explanation of the existence of such kernel shared policies and their individualistic elements may well involve various forms of social influence. And (iii) the contents of relevant attitudes of individuals can themselves be shaped by aspects of the social context.

Our construction of social rules drew on a series of ideas about explanatorily relevant dependence. There was the initial idea of pairwise dependence between intentions of different participants in small-scale shared intention. When we turned to larger-scale cases of our shared intention to J, we drew on an indirect form of dependence: the dependence of my intention in favor of our J-ing, not specifically on your corresponding intention but rather on a sufficient level of conforming intentions and actions by others. When we then turned from diachronically fragile shared intentions/policies to diachronically robust social rules, our broadly Lockean approach drew on forms of more or less direct dependence over time between shared-policy-shaped synchronic networks.

Consider then these possible forms of dependence:

	direct	indirect
synchronic	A	C
diachronic	B	D

Our central case of small-scale shared intention draws on box-A-type interpersonal, synchronic, direct intention dependence, though in simple cases of persistence over time of such shared intentions there will also be box-B-type interpersonal, diachronic intention dependence. When we turned to common cases of larger-scale shared intention, we turned to box-C-type interpersonal indirect intention dependence. When we then turned to diachronically robust social rules, we turned primarily to box-B-type diachronic dependencies across synchronic constructions that themselves involve box-C-type synchronic dependencies across individuals—though there may also be room for something like box-D-type cross-temporal dependencies across those synchronic constructions. And these different forms of dependence help support relevant functioning—of shared intentions and of social rules.

The rule content of a social rule is an abstract object with a prescriptive structure. On our theory, this abstract object is fixed both by the content of kernel shared policies and by the potential extension of range induced by further aspects of the social psychology of the kernel. Specifying this content can involve a strategy of abstraction. Return to the example of our shared policy, and social rule, in favor of wearing masks in a pandemic. Perhaps I participate in the shared policy because I judge that mask-wearing protects the wearer; in contrast, you participate because you judge that general mask-wearing protects the overall population.[38] To get the content of our shared policy, and so the social rule, we abstract away from these differences and arrive at the content *wear a mask in the pandemic*, which is something we each intend. We each participate in this shared policy, and the associated social rule, though we differ on the main justification of the activity.

A guiding conjecture has been that the kind of social rule that is central to the rule-guided infrastructure of human organized institutions involves forms of shared intention characteristic of small-scale cases of acting together. While we have significantly adjusted the details of this conjecture, we have retained a central role in these social rules for shared intentionality—for ways in which we together organize aspects of how we live with each other.

4.3 "Massively shared agency"

Let me now compare my treatment of shared intention and social rules with Scott Shapiro's discussion of "massively shared agency"—large-scale activities organized in the direction of a certain end but in which many of the participants neither have a corresponding intention in favor of the group's achieving that end nor even know or care that their own activity promotes that end (Shapiro 2014; 2011, 148–50). Think of the many workers involved in the production of iPhones. This activity is organized in the direction of the end of producing those phones. This organization is shaped by and grounded in a relevant agential background that favors that organizing end: it is not merely a pattern of strategic coordination across the many different participants. Nevertheless, many of those in the "trenches" may neither care about that end nor even know that what they are doing promotes that end. Many may simply be earning a paycheck.

This is where Shapiro appeals to the organizing role of a "shared plan" for a group G to J. There is in group G a Shapiro-type shared plan for the group to J just when

(1) that plan "was designed for members of G so that they may J by following it" and
(2) "most participants" in G "accept" that plan (2014, 283).

Further, for a participant to accept that plan is for her to accept (and so, I take it, intend) her part of the plan and to be committed to "let other members do their parts."[39] However, to accept the plan she need not intend or have as an end that the group J: she can be an alienated participant.

So, a group can have a Shapiro-type shared plan to J in the absence of an overall Bratman-style shared intention, within that group, to J.

Associated with my model of a shared intention is a conception of a shared plan as, quite simply, a shared intention. A person who does not intend that we make iPhones is not a participant in our shared intention to make iPhones and so (within my framework) is not a participant in a corresponding shared plan to make iPhones. But she may be, on my model, a penumbral participant in a social rule concerning making iPhones. In contrast, within Shapiro's framework, she may be a participant in a relevant Shapiro-type shared plan, but such Shapiro-type shared plans are not in general shared intentions as I have understood them.

Of course, what matters are the phenomena, not the words. So, to avoid confusion, when I talk of a Shapiro-style shared plan I will use a subscript: *shared plan$_S$*. Understood as a social psychological web, there can be a shared plan$_S$ for the group to J even though some relevant participants do not themselves intend or have as an end that the group J, but only have associated personal intentions.

Consider now Shapiro's conditions (1) and (2) for a shared plan$_S$ for the group to J. What is it for a plan to be "designed for members of G so that they may J by following it"? Who is doing this designing?[40] What is this designing? Is it itself an intentional activity? How is this designing related to the motivational story behind the satisfaction of the condition that "most participants" of G "accept" that plan and "let other members do their parts"?

Here I propose a strategy like our strategy concerning Hart's conditions for a social rule. We see Shapiro's (1) and (2) as together articulating a *design specification* for a shared plan$_S$ for the group to J.[41] We then ask: what social psychological structures realize this design specification?

There may be a temptation here—one against which Shapiro warns (2014, 278)—to see the designer as an Austinian sovereign and the motivation at work in (2) as deriving from sanctions and incentives set up by that sovereign. But here we can learn from Hart's insight that Austin's model undertheorized the sociality common to and important for the sovereignty central to law, since sovereignty in law characteristically involves guidance of the practical thinking of legal officials by social rules. And I think a similar thought would apply here to an appeal to such an Austin-inspired realization of Shapiro's condition (1). Such cases are possible. But the realization of condition (1) that will be common and important when we turn to human large-scale organized institutions will itself involve forms of shared thought and action.

And here I propose to appeal to a realization of (1) that involves a kernel of relevant shared policies. We can then understand the motivational story behind the satisfaction of condition (2) by appeal to extending reasons traceable to that shared policy kernel. Returning to iPhones, the thought is that the background source of organization is a kernel group that has shared intentions/policies in favor of and in support of the group's making iPhones, and that induces extending reasons that support the overall group's activity of making iPhones by supporting both conforming activities on the part of a relevant penumbra of participants and allowing others to do their parts. And this realization of conditions (1) and (2) has a structure that is isomorphic to the structure involved in hybrid social rules, as I have understood them.

Might we instead appeal to a realization of (1) that is itself a shared plan$_S$ for the group to J, and that need not involve kernel shared policies (in my stronger sense of "shared")? Well, this would be a realization of (1) that itself involves a yet further background designer. But who or what is that yet-further-in-the background designer? It seems that here we are again faced with a theoretical choice between an Austin-inspired answer and an answer that involves the kind of sociality that I have emphasized. So, to avoid embarking on a regress of background designers, I think we do best to see the basic realization of Shapiro's two conditions—the realization that is central to our model of organized institutions—as, plus or minus a bit, the kind of kernel-penumbra structure I have described. Since this kernel-penumbra structure is seen as a realization of Shapiro's two design specifications, there is here a convergence in the accounts. But in privileging this shared-policy-shaped realization, and thereby the centrality of Bratman-style shared intention, there is a divergence in the spirit of the accounts.

My thought, then, is that even given a role for shared plans$_S$ within a group whose members do not unanimously participate in the stronger form of sharing highlighted in my theory, we will want to appeal to something like that stronger form of sharing when we specify important realizations of condition (1) of such shared plans$_S$.[42] This allows us to retain the basic structure of our Hart-inspired solution to the problem of rule content: in these theoretically basic cases, rule content continues to be fixed by kernel shared policies and augmenting kernel attitudes. We thereby see the proposed kernel-penumbra structure as a theoretically privileged realization of the kind of social structure to which Shapiro's talk of a designer points. This realization involves a kernel of shared intentions and shared policies, and associated extending reasons, that help to explain relevant forms of organization and rule content, including the intentional content of the massively shared activity (e.g., making iPhones).[43] So, while I agree with Shapiro that we need a model of massively shared agency that does not identify such sharing simply with Bratman-style shared intentions, I do not think this should lead us to abandon appeal to the sequentially constructed shared policy model of hybrid social rules I have been developing.[44]

Let's step back. We might try to understand massively shared agency as a kind of strategic coordination equilibrium across the participants. But this leaves out the organizing role of a kind of sharing in the background. Following Gilbert, we might try to appeal to obligation-involving joint commitments. But that threatens to treat common but contingently present obligations as essential to the social organization. Shapiro appeals here to background shared plans$_S$. But when we ask what normally realizes the design specifications associated with such shared plans$_S$ we arrive at the structure of our sequentially constructed shared policy model of hybrid social rules. We thereby retain the centrality of shared intentionality.

4.4 Where's the normativity?

The conjecture is that in central cases, social rules involve a web of shared, doubly reflexive policies of individuals that prescribe for the group/for "us." Though in this respect these attitudes of each are like judgments about what "we" ought to do, they are not themselves ought judgments or judgments about normative reasons. These policies do, however, engage characteristic demands of plan rationality, demands that are sensitive to the interrelations built into the sharing of the policies: while not themselves normative judgments, they involve a kind of rational normativity.

In contrast, Brennan et al. 2013 and Southwood 2019 propose that a social norm in favor of action-regularity R essentially involves public clusters of normative attitudes in favor of acting in accordance with R, where these normative attitudes are dependent on a presumed R-conforming social practice (a presumption that might be mistaken).[45] Such a social practice is a public behavioral regularity that is explained by pro-attitudes of the participants. And the presumed-practice dependence goes by way of beliefs, which may be mistaken, that the (presumed) practice provides normative reason for conformity to it (Brennan et al. 2013, sec. 4.3).

Brennan et al. have a capacious understanding of what counts, for their purposes, as a normative attitude, but the central case is that of normative judgments in favor of acting in accord with R, where that includes judgments that one ought/has normative reason so to act. These normative judgments might be false, but if one had such normative judgments but acted contrary to them one might be seen as pro tanto irrational.

The shared policy model of social rules defended here highlights not normative judgments but shared policies in favor of acting in accord with R. While these policies prescribe that "we" so act, they are not judgments that we ought so to act, though they would normally be embedded in webs of judgments of value and reasons. The relevant practice dependence involves the condition that these shared policies are rationally dependent, by way of cognitive conditions on rational intention, on the actual pattern of action. In contrast with Brennan et al., this does not require that the participants in these policies see the pattern as (part of) their justifying reason for associated ought judgments. What needs to be dependent on the presumed practice is not an ought judgment but the policy. So, there can be fundamentalist participants in a social rule.

Brennan et al. emphasize that social norms are "minimally normative," where "[a] phenomenon is minimally normative inasmuch as it involves *rules* or *requirements* that permit, forbid, and require certain actions and attitudes."[46] And they think that this minimal normativity requires normative attitudes. But the policies I have been highlighting "permit, forbid, and require certain actions." They are general intentions, not merely desires or preferences; and intentions prescribe. My policy that we J prescribes that we J, and in that sense requires that we J. In analogous ways it can forbid or permit. And we can then extend this point to shared policies.

Though they are not normative attitudes, these policies are subject to norms of rationality that are separable from whether there are substantive normative reasons in their favor. And there is an interplay between the application of these norms of plan rationality and the interrelations characteristic of shared policies. In this way, the cited shared policies ensure a minimal, defeasible, rationality-based justification of associated criticisms and demands.

What about Hart's thought that the expression of "criticisms, demands, and acknowledgements" grounded in the social rule will itself normally involve "a wide range of 'normative' language" (Hart 2012, 57; see also

Brennan et al. 2013, 28–29)? Well, we have seen that multiple, potential oughts that are expressive of criticisms and demands associated with a social rule can be grounded in pressures of plan rationality, in the possibility of authority-according content, in the transmission of substantive normative reasons if such there be, in the application of extending reasons, and in relevant substantive norms of obligation, including norms of reliance-based obligations and, in certain cases, obligations to defer to certain kinds of accorded authority. So, we can explain the "wide range of normative language" in the expression of social-rule-grounded criticisms and demands without saying that the attitudes at the heart of a social rule are themselves ought judgments.[47] So, we can reject the idea that the relevant normativity of social rules must be anchored in normative ought/reason judgments of the participants.

Consider now a criticism offered by Brennan et al. of a view of social norms proposed by Cristina Bicchieri (2006, esp. 11–16). Bicchieri and I agree that at the heart of relevant social phenomena are attitudes that are not themselves normative judgments. But we develop this idea differently. With respect to a "followed" social norm, Bicchieri's proposal, roughly, is:

> If R is a rule that says how to act in S, then R is a *followed social norm* in population P if enough members of P are such that
>
> 1. Each knows of R, and
> 2. Each prefers to conform to R if
>   (a) (empirical expectations) she believes there will be sufficient conformity by others in P,
>
>   *and either*
>
>   (b) (normative expectations) she believes sufficient number of others expect her to conform,
>
>   or
>
>   (b′) (normative expectations with sanctions) she believes sufficient number of others expect her to conform, prefer her to conform, and may sanction non-conformity
>
>   and
> 3. a sufficient number of those in P satisfy 2.(a) and either 2.(b) or 2.(b′), and as a result
> 4. each prefers to conform to R.

A central condition—(b)/(b')—is, roughly, that "enough" participants think (perhaps falsely) that others expect her/him to conform. These supposed expectations on the part of others might be just empirical beliefs of those others about one's conformity. But they might be normative beliefs of those others that one ought to conform (Bicchieri 2006, 15). In either case, an important feature of Bicchieri's proposal is that it does not require that anyone actually does judge that folks ought to conform—there need not in fact be relevant normative judgments. What are needed are not actual normative judgments but only (potentially false) beliefs about the expectations of others (where those supposed expectations might be supposed normative beliefs), and a related personal preference concerning one's own conformity.[48] And a main criticism offered by Brennan et al. is in effect that, for this very reason, Bicchieri's proposal does not satisfy a minimal normativity condition (2013, 26).

It is important here to note the contrast between Bicchieri's appeal to *preferences personally* to conform to a rule and my appeal to *intentions* that *we* conform, intentions that are elements in *shared* intentions. This involves three important differences: my theory appeals to *intention*, not mere preference; the target of these intentions is *our* conformity, not just one's own conformity; and there is *shared* intention, and so an interplay of the interrelations involved in such sharing with norms of plan rationality. This appeal to *shared intentions that we* conform is how the shared policy model both satisfies a condition of "minimal normativity" and ensures a minimal rationality-based justification of associated criticisms and demands. And it does this without an essential appeal to normative judgments of the participants.

This suggests that to arrive at an acceptable version of what Brennan et al. (22) label a "clusters of *non-normative attitudes*" view (where they would understand that label as applying both to Bicchieri's proposal and to mine), we do well to draw on these further resources of the planning theory: a more complex, plan-infused psychology of practical thought and action and its associated norms of plan rationality; the potential for plural contents of those plan-infused attitudes; and the sharing of planning attitudes, sharing that involves characteristic interpersonal interrelations.[49] We can thereby carve out a theoretically illuminating space between appeal to normative judgment and appeal to a combination of personal preference with beliefs about others.

Once again, however, we should remember our strategy of sufficiency. I have described plan-theoretic structures that are sufficient for robust and extensive forms of social functioning characteristic of a kind of social rule that promises to be central to the rule-guided infrastructure of human, organized institutions. This allows that Bicchieri and Brennan et al. may have modeled different kinds of social norm involved in our social world. But my proposal nevertheless promises to support the overall conjecture that our planning capacities play a foundational role in multiple forms of human practical organization.

II RULE-GUIDED INFRASTRUCTURE OF ORGANIZED INSTITUTIONS

5 ON THE WAY TO ORGANIZED INSTITUTIONS

SOCIAL RULES OF PROCEDURE

5.1 Institutional procedural positivism

We now turn to the question of whether our shared policy model of social rules supports an illuminating model of the rule-guided infrastructure of organized institutions.[1]

Our problem is like Hart's problem of how we should understand the step from a pre-legal society infused with primary social rules to a society with a legal system. Hart's answer appealed to a structure of secondary social rules—social rules about rules. These include secondary rules of recognition, change, and adjudication; and these secondary rules induce the possibility of valid rules, within the relevant abstract-object-rule-system, that do not themselves correspond to social rules. Hart argued that a society with a web of primary social rules will likely find itself facing systematic problems of uncertainty, stasis, and inefficiency in enforcement, problems to which a solution is provided by such secondary social rules.[2] Our analogous question is: Given our model of social rules, what more is needed to provide an illuminating model of the rule-guided infrastructure of human, organized institutions? How best can we understand the step from a society infused with shared intentionality and social rules to a society with organized institutions? And, as anticipated, my answer will appeal to *social rules of procedure* that say how to resolve certain problems for an institution.[3]

This is an analogue of Hart's strategy of supposing that a basic phenomenon of social rules is at work in both the pre-legal and legal cases, but that the latter case involves social rules with a distinctive content. My appeal to social rules of procedure draws on a somewhat different social rule content. It will, however, play a role—in my account of the step from a world of social rules to a world that includes organized institutions—that broadly corresponds to the role of relevant secondary social rules in Hart's model of the step from pre-legal to legal sociality.

In seeking such a construction of organized institutions, we are not primarily seeking a just-so story of an actual historical development of these phenomena. The primary aim is to articulate conceptual, psychological, metaphysical, and normative structure that illuminates phenomena that are part of our social world.[4]

This strategy involves the Hart-friendly idea that certain kinds of actual social rules and their role in the actual practical thinking of individuals are central to rule-guided institutional organization. The specific contents of these actual social rules can be expected to vary across different institutions. We do not try to derive relevant, guiding rules directly from morality. Nor do we impose a separate moral filter on the relevant rules. Nor do we try to derive relevant rules from information about the specific substantive preferences of individual participants taken together with a normative conception of how to reason from those preferences to, as is said, a social preference.[5] We instead look directly at the actual guiding social rules.

We aim to characterize social rules whose role in guiding practical thinking is at the heart of the rule-guided infrastructure of actual institutions. This is where Hart turned to the cited secondary social rules, and where I propose that we turn to social rules of procedure. My proposal will be that the move from social rules to organized rule-governed institutions of the sort of interest here is a move to a form of actual, procedural-social-rule-structured social thinking. We can call this *institutional positivism,* since it avoids a general condition that an organized institution satisfy certain moral constraints.[6] It is an institutional *procedural* positivism that highlights social *procedural* rules.[7]

5.2 Initial model of social rules of procedure

Begin with the thought that, while there are multiple social rules at work within a so-far non-institutionalized group, there will be occasions in which problems arise that require for their solution some sort of social decision procedure. Perhaps string players in Palo Alto get together to promote music in the area, and the issue emerges of whether to collect dues and, if so, what to do with the revenue. While there are social rules that solve some relevant problems, there is, so far, no social rule that solves these problems. There is a gap in the social rules, a gap that the participants have reason to fill to solve problems of social organization.[8]

In talking here of problems of social organization, I leave open the specific contours of these problems. This contrasts with Hart's appeal to a trio of more specific problems. As I see it, different problems of social organization will arise in different cases. In the present case the problems are mundane ones about the social organization of the string players. In some cases, people may focus on higher-level problems, such as broad problems of production and distribution, or how to promote group self-governance. I seek to characterize a general form of response to multiple problems of social organization that are left unresolved by existing social rules.

And my thought is that in response to such problems, a common strategy will involve some sort of *procedure* for reaching a solution—perhaps a majority vote among participants, or a Quaker-inspired consensus procedure, or shared deliberation, or deference to a certain subgroup or to those who have a certain status conferred by that procedure or occupy a certain office created by that procedure. This will normally involve the operation of a different kind of social rule—a social rule of procedure. And my Peter French–inspired conjecture is that the introduction of such a social rule of procedure is the basic step from a cluster of social rules to a rule-guided, organized institution.

To develop this idea, I begin with an initial model of social rules of procedure and then add further complexities. In this chapter I talk informally of a social procedural rule of a specific institution. In the next chapter, I seek a more precise understanding of the relation between multiple social procedural rules and a particular organized institution.

I will focus on the central case of a social rule with a cotemporaneous kernel. My conjecture is that this central case is fundamental to a theoretically illuminating specification of sufficient conditions for human rule-guided organized institutions. What is special about a social rule of procedure is its content: a specification of procedures for resolving certain problems. And these procedures are tied to relevant follow-through. So, the content of a social rule of procedure will be, roughly:

Given relevant intentions to solve a certain problem,

(i) proceed in such-and-such ways for arriving at a resolution of that problem, and then

(ii) follow-through in such-and-such ways with the outputs of those procedures.⁹

This is a more complex content than that of a social rule that simply says that the first violinist sets the tempo. But its social-psychological structure remains that of a social rule, as understood by our shared policy model.

These problem-solving procedures can be more or less pure procedures, as in a majority vote. In contrast, they can privilege certain substantive considerations by assigning weights for relevant deliberation (Bratman 2014a, chap. 7). For example, a department's social rule of procedure concerning graduate admission might assign certain weights to letters of recommendation. A related possibility is that the social rule specifies how risks are to be treated within relevant deliberation. This would specify a social "risk function" of the sort that has been highlighted in the individual case by Buchak (2013) and by Murray and Buchak (2019).

Such specified procedures may involve differing roles to be played by different participants. For example, a department's social rule of procedure for solving its problem of graduate admissions might designate a subcommittee with a specific role in solving this problem. Certain individuals—those who are at a given time members of that admissions subcommittee—are accorded a distinctive status within the processes that respond to this problem. In this way such social procedural rules can induce a structure of *institutional roles and offices*, a structure that is a common feature of human organized institutions.

A social rule of procedure can involve views about who has relevant expertise. Think of a university's procedures for evaluating a candidate for tenure, or a religious institution's commitment to treating certain participants as having religious expertise, or a government's procedures for incorporating scientific expertise. Again, this means that certain individuals are accorded a distinctive role or status within processes that aim to solve a relevant problem.

In summary: social rules of procedure can concern more or less pure procedures, substantive weights for reasoning, attitudes to risk, and/or designated roles and related statuses.

A social rule of procedure will involve a kernel whose time-slice projections involve shared policies. The associated pattern of activity involves conformity both to specified procedures and then to their outputs. So, the social rule kernels will involve both shared policies that favor the procedure in relevant contexts (for example, a voting procedure), and associated shared policies that favor follow-through with the outputs of the procedure (for example, the results of the vote). So, hybrid social rules of procedure can involve two kinds of penumbra:

(a) a penumbra of the aspect of the social rule kernel that favors following the cited procedures, and
(b) a penumbra of the aspect of the social rule kernel that favors downstream follow-through with outputs of those procedures.

Let's call (a) the *procedural penumbra* and (b) the *output penumbra*. Those in the procedural penumbra will normally also be in the output penumbra—for example, Shapiro's judge. But there can be those in the output penumbra who play no role in the background procedures and so are not in the procedural penumbra. Ordinary citizens, within Hart's theory, may be such persons with respect to certain secondary social rules.

We now need to say more about outputs of such procedures.

5.3 Outputs: Two distinctions

In some cases, the output of a social rule of procedure specifies a type of *action*—for example, sending medical supplies to a certain city, or performing works by Schubert, or accepting certain applicants to a graduate program. In other cases, the output specifies a certain proposition—for example, a proposition of climate science, or of a certain doctrine—to be *accepted* in relevant thinking (Bratman 1999d).

Acceptance is relativized to certain (perhaps broadly characterized) contexts and can be shaped by practical concerns. Acceptance can diverge from belief: I might believe the ladder is safe but, given the risks, not accept that proposition in my reasoning about cleaning the roof. And in the case of an acceptance output of a social rule of procedure there can be complex relations between what is accepted and the beliefs of those who participate in that rule—a point to which I will return.

In one sense, outputs of a social procedural rule will be *events* that are the result of the operation of the social rule—for example, the result of a vote. These events will have an action-focused or acceptance-focused content. These output events will normally be public and occur within a context of persisting social procedural rules and related activities and processes (e.g., counting votes). Given the nature of this persisting, background social structure, and the nature of the output event, there will normally be a thick, temporally extended social-psychological web that is, I will say, *crystallized* by that output event. For example: the vote favors action A (or acceptance of proposition P) and, in the context of the persisting social procedural rule, that event output crystallizes a temporally extended social-psychological web that favors performing A or accepting P. That web will include the continued role of the relevant social rule, now in support of follow-through. This crystallized, temporally extended social web is, in a second sense, an output of the procedure. This *crystallized output* is a temporally extended social web that involves both persisting social rules—including social subrules of follow-through—and embedded, public output events; and it has an induced content along the lines of "accept P" or "perform A."

So, we have a 2×2 matrix of kinds of social-procedural-rule output:

	Action focused	Acceptance focused
Event output	1	2
Crystallized output	3	4

An event output (as in boxes 1 or 2), together with a persisting background of relevant social rules of procedure, helps constitute a corresponding, crystallized output (as in boxes 3 or 4). In the case of box 4, if all goes well this crystallized output will tend to lead to a web of thinking within which the favored proposition is accepted. In the case of box 3, if all goes well this crystallized output will tend to lead to a web of activities associated with the favored action.

The activities/modes of thinking supported by such crystallized outputs will include activities/modes of thinking of relevant individuals and/or groups of individuals who think/act in shared intentional ways.[10] Since there may be participants in an output penumbra of the social rule of procedure, we cannot assume that these activities/modes of thinking will include shared intentionality on the part of all participants in the underlying social rules of procedure.

5.4 Acceptance-focused outputs

Consider now box 4. A social rule of procedure that issues in acceptance-focused crystallized outputs will involve a social subrule of follow-through concerning the role of the favored proposition in downstream thought and action. This social subrule will support downstream thought and action that involve accepting the favored proposition in relevant contexts—for example, using that proposition as a premise in certain further decision procedures.

Such a social-rule-generated acceptance-focused crystallized output is distinguishable from a condition of broad agreement in belief concerning the favored proposition. While these phenomena many times go together, such broad agreement by itself neither guarantees nor is necessary for a corresponding social-rule-generated acceptance-focused crystallized output. It is possible, however, that a specific social procedural rule supports one or both of these tight connections between broad agreement in belief and acceptance-focused output. And significant divergence between acceptance-focused output and what is broadly believed in the relevant, overall population can be a source of instability.[11]

An acceptance-focused crystallized output will be temporally extended. It will involve a web of social rules concerning both background procedures and follow-through. This structure will support downstream functioning in which the acceptance of a favored proposition plays characteristic roles in further practical thinking. Perhaps a company's procedural-social-rule-generated acceptance-focused crystallized output endorses certain propositions about climate change, and so these propositions are set to appear as premises in further reasoning—individual, shared, and/or institutional[12]—concerning its business practices. If all goes well, this downstream functioning will emerge from the proper functioning of the background, persisting social rules of procedure—now in follow-through mode—taken together with relevant event outputs. So, these acceptance-focused crystallized outputs will play relevant, downstream functional roles, and we again ground functioning in construction.

5.5 Action-focused and rule outputs

Consider now box 3: action-focused crystallized outputs. As noted, such social-procedural-rule action-focused crystallized outputs need not correspond to shared intentions across all participants. Such crystallized outputs are temporally extended and robust in a way in which shared intentions need not be. But even if we focus on temporally persisting shared intentions, our theory continues to support a separation between crystallized outputs and corresponding shared intentions. A primary reason for this[13] is that these crystallized outputs can be outputs of a social procedural rule with a kernel-penumbra structure, one whose output penumbra includes alienated participants. Such penumbral, alienated participants will have personal intentions to conform to the outputs. However, since they do not intend the general conformity to the procedures or the outputs, they may well not themselves participate in corresponding shared intentions.

Some action-focused crystallized outputs can be general and thereby *rule-like*: they can favor a general way of acting in certain general circumstances. Think of an output that says quite generally to wear masks, or to follow a majority-rule procedure to settle certain issues. This gives us the idea of an action-focused crystallized *rule output* of a social procedural rule. A crystallized rule output is a construction that consists of relevant social rules of procedure (including their subrules of follow-through) and event outputs. The follow-through aspect of the background social procedural rules is set to engage with the event outputs in shaping downstream activity. So, we can see such crystallized rule outputs as, indirectly, themselves a kind of social rule in favor of follow-through activities, one that need not correspond to a shared intention or shared policy among all the participants.

5.6 Authority-according social rules of procedure

I have so far associated social rules of procedure with regularities in following certain problem-solving procedures and in following through with their outputs. These social rules of procedure can go beyond a concern with pure procedures and include specification of substantive weights and/or "risk functions" and/or specification of who has relevant expertise. And these social rules can specify relevant roles and statuses. I now want to recall our earlier discussion (in Section 1.2.4) of authority-according shared intention and turn to an analogue in the case of social rules of procedure.

The shared policies that help constitute a social rule of procedure involve interlocking policies of each, and so policies of each that favor relevant thought and action in part by way of the workings of relevant policies of each. Consider now social rules of procedure in which these policies of each favor the roles of the policies of others by way of according authority to play those roles. This authority may be accorded to certain persons or subcommittees, or to those seen as having a certain expertise, or to the occupants of a certain office or status. These are *authority-according* social rules of procedure.

In according such authority, a social rule of procedure supports distinctive forms of practical thinking within a domain, practical thinking that goes beyond guidance by basic norms of plan rationality. Insofar as the social rule is effective, within the relevant domain participants will be set (defeasibly) to treat some as having an associated, accorded *right* to settle certain matters, and participants will be set (defeasibly) to see some as having accorded *duties* of deference to authoritative decisions. This can induce forms of authorized *hierarchy*: those in certain roles are authorized to make decisions to which others are to defer.

This will, then, involve practical thinking with contents along the lines of:

Within the domain of this authority-according social rule, P has the accorded authority/right/duty/permission to A.

However—to return to an earlier thread—the existence of a social rule supporting this structure of practical thinking would not by itself entail that there are normatively substantive rights and duties. There may only be *de facto* rights and duties that are *relativized* to a domain associated with this contingent social rule.[14] Nor need the existence of this authority-according social rule entail that the participants believe there are corresponding normatively substantive rights and duties, though such beliefs will be common. Nevertheless, authority-according social rules of procedure do involve intentions and policies in favor of forms of practical thinking that essentially involve this web of concepts of relativized authority, rights, and duties.

In Section 1.2.4, I generalized Darwall's appeal to "conventional authority relations" to an appeal to shared-intentional authority relations. I am now generalizing further with an analogous appeal to *social-procedural-rule authority relations*: authority relations that are relativized to a domain of thought and action associated with a specific, contingent authority-according social rule of procedure.

Small-scale shared intentional activity involves interlocking intentions: each intends that the relevant intentions of others play relevant roles. But it need not involve an interlocking that favors the role of acceptance of the authority of others. Similarly, social rules of procedure, while involving interlocking, need not in general be authority according. However, given the hierarchical complexity that is common within organized human institutions we can reasonably suppose that at least normally such institutions will involve authority-according social rules of procedure. This is the *institutional centrality of authority-according social rules of procedure*.

Associated with authority-according social rules of procedure will be not just a pattern of coordinated action but also an associated pattern of *authority acceptance* within relevant practical thinking—for example, a pattern of acceptance of the authority, within the relevant domain, of a certain subcommittee to make a certain decision for the institution, where this will involve, inter alia, a pattern of deference to and conformity to its authority-accorded decisions. This involves acceptance, within the relevant domain, of an associated, accorded right and a corresponding, accorded permission of an authorized subcommittee to make relevant decisions, and of accorded duties on the part of others to defer to that right. So, in such an authorized hierarchy there is acceptance of something in the spirit of what John Searle (2010, 8–9) calls "deontic powers."

Such authority-according social rules of procedure, then, prescribe (a) patterns of coordinated action (e.g., conforming to a subcommittee's decision), (b) associated patterns of authority acceptance (patterns of acceptance of accorded relativized rights, permissions, and duties), and (c) coordination between (a) and (b). Authority-according social rules of procedure will have a *coordinating dual aspect*: they will prescribe both deontic-structured practical thinking and associated patterns of action; and they will prescribe coordination across these forms of thought and action.

I take it that the Hohfeldian thinking involved in (b) is not reducible to thinking simply about patterns of action, as in (a). Maintaining this distinction between the aspect of such social rules of procedure that accords, as Searle would say, deontic powers (albeit relativized, *de facto* deontic powers) and the aspect that directly prescribes relevant action does not, however, require that we go on to say, as Searle seems to go on to say, that a social rule that accords these deontic powers entails the existence of new normative reasons for action (Searle 2010, 9).[15] After all, there may be social acceptance of authority to do very bad things—for example, accorded authority in the story "The Lottery" to designate who is stoned. There are further normative questions concerning the conditions under which such structures of socially accorded relativized authority support normatively defensible, substantive authority. We need to distinguish the "is" of authority-according social psychological structures from the "oughts" of normatively substantive authority relations.

Would Hart agree? Consider his observation:

> Rules that confer rights, though distinct from commands, need not be moral rules or coincide with them. Rights, after all, exist under

the rules of ceremonies, games, and many other spheres regulated by rules which are irrelevant to the question of justice or what the law ought to be. Nor need rules which confer rights be just or morally good rules. The rights of a master over his slaves show us that. (Hart 1958, 606)

A social practice of slavery involves social rules that "confer rights" to a master and correlative duties to a slave. We can observe these right-/duty-conferring social rules, and their associated practical thinking, but still ask whether there are good normative reasons for a slave to defer to a master. Hart is clear in these comments that there need be no good moral reason to defer. And a plausible reading of these comments—though one that goes beyond Hart's explicit comment—is that in such a case of a right-conferring rule that is morally unjust and morally bad, there may be *no good normative reason at all* for a slave to accede to an exercise of the rule-conferred right on the part of the master. This is so even though there is a structure of conferred rights and duties, and associated pressures of wide-scope plan rationality. The conferred rights and duties are in this case relativized to a morally abhorrent practice, and so would normally not ensure normatively substantive rights and duties.[16]

Finally, we can put these comments about authority-according social rules of procedure together with our earlier observations about social rules of procedure more generally. Authority-according social rules of procedure can in some cases be hybrid. There is a distinction between procedural and output penumbras of an authority-according hybrid social rule of procedure. And the outputs of an authority-according social rule of procedure can in some cases be action-focused and in other cases be acceptance-focused.

We are almost ready to make the next step, the step from our shared policy model of (authority-according) social rules of procedure to a model of an organized institution. But first, some loose ends.

5.7 Further ideas

5.7.1 Induced teleology

A social rule of procedure can sometimes issue in an output that specifies a course of action *with a certain, further aim*. Perhaps the output is not simply that medical supplies be sent to a given city but that they be sent in order to reduce fatalities or, in a different case, in order to support the local government. Call this *induced further teleology*. When the social-rule-induced output has this further teleological structure, the activity that is guided by this output will be constrained to be responsive to that built-in further aim.

Induced further teleology should be distinguished from reason-grounded extension. In a case of induced further teleology, a further aim is built into the output of the procedural social rule. In a case of reason-grounded extension of policies in favor of following through with outputs of certain procedures, a kernel shared policy helps induce reasons—for example, incentives—that favor the conformity of various individuals to those outputs, outputs that need not (though they may) have a further, induced teleological structure.

In the case of outputs that involve induced further teleology, reason-grounded extension may support an individual doing what counts as her part in the output even though in doing this the individual need not herself be acting in pursuit of that further aim. Perhaps the output of the hybrid social rule of procedure is sending the medical supplies as a way of relieving suffering, but in doing her part in response to extending reasons (e.g., her salary) the driver of the delivery truck (who is in the relevant output penumbra) may not herself be guided by that further aim (though ways of driving that block the relief of suffering will be precluded by that further aim). It can still be true that the supplies are sent in order to relieve suffering.

5.7.2 Historical thickness

These processes of social-procedural-rule-guided thought and action may be *historically thick*. They may include procedures undertaken in the past by those who have departed from the scene prior to the final social-procedural-rule-based resolution of a relevant issue. After all, these can be complicated matters whose resolution takes a lot of time. Further, social rules of procedure can have contents that support a role of the earlier history in determining a given output. There can be, say, a social rule of procedure that requires that the procedures conform to conditions articulated in a document created years ago. This is a way in which a social rule of procedure may appeal to external vehicles (Epstein 2015).

At each time along the way the procedures, and their outputs, need to be grounded in operative social rules that themselves involve shared policy kernels. In the central cases highlighted here these kernels will be cotemporaneous. There can also be cases in which these kernels are non-cotemporaneous. But in such cases, as the procedures unfold, there needs to be, at the least, a currently functioning penumbra that involves extending reasons—for example, reasons induced by a diachronic snowball of reliance—traceable to the kernel.

This helps us see two different ways in which historical, external vehicles—for example, documents written at t_1 as an issue of the functioning of a shared policy kernel at t_1—might play a role in downstream social-procedural-rule-guided thought and action. In a basic case, there is at t_2 a shared policy kernel that says to use these historical documents as part of relevant procedures. In a second case, the production of these documents by the t_1-kernel is part of the way in which that kernel induces a relevant penumbra at t_2 even though there does not remain at t_2 a corresponding shared policy kernel. The documents help explain why, in this case, the withering away of the kernel does not induce the withering away of the social procedural rule.

5.7.3 Continuity, discontinuity, and core capacity

Our theory posits theoretical continuity—conceptual, metaphysical, psychological, and normative—in the move from individual temporally extended planning agency to shared intention and shared intentional activity. One aspect of this continuity is that our construction of shared intention, like our model of temporally extended planning agency, does not essentially involve interpersonal authority acceptance. And we have then used such shared intentions in the move to social rules.

However, I have conjectured that a model of social rules of procedure central to the rule-guided infrastructure of organized human institutions should appeal, in the content of relevant policies, to accorded and accepted, relativized *authority*. There is here a discontinuity in the step from the basic case of a social rule to the social rules of procedure central to organized institutions. So, there is continuity in the steps from individual temporally extended planning agency to shared intention and then to basic social rules. But there is an authority-focused discontinuity when we turn to human organized institutions, given the centrality to such organized institutions of authority acceptance and associated acceptance of, as Searle would say, "deontic powers" (albeit relativized, *de facto* deontic powers).

This combination, of continuity in the steps to shared intention and then to basic social rules, and then a discontinuity in further constructive steps, contrasts with views of both John Searle (1990) and Margaret Gilbert (2009). Both these philosophers aim to understand larger institutions in part by way of a distinctive new element they directly introduce in the initial step from the individual case to SIA. In Searle's case this is the introduction of non-reducible "we-intentions"; in Gilbert's case it is the introduction of non-reducible, obligation-involving "joint commitments." On my proposal, in contrast, the relevant discontinuity occurs later in the sequence of constructions: we appeal to accorded authority and authority acceptance in the step to the social rules of procedure characteristic of human organized institutions.

This is also in tension with the view of Abraham Sesshu Roth (2004) that even small-scale cases of shared intention essentially involve relations of "non-dictatorial" authority between the participants. Roth does not argue that since authority is needed at the institutional level it will seep into the small-scale case. Instead, he thinks this authority is directly needed to explain "contralateral commitments" that are systematically present in small-scale cases. In contrast, my claim is that we get robust sufficient conditions for small-scale shared intentional activity by way of our plan-theoretic model without an appeal to authority. Relations of authority can appear in specific cases of authority-according shared intention, but are not essential to the basic case of shared intention.

As this point, however, we need to address a question from the other direction, a question from Elise Sugarman. The discontinuity I have noted involves special contents of policies that are central to human organized institutions: these contents appeal to relativized authority and "deontic powers." But given that what we are appealing to is not a new attitude (as in Searle's theory of we-intention) or a new substantive normative relation built into SIA (as in Gilbert's theory of joint commitment), why say that this is an important form of discontinuity? After all, we know we need to expand relevant intention contents even in the move from individual intentional agency to SIA, yet in that case I have emphasized the continuity.

The answer is that appeal, within the contents of relevant policies, to according and accepting authority, rights, and duties involves appeal to distinctive forms of practical thinking that go beyond the coordination-tracking and broadly instrumental thinking associated with ordinary intentions and plans and basic norms of plan rationality. In the basic move to SIA, we exploited plan-rationality-guided coordination-tracking and instrumental thinking with respect to social ends—for example, our playing the quartet by way of interlocking intentions and meshing subplans. But we did not need to appeal to thoughts about who has, for example, an accorded right, within the SIA, to set the tempo. When we turn to complex human organized institutions, however, we do need to put acceptance of "deontic powers," within a given institution, front and center. This is the institutional centrality of authority-according social rules of procedure. So, though we are not appealing to a new psychological attitude (as does Searle) or a new normatively substantive interrelation built into SIA (as does Gilbert), we are embracing a discontinuity in the nature of the involved practical thinking: that practical thinking will be shaped not only by basic norms of plan rationality but also by accorded, relativized authority, rights, and duties.

5.7.4 Social rules of procedure and secondary rules

Return to Hart's view that the move from primary social rules to a legal system involves the introduction of certain secondary social rules. Hart highlights three such secondary social rules: a rule of recognition that specifies conditions for being a valid rule within a privileged system of rules; a rule of change that says how to change what those valid rules are; and a rule of adjudication that says how to settle disagreements about what the valid rules are or how to apply those rules. A theme in Chapter 6 will be that social rules of procedure play an overall role in our model of organized institutions that in a way parallels the overall role of these secondary social rules in Hart's model of law. Let me here briefly note some more specific commonalities.

A social rule of procedure might authorize a group to solve certain problems by following certain procedures for settling on certain rule outputs or the acceptance of certain propositions. This would be analogous to a Hartian secondary social rule of change. There can also be cases in which a social rule of procedure authorizes a group to adjudicate disputes by following certain procedures. This would be analogous to a Hartian secondary social rule of adjudication.

What about a Hartian secondary social rule of recognition? A rule of recognition is a rule for settling whether a particular rule, L, is valid within the relevant system of rules. Here we can draw on the point that a social rule of procedure can concern what propositions to accept. And we can focus here, in particular, on the acceptance of the proposition that a given rule is valid within the relevant system of rules. We can then go on to note two possibilities. The first is that a social rule of procedure might authorize a group to apply certain temporally extended procedures (e.g., court proceedings) in order to arrive at the acceptance of propositions concerning what the relevant valid rules are. The second is that a relevant social rule might directly combine with background facts, without a need for yet further temporally extended procedures, directly to set the stage for acceptance that L is (or is not) valid in the relevant system of rules. These are, then, two ways in which a Hartian social rule of recognition can be associated with a social procedural rule concerning acceptance of propositions about validity.

6 A PROCEDURAL SOCIAL RULE MODEL OF ORGANIZED INSTITUTIONS

Our next step is from our shared policy model of (authority-according) social rules of procedure to a model of organized institutions. Following Hart, we see an organized institution as rule-guided, and we seek to understand the social realization of these guiding rules. We consider *social* rules, where a social rule is social not just in its content but also in its realization in the interpersonal causal order. We then seek a model of the rule-guided infrastructure of human organized institutions. To do this, we build on our shared policy model of social rules by first characterizing, in Section 6.1, an *institutional web* of social procedural rules, one associated with a given institution, and then explaining, in Section 6.2, when outputs from rules in that web are *institutional outputs*.

6.1 An organized institution's web of social procedural rules

An organized institution involves a web of social rules of procedure.[1] It will also involve other social rules; it will involve outputs of relevant social rules of procedure; and at a given time, it will involve certain individuals. But the first step is to focus on a web of relevant (authority-according) social rules of procedure. These social rules will normally define certain roles—for example, being a member of the admissions committee, or of the tenure review committee, or of the finance committee, or of a marketing subgroup, or of the membership committee, or of a legislature, or being chief scientific officer or chief general counsel. They can thereby define offices that different people can fill at different times—for example, chair of the admissions committee.

They define procedures associated with these roles and offices. And these procedures, roles, and offices can be hierarchically related: the outputs of the tenure review committee can be subject to approval by the overall department, whose approval might then be subject to social-rule-supported approval by a school-level committee.

An organized institution will normally involve multiple social rules of procedure and multiple associated offices and roles. These may concern different practical problems. For example, there may be a social rule of procedure for deciding what goods to produce, and a different social rule of procedure for deciding on investment policies, or on ways of advertising, or on hiring policies (Strudler n.d.) Our question now is: when are different social rules of procedure in the web of one and the same institution?

For certain institutions, perhaps we can appeal to a single overarching social rule at the top of a hierarchy of social procedural rules and say that this single overarching rule is what individuates and unifies the web of social procedural rules associated with a specific institution. This may be how we should think about the role of Hart's social rule of recognition in unifying a legal system. But note that what is needed is not just an abstract object rule but a *social* rule. And the social realization of an overall, unifying abstract object rule may itself be complex and involve multiple social rules of procedure. In such cases we need to explain why those multiple social rules of procedure are elements of a single, overarching *social* rule of a single institution.

Further, we should leave room for organized institutions with a web of interconnected and interdependent social procedural rules—perhaps including higher-order social rules that potentially adjudicate certain kinds of conflict—but without a single, overarching social procedural rule that ties together the functioning of those social procedural rules. Perhaps a loosely knit start-up or an academic research group or a chess club or a music club or a neighborhood association might look like this. Here a Lockean image of sufficiently overlapping strands of interconnection and interdependence may be more apt than the image of a single overarching social rule. Perhaps a chess club has interrelated social rules for settling issues of membership, of game etiquette, of game scheduling, of ranking of players, and of the use of funds. These may include higher-order rules that can adjudicate certain conflicts—for example, between outputs concerning game scheduling and those concerning the use of funds. But this can be in the absence of a single, overarching social procedural rule that ties this all together.

If all goes smoothly, we may be able to abstract from the functioning of such an institution a single, complex, overarching abstract object rule implicit in that functioning. But even then we should be prepared to allow that such an abstracted rule may be partial and not address certain potential but not actual conflicts. And we should be prepared to allow that the actual social realization of that (perhaps partial) abstract object rule involves the functioning of a web of multiple social procedural rules—in which case we would need to explain why those social rules are elements of a single institution.

So, while there may be cases of organized institutions unified by a single overarching social rule at the top of a hierarchy, other more loosely knit institutions are in the neighborhood. And recall that our aim is not to chart in detail the many specific ways in which different organized institutions function. Instead, our aim is to articulate an abstractly specified but illuminating structure that is common to and important for a broad range of human organized institutions, despite variability across those institutions. So, let's ask whether we can usefully see the case of unification by a single overarching social rule as a special case of a more inclusive genus of more or less unified webs of social rules of procedure, webs that are characteristic of human, rule-guided organized institutions.

The search for such a genus would leave open important details about specific rule-guided institutions—details that will vary across different institutions. But the hope would be that we can arrive at a level of abstraction that is apt for our central theoretical concerns here, namely: defending the foundational roles of planning and shared intentionality in human rule-guided institutions; exploring the possibilities of institutional intention and intentional agency; and providing a framework for further investigation of specific institutions.

Begin by noting that multiple social rules of procedure might each at least implicitly require the co-possibility of the procedural functioning of each of the social rules in a given web. For example, the social procedural rule concerning advertising and the social procedural rule concerning production decisions may each at least implicitly include a condition of co-functioning alongside the other. I will say that such social procedural rules *interlock*.

Such social-rule-endorsed mutual co-functioning will in many cases also ensure that the different actions and/or propositions favored in the crystallized outputs of these different procedures will be consistent/co-possible as well. And a requirement of consistency across different crystallized outputs can sometimes be specified in each rule. For example, the social procedural rule concerning advertising might at least implicitly require that the content of its crystallized outputs be consistent with the contents of the crystallized outputs of the social procedural rule concerning what goods to produce, and vice versa.

Can we say, then, that a web of social rules of procedure characterizes a single institution just when the different rules in this web at least implicitly

(b) interlock and
(c*) require consistency in output across the web?[2]

Well, there are two problems.

First—and as noted by Sarah Paul and Axelle Marcantetti—an institution might involve multiple social rules of procedure whose procedural functioning is co-possible but whose outputs are potentially not consistent with each other. Perhaps the social rules of procedure set up multiple subcommittees with procedural rules whose functioning is co-possible but whose outputs may not be co-realizable. Perhaps this is a useful competition within the institution. In some such cases, there will be a further, higher-order social rule for adjudicating such conflicts and authorizing certain outputs. And the multiple procedural rules may each point to that background adjudicative rule. But perhaps there is a gap in the actual social procedural rules of an institution such that were certain conflicts to occur they would not be resolved by social rules already in place. (This allows that there may be more or less intelligent, or morally sensitive, or distributed approaches available for responding in the face of such conflicts. It also leaves open the possibility that in the face of certain conflicts the institution would falter.) So, condition (c*) seems too demanding. That said, we can expect that there will be significant pressures within the web of social procedural rules associated with an institution for limits on the extent of inconsistency of outputs of those rules, given needs for coordination within the institution—pressures that can in some cases be satisfied by background adjudicative rules.

Second, even if a web of social rules does satisfy (b) and (c*), it might still involve social rules of different institutions. After all, different medical schools might coordinate admissions. However, even if different schools coordinate admissions, they probably do not coordinate faculty hiring, or tuition, or building construction, or grant applications, or allocation of medical resources. In contrast, the social rules that lie behind multiple forms of institutional coordination within a *single* medical school set up a rich web of interrelated procedures, roles, and offices.

I propose to combine this idea of a rich web of social procedural rules with a condition of interlocking and a qualified consistency condition. What constitutes a social rule web of a single institution is:

(a) a sufficiently rich web of social procedural rules that
(b) interlock and
(c) to a significant extent defeasibly require consistency of outputs (perhaps by way of relevant higher-order adjudicative social procedural rules).

Condition (a) allows for vagueness about whether a web of interrelated social rules is sufficiently rich to be associated with a single organized institution. And what constitutes such sufficient richness of web may differ for different kinds of institutions. In a case of unification by a single overarching social rule at the top of a hierarchy of social procedural rules, the hierarchical structure helps constitute sufficient richness of web. Even in the absence of a single, overarching social rule, there may be higher-order social rules of procedure that help constitute sufficient richness of web. In some cases, there can be sufficient richness of web of interlocking social rules even if there are gaps in the social rules for resolving certain possible conflicts. And richness of web may be a matter of multiple, overlapping strands of interlocking and defeasible requirements of output consistency. In general, sufficient richness of web will not be simply a matter of the number of social rules involved but will reflect the importance of different kinds of social rules in the functioning of the institution, and our measure of importance will be sensitive to the kind of institution at issue. Such judgments of importance may involve certain evaluative views. In such cases, our model of the institutional web of social rules—though not our model of the social rules themselves—will incorporate these evaluative views.[3]

An important complexity is that certain organized institutions will not only exploit the machinery of legally binding contracts but be individuated by background structures of law. An example from Barry Maguire: the law might distinguish between a merger of institutions A and B into a new, single institution, and a subcontracting arrangement between A and B that involves interlocking social rules of procedure across A and B.[4] For organized institutions that are creatures of law, such as a limited-liability corporation, these background legal structures may unify multiple, interlocking social procedural rules within the web of a single institution—or alternatively, as in subcontracting, disunify. In both the case of merger and the case of subcontracting, we can suppose that there are extensive webs of interlocking social procedural rules that to a significant extent require consistency of outputs. The key difference is in how these webs are treated within the background legal structures. For such creatures of law, then, differences in the legal background and the way the social rules are connected to that background shape our assessment of sufficient richness of web.

The appeal to sufficient richness of web is, then, an abstract organizing idea that allows us to see different kinds of institutions as involving different forms of richness of web of interrelated social rules of procedure. Potentially overlapping examples include corporate creatures of law; Hart-type hierarchies; not fully hierarchically specified webs of interlocking social rules that nevertheless involve higher-order, adjudicative social procedural rules; or simply extensive webs of interlocking social rules, as perhaps is the case with a music club. In each case interlocking social rules of procedure support associated procedures, roles, and offices, and thereby support organized institutional functioning that is robust with respect to changes in participants. But different kinds of institutions—examples include a democratic state, a corporation, a family business, a religious congregation, a neighborhood association, a private club, and a scientific research lab—can involve different forms of richness of web. We try in this way to point to an overarching genus while leaving room for different forms of richness of web involved in different species of organized institution.

In a way, this is theft over honest toil: much of the work of understanding a specific institution will be in articulating how in particular its web of interlocking social procedural rules is sufficiently rich. But this is a feature, not a bug. We want to explore the theoretical fecundity of shared-intention-involving, robust constructions of organized rule-guided institutions. We want to see whether such constructions support institutional intention and intentional agency. And we want to articulate an abstract framework for further research on multiple kinds of organized institutions.[5] In light of these theoretical aims, I propose to appeal to a sufficiently rich web of interlocking social procedural rules that involve defeasible pressures toward consistency of output, while highlighting the possibility of multiple forms of sufficient richness of web. And we associate a particular institution with a web of social procedural rules that satisfies conditions (a)–(c): this is the *institutional web* associated with that institution.

Consider now a particular social rule of procedure, R, that is in the institutional web of a specific institution. R will normally involve both a kernel and a penumbra. And it will at a given time specify a population, namely: those who are in either the kernel or the penumbra at that time. Call this the *population-base of R at a given time*. Given an institutional web of social rules of procedure, we can consider the population bases of each of these different social rules at a given time. The population base of one of these social rules may be different from that of another one of these social rules. After all, a participant in one of these rules may have no part to play in the procedures or outputs of a different, though interlocking, social rule. But given that these social rules interlock there will be rational pressure on an individual in the population base of one of these rules to be set, other things equal, not to interfere with the procedural functioning of the other rules in the web. And insofar as these social rules require consistency across different outputs, or there are in the web higher-order interlocking, adjudicative social rules that resolve certain conflicts, there will be rational pressure on an individual in the population base of one of these rules not to interfere with the outputs of other rules in the web or, in cases of adjudicated conflict, to defer to an adjudication-favored output.[6]

I will say that a person who is in the population base of a social procedural rule in an institutional web of social rules and is set to conform to these rational pressures is *minimally cooperative* with respect to that institutional web. An organized institution will involve an institutional web of social rules of procedure—a web that satisfies conditions (a)–(c)—together with relevant outputs and, at a given time and assuming relevant rationality, a set of minimally cooperative individuals each of whom is in the population base of at least one of the involved social procedural rules. This allows for the possibility of someone who is in the population base of one of the social rules in the institutional web but, despite the rational pressures, is not minimally cooperative. However, pressures both of rationality on individuals and for coordination within the institution will limit the extent of such breakdowns in cooperation. So, to characterize the basic structure of an organized institution that is at work in its normal rule-guided functioning I will highlight those individuals who are in fact minimally cooperative.

6.2 Institutional outputs

We have, then, the idea of an institutional web, and we have the idea of outputs of social rules within that web. Our next question is: when are such outputs *institutional outputs*? Suppose that a subcommittee of Medic Supply follows its rules of procedure and arrives at an output that favors sending supplies to C. What is it for such an output to be an output *of the institution*, Medic Supply?

If we thought an institution always involves a single, overarching social procedural rule, then we might try to say that all and only the outputs tied to that single overarching social rule are institutional outputs of that institution. But we have instead appealed to an institutional web of multiple social rules. So, we are faced with another question: when, more generally, is an output of a social rule of procedure attributable to an institution in whose institutional web that social rule of procedure is located?

One condition concerns consistency across outputs. Given an institution's web of social procedural rules, a crystallized output, O, of one of those social rules is an *institutional* output only if either

(i) it is consistent with the other outputs of social procedural rules that are in this institutional web, or
(ii) while O is not consistent with certain other outputs of other social procedural rules in the institutional web, there is in that institutional web an unconflicted, interlocking adjudicating social rule of procedure that authorizes O.

I will say that O satisfies the *consistency/authorization condition* just when (i) or (ii). If social procedural rules of an organized institution issue in outputs that do not satisfy this consistency/authorization condition, these are not *institutional* outputs.

A second condition appeals to the functional role of an institutional output. We can begin by saying that a crystallized output, O, that satisfies the consistency/authorization condition will be an institutional output only if

(iii) O tends to shape relevant downstream thought and action in relevant ways.

What ways? In a basic case, an action-focused output will combine with an acceptance-focused output of one of the social rules of procedure in the institutional web, an acceptance-focused output that is a cognitive *correlate*. Perhaps the action-focused output is to send the medical supplies to C, and a correlate acceptance-focused output concerns means to that. And analogously in a basic case of an acceptance-focused output: that acceptance-focused output pairs with a correlate action-focused output, of one of the social rules of procedure in the institutional web, on its way to action.

Alternatively, an action-focused output might combine not primarily with acceptance-focused outputs but with a distributed web of relevant beliefs or acceptances among participants. Perhaps some know the train schedule and others know the truck schedule, but both are needed for delivery of the medicine.[7] Again, perhaps an acceptance-focused output concerning the significance of human contributions to climate change interacts with a distributed web of intentions of individual participants (or small-scale shared intentions) and thereby leads to action.

So, concerning both action-focused and acceptance focused outputs, we can appeal to two kinds of correlates: output correlates and distributed-web correlates. And we can say that output O satisfies condition (iii) for being an *institutional* output only if it is set to function together with either (or both) a relevant output correlate or a relevant correlate web of distributed individual beliefs and/or acceptances and/or intentions and/or a web of small-scale shared intentions or acceptances.

Satisfaction of condition (iii) will normally involve satisfaction of the consistency/authorization condition since unresolved inconsistencies in outputs will tend to block relevant functioning. But even in a case in which an unresolved output inconsistency does not block downstream functioning, that unresolved inconsistency will baffle institutionalization of the output.

Suppose now that social procedural rule S_1 is an element in the institutional web of social rules $S_1, \ldots, S_n$ that is associated with institution I. Suppose S_1 issues in crystallized (acceptance-focused or action-focused) output O_1. I propose that O_1 is an *output of institution I* just in case

1. with respect to $S_1, \ldots, S_n$, O_1 satisfies the *consistency/authorization condition* and
2. it satisfies the *functional role* condition: O_1 tends to organize downstream thought and action in partnership with output and/or distributed web correlates.

If multiple O_i's satisfy conditions 1 and 2 with respect to a given institution, there will be a *web* of *institutional* outputs—action-focused and/or acceptance-focused. So, though we began by thinking of output correlates as outputs simply of a specific S_i, we can now see institutional outputs as themselves, potentially, output correlates for other outputs. We can now say, for example, that an action-focused institutional output in favor of sending the supplies may help organize downstream thought and action in partnership with institutional acceptance-focused outputs concerning means.

The functional role condition leaves room for disagreements within the institution. There is room for disagreement about what would be the best course of action, so long as, despite this disagreement, O_1 emerges as the relevant crystallized action-focused output. Further, even if O_1 is a crystallized output, there can be disagreements about the underlying rationale for O_1. For example, in a case in which O_1 is sending a vaccine to C, it remains open that some highlight the health benefits while others highlight the public relations benefits. There is also room for disagreements about relevant factual matters. Disagreement about certain downstream effects of sending the vaccine to C may not block the functioning of an action-focused output in favor of sending the vaccine to C; nor need such disagreement block the functioning of an acceptance-focused output that sending the vaccine to C will reduce fatalities.

Nevertheless, in some cases disagreement may block relevant functioning of output. Suppose that O_1 is the option of sending whatever vaccine has been shown by the science to be most effective. Disagreement about which vaccine that is might undermine satisfaction of the functional role condition by that output. But matters are complex. Even if there is this disagreement among participants, there may be an acceptance-focused output of a social rule in the institution's web that settles this matter. And it may be that, given certain contingent features of the institution, this acceptance-focused output is set to ensure relevant functioning of O_1 even given the cited disagreement among participants. Such an acceptance-focused output, we can say, *compensates* for the disagreement across participants.

The functional role condition will, then, allow for some disagreement but preclude certain cases of non-compensated disagreement. In this way the functional role condition induces a condition of *limited functionally relevant non-compensated cognitive divergence*. So, if condition 2 is satisfied it will also be true that

3. with respect to O_1, the institution satisfies a condition of *limited functionally relevant non-compensated cognitive divergence*.

So, we have three conditions of institutionalization of output, where condition 3 is induced by condition 2. The next question is whether conditions 1 and 3, taken together, ensure condition 2, the functional role condition. Suppose that a crystallized output, O, of a social rule of procedure, R, in an institution's web satisfies both the consistency/authorization condition and the condition of limited functionally relevant non-compensated cognitive divergence. Will it follow that O also satisfies the functional role condition?

Yes. Focus first on action-focused outputs of a non-hybrid social procedural rule R in the institutional web. We consider those who are either participants in an associated shared policy in favor of relevant procedures and follow-through or, while not in the population base of R, are in the base of some other social rule in the institutional web and are minimally cooperative. Suppose that the crystallized output of R is to send medicine to C. Suppose that the involved shared policies concerning follow-through—in the context of minimal cooperativeness and satisfaction of conditions of consistency/authorization and limited functionally relevant non-compensated cognitive divergence—function successfully in accord with norms of plan rationality. Then, if there are needed cognitive correlates (e.g., concerning means), there will be, within the institution, coordinated, temporally extended thought and action in the direction of sending medicine to C.

An analogous point holds for cases in which the social rule of procedure is hybrid. Consider a social procedural rule with alienated participants in its output penumbra.[8] Suppose that the crystallized output of this rule favors sending medicine to C. Suppose that, whereas some participate in a resulting shared intention in favor of that output, others—in the output penumbra—only intend to do their part (e.g., drive a delivery vehicle) for extending reasons (e.g., a salary). And suppose that there are needed cognitive correlates. If these different elements function in accord with plan rationality, and in a context of minimal cooperativeness and satisfaction of conditions of consistency/authorization and limited functionally relevant non-compensated cognitive divergence, there will be a coordinated complex of thought and action in the direction of sending medicine to C. After all, though those in the output penumbra do not buy into the overall institutional activity of sending medicine, they do, for extending reasons, buy into doing their own parts in that overall activity, and so into what on their part is needed for that overall activity. So, if they function successfully in accord with norms of plan rationality, they will contribute appropriately to sending medicine to C.

So, given the crystallized action-focused output, there is, within the institution—given minimal cooperativeness, satisfaction of conditions of consistency/authorization and limited functionally relevant non-compensated cognitive divergence, and needed cognitive correlates—temporally extended rational guidance of socially embedded thought and action. This guidance is supported by the social output structures crystallized by a relevant event output of a social rule of procedure in the institutional web. This guidance goes primarily by way of the rational dynamics induced by relevant social subrules of follow-through. This will involve some combination of rational functioning of relevant kernel shared policies and roles of extending reasons and induced penumbral intentions. So, relevant crystallized action-focused outputs will play relevant downstream functional roles if there are needed cognitive correlates. And by way of an analogous line of reasoning we could extend this conclusion about the role of crystallized outputs in downstream functioning to the case of acceptance-focused outputs.

So, crystallized outputs of a social procedural rule in an institution's web—given satisfaction of the consistency/authorization condition and the condition of limited functionally relevant non-compensated cognitive divergence—will, given minimal cooperativeness, satisfy the functional role condition in our theory of institutionalization of output. Therefore these crystallized outputs will be institutional outputs.

We have, then, our theory of institutional outputs. Suppose social procedural rule S_1 is an element in the institutional web of social procedural rules $S_1, \ldots, S_n$ that is associated with institution I. Suppose S_1 issues in crystallized (acceptance-focused or action-focused) output O_1. O_1 is an output *of institution I* just in case it satisfies a trio of further conditions:

1. consistency/authorization,
2. functional role, and
3. limited functionally relevant non-compensated cognitive divergence.

Further, satisfaction of condition 3 is needed for satisfaction of condition 2; and, assuming minimal cooperativeness, satisfaction of conditions 1 and 3 together suffices for satisfaction of condition 2.

We observed earlier that the kernel-penumbra structure of social rules of procedure induced the possibility of a separation of social-procedural-rule action-focused crystallized output from corresponding shared intention on the part of all participants in the social rule. We now note a second potential source of an analogous separation: it is possible that, for a specific social rule of procedure, R, in the institutional web of institution I, there is a participant in I, P, who is not in the population base of R, though P is in the population base of some other social rule of procedure in I's web. So, P will likely not participate in a shared intention in favor of an action-focused output of R (even if P is minimally cooperative). And this may be so even if that output is an institutional output. So, there are these dual sources of separation of institutional action-focused crystallized output, on the one hand, and, on the other hand, corresponding shared intention.[9]

6.3 The rule-guided infrastructure of an organized institution

We have, then, a shared policy model of social rules of procedure, including authority-according social rules of procedure. We have the ideas of an organized institution's *institutional web* of social procedural rules and of an associated set of minimally cooperative individuals who are in the kernel or penumbra of at least one of the social rules in an institutional web. And we have a model of *institutional outputs* of an institutional web of social procedural rules. We thereby have building blocks for our model of the rule-guided infrastructure of an organized institution.

We model an organized institution as involving an institutional web of social rules of procedure. This web involves a mix of non-hybrid and hybrid shared-policy-shaped social rules of procedure, including authority-according social rules of procedure. These social procedural rules satisfy conditions set out in Section 6.1 for being in that institutional web. We also associate with the institution relevant institutional outputs—understood by way of our account in Section 6.2 of institutionalization of output. And we keep track of the potential roles of hybrid social rules. We thereby highlight the role of shared intentionality in our organized institutions without supposing that the normal functioning of those institutions involves shared intentions across all participants.

Though our initial focus is on procedural rules, our model also allows for important roles of substantive institutional values.[10] We have noted that social rules of procedure can concern substantive weights in relevant reasoning. Such commitments to weights can constitute a form of institutional valuing. We can now add that social procedural rules can have institutional acceptance-focused outputs that favor certain substantive values, and that can be a second form of institutional valuing. Both forms of institutional valuing are connected to relevant social rules of procedure in a way that clarifies how substantive institutional value commitments can shape institutional functioning.

My aim has been to identify an abstractly specified infrastructure that is common to and important for a wide range of human organized institutions, despite variability across those institutions. Here, again, I take my cue from Hart. He sought to draw on social rules to construct a rule-governed infrastructure involving certain secondary social rules, an infrastructure that is common to legal systems despite variations across different systems. I seek to draw on planning and shared intention—and associated constructions of Hart-type social rules—to construct a rule-governed infrastructure that involves social rules of procedure, an infrastructure that is characteristic of a wide range of human organized institutions despite variation across such institutions.

This involves a strategy of sufficiency, one that leaves open the possibility of multiple realizations as well as cases that are in some ways weaker. But the conjecture is that this model of the rule-guided infrastructure of organized institutions helps us see how our planning capacities, and their role in our shared agency, can lie behind important forms of human rule-guided institutional organization.[11]

A final concern is that the set of minimally cooperative individuals who are in the kernel or penumbra of at least one of the social rules in an institutional web will be large. Within certain contexts of inquiry—for example, questions about institution-based individual accountability—we may want to focus on narrower groups of individuals. What narrower groups?[12]

There are multiple strategies available here. In some contexts, we might focus on kernel participants in central social rules in the institutional web—where the criteria for centrality of social rule will be sensitive to the specific kind of institution at issue. In other contexts, we might appeal to those social rules of procedure in the institutional web that articulate conditions for membership in the institution.[13] Perhaps membership is tied to payment of dues, or to conditions of citizenship. Here, however, we would need to allow that some non-members can play central roles and some members may not play a role and may not even be minimally cooperative. Again, we might draw on the idea that certain penumbral participants "ascribe . . . authority" (Pettit 2017, 22) to certain kernel participants. This would filter out those in the penumbra who see themselves simply as coerced by those in the kernel. Here, however, we need to recognize that the ascribed authority can be limited (Strudler n.d.): we would be including many who play only a peripheral role—for example, some drivers who deliver medical supplies because they ascribe some such limited authority. Yet again, we might appeal to penumbral participants whose role in the penumbra can be terminated by decisions by those in the kernel—they can be fired (Wenar in correspondence). But, again, this may include many who play only a peripheral role in the institution's functioning. Finally, we might focus on those who are minimally cooperative kernel or penumbra participants in a sufficiently extensive subset of the social rules in the institutional web. Here the criteria for sufficient extensiveness can be sensitive to the specific kind of institution at issue, and to the context of inquiry; we might also go on to limit the relevant penumbral participants to those who are responding in particular to intentionally induced extending reasons.

Perhaps yet further strategies are available for focusing on certain subsets of individuals who are in the kernel or penumbra of at least one of the social rules in an institutional web. Our account of organized institutions allows us to draw on some or all these further theoretical resources: we do not need to single out one of these strategies as uniquely apt. In each case we will be guided by our specific theoretical interests and by reflection on the details of the institution at issue.

6.4 Searle on institutional roles

Social rules of procedure many times set up institutional roles. This takes us into territory explored by John Searle (1995, 2005, 2010). Part of Searle's focus is on informal institutional phenomena, such as informal systems of exchange or informal borders. But he also intends his theoretical framework to apply to organized institutions of the sort that are of interest here. Searle emphasizes ways in which a background of "collective acceptance"[14] induces social roles and statuses (for example, being a University of California faculty member, or being a Palo Alto police officer). This makes possible certain functions—"status functions"—that one can perform by virtue of occupying such roles or statuses (for example, assign grades, or make an arrest). This background of collective acceptance involves contents of the form "X counts as Y in C"—for example, X counts as a University of California faculty member, or a Palo Alto police officer, in certain contexts. And Searle supposes that collective acceptance whose content is "X counts as Y in C" assigns associated "deontic powers"—for example, a *right* to assign grades, or to arrest someone.

This connection between collective acceptance with content "X counts as Y in C" and deontic powers may be overstated. Suppose there is collective acceptance of "this counts as a pirouette." This might help constitute what Searle calls a "constitutive rule"—a rule that constitutes a specific form of activity rather than merely regulates a form of activity specified independently of the rule.[15] But it does not seem necessarily to assign rights or duties. Granted, if you accept that this is what counts as a pirouette and aim at dancing a pirouette you will be rationally constrained in your dancing. But rational constraint is not the same as deontic powers.

This contrasts with one of Searle's main examples: a constitutive rule along the lines of "X counts as money in context C." Here the rule is associated with certain institution-relative *de facto* rights—for example, to use X to discharge a debt.[16]

So, some—but not all—such constitutive rules assign institution-relative deontic powers. But we can still accept Searle's insight concerning many institutional cases. There is, for example, a tight connection between counting as a University of California faculty member and having associated, institution-relative, *de facto* rights and duties. And our procedural social rule model of organized institutions can here draw from Searle. It can say that certain social procedural rules will have such "counts as" contents and accord special roles to those with a certain status or in certain offices—as in our earlier example, members of an admissions committee—and thereby associated deontic powers. Further, such a social rule of procedure can be associated with an acceptance-focused institutional output that specifies conditions, for example, for who "counts as" a committee member who has associated institutional rights or duties.

A further qualification, however, is that even role-according social rules of procedure are not necessarily authority-according. Consider a social procedural rule that, for reasons of efficiency in a census, samples a population by identifying views of every tenth person on a voter list and uses that information in its policy recommendations. If you are one of those identified persons you "count as" one of the chosen people, and you thereby play a special role in the procedure set up by the rule. But it does not follow that you have been accorded a right to play this role.

That said, it will frequently be true that a role-according social rule of procedure does accord relevant institution-relative, *de facto* authority or rights or duties to those who "count as" being in the designated role—for example, a member of the admission committee, or of the Palo Alto police force, or of the University of California faculty. In this qualified way, then, we can agree with the Searle-inspired connection between social rules that spell out who "counts as" occupying a given role and associated, accorded deontic powers.

There do remain important disagreements between Searle and yours truly about the theoretical background. First, my planning theory of shared intention is reductive in a way in which Searle's appeal to purportedly irreducible we-intentions is not.[17] Second, in his appeal to a general background of "collective acceptance," Searle does not highlight interrelations across those in this background. He writes: "Once you have collective intentionality then, if it is *in fact* shared by other people, the result is more than just yourself and other people: collectively you now form a social group."[18] In contrast, I have agreed with Gilbert about the importance of such interrelations—though Gilbert and I understand them differently. Third, Searle says that a person in an institutionally defined role thereby has a reason—as I understand Searle, a normative reason—to act in accordance with that role; and, as noted earlier, that risks moving too quickly from an "is" of institutional organization to a substantive "ought." Even given these differences, however, we can incorporate a version of Searle's emphasis on "counts as" social rules and associated ideas of institutional roles and statuses, and we can make room for the Searle-friendly idea that in some cases social rules accord (relativized, *de facto*) authority to those with a certain accorded status.

That said, I have argued that to get from shared intention to social rules, and then from social rules to organized institutions, we do well to draw on a web of further ideas—ideas spelled out in Chapters 3–6—that in multiple ways go beyond Searle's appeal to collective acceptances with "counts as" contents. And I now proceed to argue that the resulting model of a rule-guided organized institution supports appeal to forms of institutional intention and agency that are in tension with Searle's thought that "there is nothing that need count as the corporation itself."[19]

III INSTITUTIONAL INTENT

7 INSTITUTIONAL INTENTION

According to our procedural social rule model of rule-guided organized institutions, social procedural rules in an institutional web normally issue in crystallized outputs that shape downstream thought and action. These outputs can be action-focused or acceptance-focused. In each case, they may satisfy conditions for being institutional outputs. Even when these institutional outputs are action-focused, they need not directly correspond to shared intentions on the part of all participants in the involved social rules. This potential break between these institutional crystallized outputs and overall shared intentions is an impact both of the possibility of hybrid social rules of procedure and of the complex relations between multiple social rules of procedure within the web of a single institution.

Return now to the second main question from our overview: given our theoretical resources,

> (B) can we thereby explain in what sense, if any, such organized institutions can themselves have *intentions* and be *intentional agents*?

I proceed to answer (B) in a way that sees institutional intentions as institutional outputs of the procedural-rule-guided institutional functioning we have been characterizing.

Return to Medic Supply. Suppose that an action-focused output of a social procedural rule of a subcommittee says: send medical supplies to C. And suppose this is an institutional output. My claim will be that this crystallized, institutional output will be set to function in ways characteristic of intention. We thereby infer that it is, functionally speaking, an intention of Medic Supply. It is a construction that is an institutional intention because it satisfies the functional specification for such an intention.

As discussed in Section 6.2, when there is an institutional crystallized action-focused output there normally is, within the institution, temporally extended coordination-inducing rational guidance of socially embedded thought and action. This guidance is supported by thick social output structures crystallized by a relevant event output of a social rule of procedure (e.g., the result of an authorized deliberation procedure on the part of a subcommittee), together with minimal cooperativeness and satisfaction of conditions of institutionalization of output.[1] This guidance goes primarily by way of the rational dynamics induced by relevant social subrules of follow-through. This will involve some combination of rational functioning of relevant kernel shared policies and roles of extending reasons and induced penumbral intentions. In this way, such institutional, crystallized action-focused outputs will play the downstream functional roles highlighted within our theory of institutionalization of output: they will be set to organize thought and action in partnership with relevant correlates in the direction of what is favored by the output (e.g., sending the medical supplies to C).

The next point is that this guidance, while it does not ensure corresponding *shared* intention, does have the structure of guidance, in the actual circumstances, that is characteristic of *intention*. These crystallized institutional output social structures, when functioning in accordance with the rational dynamics of planning agency, support temporally extended coordination-inducing, cognitively sensitive guidance of socially embedded thought and action in the direction of what is seen as favored by the output event in ways that avoid what is seen as incompatible with that output. So, these institutional crystallized output structures normally play the functional roles characteristic of intention—for example, an intention to send the supplies to C. So, within our functional specification approach, we can say that these institutional crystallized outputs are *institutional intentions*. The institutional background of such an institutional intention will involve various shared intentions/shared policies. But such an institutional intention need not itself involve a strictly corresponding shared intention across all the participants. Institutional intention is not shared intention.[2]

Such an institutional intention is a temporally extended phenomenon that involves the ongoing operation of social subrules of follow-through. There is a contrast here with the intentions of individuals. I have treated the intentions of individuals as attitudes at a given time (or small time interval), though their functional characteristics involve roles in shaping temporally extended thought and action. And this induces an analogous view of shared intention at a given time. But the cited intentions of an institution are not just functionally connected to temporally extended thought and action; they are themselves temporally extended and involve persisting social rules of procedure and their social subrules of follow-through. The persistence of these social rules underlies the continuities of functioning over time that are characteristic of intention. And such institutional intentions are normally robust in the face of certain changes—actual or counterfactual—in individual participants. In these ways, institutional intentions are more like social rules than they are like shared intentions.

The kernel shared policies involved in these institutional intentions, by way of their involvement in the underlying social rules of procedure, include shared policies in favor of follow-through and so in support of tracking what is favored by relevant outputs and adjusting as need be in the direction of promoting what is favored by those outputs. These shared policies in favor of follow-through induce rational pressure on those who participate in the shared policy in the direction of supporting relevant means and preliminary steps and avoiding further outputs that are not co-possible with the output being tracked. And, in a hybrid case, this rational pressure will extend, by way of reason-grounded extension, to a broader, penumbral population. The crystallized action-focused output will thereby support functioning in the direction of means to what is favored by the output and avoiding what is incompatible with what is favored by the output. And this helps support the idea that this crystallized, temporally extended structure is, functionally speaking, an institutional intention (Bratman forthcoming c).

A temporally and socially thick action-focused crystallized output of a social-rule-based procedure constitutes an intention of the institution only if it satisfies the consistency-authorization condition for being an institutional output. In a basic case this will mean that this output is consistent with other such outputs. We now see that, given the functional nature of the underlying social rules, there is a social, rational dynamics in support of *continued* output consistency. Further, we have seen that, given the underlying social rules, there is a social, rational dynamics in support of filling in with means to what is favored by the institutional output, and so in support of various forms of social thinking—including bargaining and shared deliberation, and including a web of distributed attitudes of individuals—aimed at settling on relevant means. Since such consistency-supporting and means-end-coherence-supporting forms of ongoing functioning are part of the characteristic functioning of intention, this further supports the idea that these crystallized, socially thick, action-focused institutional outputs are, functionally speaking, intentions of the institution.

The cognitive background for the functioning of an institutional intention can involve a mix of acceptance-focused outputs as well as a distributed web of beliefs and/or acceptances of multiple, relevant individuals. And some of these acceptance-focused outputs can themselves qualify as institutional outputs.

The downstream functioning of such institutional intentions may involve a cascade of yet further institutional intentions. One way this can happen is that an institutional intention itself becomes input to a further, social-rule-guided procedure that issues in yet a further institutional intention. For example, the institutional intention to send medicine might then be an input to a procedure that issues in a further institutional intention to announce this activity publicly.

Given the underlying rational dynamics, these crystallized, temporally extended, institutional, action-focused outputs of social rules of procedure settle practical problems for the institution (e.g., problems of allocation of resources), pose further problems of means and preliminary steps (e.g., how to transfer the resources to intended recipients), and constrain solutions to other, related problems (e.g., concerning other uses of institutional resources). In these ways these institutional crystallized action-focused outputs, in a context of minimal cooperativeness, involve a more or less stable, cognitively sensitive network that helps organize—and thereby make sense of—relevant temporally extended, socially embedded thought and action. This network will involve a complex mix, on the part of relevant individuals, of relevant intentions, a mix that will, in this context, normally guide in the direction of what is favored by the output of the procedure. And it will involve Lockean cross-temporal continuities and connections between relevant plan states at different times, where this will help support the cross-temporal organization of relevant temporally extended activity.

These roles in temporally extended thought and action—roles of stably posing problems and filtering solutions to these problems in ways that help to frame, to guide, to coordinate, to unify, and to organize, all potentially in response to new information—are what the planning theory sees as essential to intention. And such framing, guidance, coordination, organization, and unification help make sense of the temporally extended thought and action.[3] So, there is reason to see these institutional crystallized action-focused outputs as, functionally speaking, intentions of the institution, intentions that are not in general shared intentions.[4]

This model of institutional intention appeals not only to institutional action-focused outputs but also to institutional acceptance-focused outputs that may be among the cognitive correlates that operate in tandem with institutional intentions. (As noted, however, those cognitive correlates can also include acceptance-focused outputs that are not institutional outputs, and webs of beliefs/acceptances of relevant individuals.) Without trying to argue for this in detail, I think we can see that considerations analogous to those we have explored concerning institutional action-focused outputs will support the idea that such institutional acceptance-focused outputs themselves function in ways characteristic of acceptance. This puts us in a position to say that such institutional acceptance-focused crystallized outputs are themselves *institutional acceptances*, functionally speaking. Such institutional acceptances are a distinctive cognitive aspect of organized institutions. So, we have parallel and coordinated models of institutional intention and institutional acceptance; and in each case, functioning is grounded in construction.

Will such institutional acceptances function in ways characteristic of *belief*, and so be *institutional beliefs*, functionally speaking?[5] Well, as in the case of individual acceptances, such institutional acceptances are characteristically tied to various practical considerations. The procedures of a firm that issue in an institutional acceptance of a proposition about climate change may be sensitive to various economic considerations over and above a sensitivity to the evidence (Lackey 2021, chap. 1). This tie to practical considerations is a mark of the contrast between acceptance and belief. So, while institutional acceptance-focused crystallized outputs will normally function in ways characteristic of acceptance, they will not in general function in ways characteristic of belief. So, they will not in general be beliefs of the institution.

That said, there can be cases in which an institutional acceptance is an output of a social procedural rule that is tightly tied to consideration of evidence. Perhaps this is true about the Food and Drug Administration's acceptance concerning the implications of certain drug trials. In such cases it may be reasonable to classify this institutional acceptance as an *institutional belief*. Such a classification would depend on our assessment of the extent to which the underlying procedures are evidence-tracking. We thereby highlight the basic construction of institutional acceptance but make room for a classification of a subset of those acceptances as institutional beliefs.

Now, the cognitive background for the functioning of intentions of an individual will be the beliefs and/or acceptances of that individual. In contrast, in the institutional case the cognitive background of an institution's intention can include *both* acceptances of that institution, some of which may qualify as institutional beliefs, and beliefs and acceptances of individuals. This is a difference between the underlying, function-specifying theory for institutional intention and that for individual intention. As I see it, however, this is a feature, not a bug. We can recognize this difference concerning cognitive correlates of intention—individual or institutional—while highlighting the basic functional commonality of shaping downstream thought and action in tandem with relevant cognitive correlates. We thereby retain the idea that relevant crystallized institutional outputs are, functionally speaking, intentions of the institution. But to do this we need to avoid an overly simple extension from the individual to the institutional.[6]

We are modeling institutional intentions as crystallized cross-temporal action-focused institutional outputs that involve ongoing shared-policy-shaped social rules of procedure, including subrules of follow-through, together with thereby supported conforming intentions on the part of individuals. This to some extent coheres with Philip Pettit's observation concerning group intentions that "individual intentions will follow on the formation of the group intention, of course, since the group can only act through the actions of its members" (2003, 183). But our theory offers primarily a constructivist account of the relation between the group/institutional intention and the intentions of individual actors. The central idea is not that the group/institutional intention precedes and leads to later, relevant individual intentions, though this can happen.[7] The central idea, instead, is that the crystallized, temporally extended social construction that constitutes the group/institutional intention already itself involves interconnected intentions and policies of relevant individuals.

While our sequential construction respects the modesty and potential modularity of the role of shared intention in institutional functioning, it nevertheless draws in basic ways from the plan-theoretic model of shared intention. So, we have a path to "scaling up" our plan-theoretic model of shared intention in part by way of a merger with Hart-inspired ideas about social-rule-based institutions. We have uncovered a social-rule-based way in which an organized institution can have intentions of its own, intentions that can cascade through the institution and provide a supporting network for a wide range of institution-related activities, individual and shared.

So, we have a social-procedural-rule construction of institutional intention. Our construction legitimizes our thought and talk of institutional intention by showing how such intentions can constructively emerge within our model of rule-guided, organized institutions.

We thereby have what we wanted. We have a merger of the planning theory of shared intentionality and Hart-inspired ideas about social rules, a merger that provides a model of the rule-guided infrastructure of organized institutions. And this merger then generates a model of institutional intentions—Medic Supply's intention to send the drugs, or the intention of the Philosophy Department to admit Jones to its Ph.D. program, or General Motors' intention to phase out production of gasoline-powered cars, or a legislature's intention to criminalize a certain kind of action, or the intention of the Food and Drug Administration to approve a certain drug. In the spirit of Gricean creature construction, we build sequentially on the planning theory of shared intention and SIA. We "scale up" that theory to help us better understand organized institutions. We thereby lend credence to the fundamental idea that our planning capacities not only support our temporally extended and shared intentional agency but also support, in part by way of their support for shared intentionality, the rule-guided infrastructure of our organized institutions and, thereby, institutional intention.

But now we need to consider an objection from Donald Davidson's work on mind and agency.

8 A DAVIDSONIAN CHALLENGE

The objection begins with the thought that an intention needs to be embedded in a dense holistic web of attitudes, a web of a sort essential to there being a *subject* whose intention it is. However, given the normally wide range of disagreement within our organized institutions, especially given our pluralistic culture, there is little reason to expect that the outputs of social rules of procedure will normally be embedded in an overall dense holistic institutional web. So, these outputs are not, strictly speaking, intentions of the institution. Or so the objection goes. To assess this objection, I turn to its roots in work of Donald Davidson.

8.1 Davidson on interpretation, content, and the holistic density of mind

The key is the set of connections that Davidson thought he saw between agency, intentional agency, mind, and a dense holistic subject. Davidson argued that there is agency, strictly speaking, only when there is intentional agency; and intentional agency is the agency of a minded subject, one who is the locus of a dense holistic, broadly coherent web of attitudes. On Davidson's view, these pressures for coherence and holism come from the nature of interpretation of a subject.[1] We understand mind in part by understanding essential elements of our interpretation of a system as minded.[2] And when we reflect on those essential elements, we see that sensibly to attribute minds we cannot simply attribute, in piecemeal fashion, individual local elements. What such elements amount to—where that includes what their content is—can only be specified by locating them in an overall, dense and coherent web.

There are two interrelated ideas here. The first concerns the need for a kind of density in attributing belief:

> Beliefs are identified and described only within a dense pattern of beliefs. I can believe a cloud is passing before the sun, but only because I believe there is a sun, that clouds are made of water vapor, that water can exist in liquid or gaseous form; and so on, without end. No particular list of further beliefs is required to give substance to my belief that a cloud is passing before the sun; but some appropriate set of related beliefs must be there. If I suppose that you believe a cloud is passing before the sun, I suppose you to have the right sort of pattern of beliefs to support that one belief. (Davidson 2001a, 200)

And again, in a different essay:

> There is probably no definite list of things that must be believed by someone who understands the sentence "The gun is loaded," but it is necessary that there be endless interlocked beliefs. (Davidson 2001b, 158)

Attribution of belief involves attribution of a "dense pattern of beliefs"—"endless interlocked beliefs"—where that dense pattern of interlocked beliefs provides "support" for that attributed belief. And the support at issue includes support for attributing the cited content: to suppose your belief is about clouds I need to suppose you have some thick, dense web of further beliefs that "give substance to" the attribution of this content to your belief.

We can expect this need for density to generalize to other attitudes. But the generalization is delicate. Suppose we attribute an intention to load the gun. It seems that the involved "endless interlocked" attitudes will primarily be beliefs, not other intentions. The intention to load the gun will need background beliefs about guns and loading, for example. These may include beliefs that do not directly correspond to intentions—for example, beliefs about side effects of gun loading. So, the initial density associated with an intention to A will involve a web of associated *beliefs* about the nature of A and how it would be embedded in the world. We need this further belief web to support our attribution of an intention with this content.

However, we go beyond this belief web when we turn to Davidson's further idea that to attribute an attitude to you appropriately, I need to see it as part of a web of multiple kinds of attitudes that "cohere" in ways that "make sense" of that attitude:

> We make sense of particular beliefs only as they cohere with other beliefs, with preferences, with intentions, hopes, fears, expectations, and the rest . . . the content of a propositional attitude derives from its place in the pattern.
> . . . [This is] the constitutive ideal of rationality. (Davidson 1980e, 221, 223)

It follows, I take it, that we make sense of particular *intentions* "only as they cohere with other beliefs, with preferences, with intentions, hopes, fears, expectations, and the rest."

Attributions of intention, then, need to be embedded in a dense web of "endless interlocked" associated beliefs that are themselves embedded in a broad multi-attitude web of attitudes, a web that both shapes the content of those attitudes and provides an underlying holistic rational coherence that is needed to make sense of those attitudes. And finally—though to my knowledge this is not developed explicitly by Davidson—an underlying thought seems to be that this embedding of these attitudes within a dense holistic web helps explain why guidance by such *attitudes* can be guidance by the *agent* and so the agent's *action*.

Of course, individual humans are all too human, and there can be local breakdowns in coherence. Some of these breakdowns are the concern of Davidson's work on weakness of the will and self-deception (1980b, 2004). And there are questions here about why guidance by a weak-willed intention can constitute, even given the involved incoherence, not just a process of motivation but also intentional guidance by the agent. But the underlying thought is that such breakdowns need to be embedded in a broadly coherent, dense multi-attitude background if they are to be breakdowns in attitudes of belief, intention, and the like, attitudes with more or less determinate contents.

On this Davidsonian view, then, to be an intentional *agent* one needs to be a dense holistic *subject* of relevant attitudes. When an intention to A is, as it needs to be, an intention of such a holistic subject, that subject will also have

(i) a dense web of beliefs³ about what A would involve, and
(ii) a web of intentions, evaluations, desires, and emotions—together with a dense web of associated beliefs—that provide a holistic background against which so intending makes rational sense.

Note that (i) and (ii) are not just a matter of consistency across the intentions and beliefs of the subject. Consistency can come cheap and does not ensure density. Consistency by itself is compatible with the absence of many of the beliefs, intentions, and evaluations at stake in (i) and (ii). What is required by (i) and (ii) is not just consistency but a dense coherent pattern of attitudes that helps fix contents and provides the background needed to make sense of the attitudes.

This idea of a dense holistic subject is close to Carol Rovane's idea of a "rational point of view" (1998, 21). On her view, such a rational point of view involves the subgoals of

> resolving contradictions and other conflicts among one's beliefs and other psychological attitudes, accepting the implications (both logical and evidential) of one's attitudes, ranking one's preferences, assessing opportunities for action, assessing the probable consequences of performing the actions that are open to one, determining what means are available for achieving one's ends, evaluating one's ends . . . in the light of both the available means to achieving them and the probable consequences of acting upon them.⁴

A dense holistic subject is one with a more or less successful, Rovane-type rational point of view, one that involves an "overall rational unity" (164).⁵

These are important ideas about the kind of dense holistic subject that is involved in individual human intentional agency. Before exploring these Davidsonian ideas further, though, I want to note a somewhat different approach to agency developed by Harry Frankfurt.

8.2 Frankfurt on "the structure of a person's will" and where "the person himself stands"

Davidson's appeal to dense holism is a response to pressures on articulating, within interpretation, "the content of a propositional attitude." It is also a response to the need to "make sense" of an attitude by embedding it in a dense holistic structure of attitudes of multiple sorts. This is needed to explain why the attitude is the kind of attitude it is said to be—a belief, say, and not a conjecture or a fantasy. While we make room for occasional breakdowns in coherence, such breakdowns need to be embedded in a broadly coherent, dense multi-attitude background.

I will, for present purposes, grant these ideas about the dense holism of individual subjects, plus or minus a bit. There remain, however, questions about agency that go beyond a Davidson-inspired focus on questions about the content of attitudes.

Harry Frankfurt highlights cases of motivation by desire in which the agent is not fully identified with what she is doing. In Frankfurt's example, one is moved by a desire for a drug to which one is addicted. Frankfurt argued that in some such cases the agent may act intentionally but not "of his own free will" (1988a, 25). To understand the stronger form of agency involved in acting of one's own free will, we need to say more about "the structure of a person's will" (1988a, 12). Here Frankfurt appeals to higher-order desires: in acting of one's own free will one is moved by a desire by which one wants to be moved. In contrast, one might be moved by a desire for the drug even though one desires not to be moved by that desire. A higher-order desire in favor of being moved by a certain first-order desire can constitute, as Frankfurt later puts it, where "the person himself stands" (1988b, 166). Action of one's own free will is action motivated by where one stands.

This appeal to the agent's standpoint is not an appeal to a single privileged attitude. In this way it contrasts with J. David Velleman's appeal to an aim of self-understanding, an aim that plays "the role of the agent" (1992, 480). Frankfurt's idea is rather that the agent's standpoint has a certain—as he understood it, hierarchical—organized structure that can be realized by different attitudes in different cases.[6]

Davidson saw his reflections on interpretation, the dense holism of mind, and subjecthood as also providing the basic elements for a theory of agency. Frankfurt's reflections on structures of will and agential standpoints provide further theoretical resources for understanding important forms of agency. In accepting a suitably qualified Davidsonian dense holism about the attitudes of an individual human subject I leave open (and will return to, in Chapter 10) the possibility of appeal to such further Frankfurt-inspired structures in understanding important forms of agency, including institutional agency. That said, let's first look more closely at Davidson's proposals about the dense holism of mind and how they seem to challenge our model of institutional intention.

8.3 Davidson meets pluralism

The challenge is that, given common forms of pluralistic disagreement, there will not in general be a dense holistic institutional subject that satisfies versions of (i) and (ii) (in Section 8.1). So, what I have characterized as institutional intentions will not in general be embedded in a dense holistic, Davidsonian web of attitudes of that institution.[7] But then the application of Davidson's model of interpretation to organized institutions challenges the idea that the institutional action-focused crystallized outputs of relevant social rules of procedure are *intentions* of the institution.

Let's spell out the tension between my proposed model of institutional intention and Davidson's dense holism. Suppose that Medic Supply intends (in the sense I have proposed) to send medical supplies to a certain country. While there needs to be relevant intention consistency, there may still not be a single, dense framework of intentions, beliefs, acceptances, and evaluations of that institution that substantively makes sense of this intention. Perhaps some in the institution support sending the supplies because they think it will reduce human suffering. Perhaps others are skeptical about this but favor sending the supplies to support the local government, or because of promises made to donors, or because it is a way of discharging certain legal requirements on non-profit organizations. Perhaps some see sending the aid as a response to certain religious commitments, whereas others reject those religious commitments. These differences may remain in place even given the institutional intention (in the sense I have articulated) to send the supplies. And there may be no need for the institution itself to take a stand about which, if any, of these potential rationales is to be incorporated within its institutional commitments. In this respect the situation can be like our earlier case of a shared intention to paint the house, where your concern is the mildew and mine is the color. Indeed, it may be important to the successful functioning of Medic Supply that the institution prescind from taking sides with respect to some of these differences. Perhaps a majority of the group judges that sending the supplies is required by their religious beliefs, but a minority does not want to be involved in a religiously shaped institution. So, the group avoids taking a group stand, one way or another, on that religious consideration. Thus the institution itself may not be committed to a single overall view about the substantive grounds for that purported institutional intention. There is a sensible incompleteness in the institutional background of the institutional intention.

This is a smaller-scale version of a claim of Cass Sunstein's:

> Well-functioning legal systems often tend to adopt a special strategy for producing agreement amidst pluralism. *Participants in legal controversies try to produce incompletely theorized agreements on particular outcomes.* They agree on the result and on relatively narrow or low-level explanations for it. They need not agree on fundamental principle. . . . This is an important source of social stability and an important way for diverse people to demonstrate mutual respect, in law especially but also in liberal democracy as a whole.[8]

Medic Supply can have institutional intentions (in the sense I have articulated) even though its web of supporting institutional attitudes is "incompletely theorized."[9] And the efficiency of Medic Supply's efforts might depend on this incompleteness, given the pluralistic divergence within that institution.

A complication is that social rules of procedure can sometimes issue in outputs that involve further aims. This is the phenomenon of induced further teleology. Perhaps Medic Supply arrives at an institutional output *to send the supplies in order to support the government*. This output would be more completely "theorized" than one that only involves sending the supplies. Whether an organized institution arrives at more or less completely theorized outputs of its social rules of procedure will vary case by case. It will vary both with differences in the contents of the social rules of procedure and with differences in how the procedures work their way through in the particular case. The central point here is only that such organizations *can* arrive at relatively thin institutional intentions whose background is substantially "incompletely theorized," and that this may result given common forms of pluralistic disagreement within such institutions and the advantages in certain cases of such disagreement of leaving relevant matters "incompletely theorized."

This shows how purported institutional intentions (of the sort I have articulated) may fail to satisfy Davidson's condition (ii) at the level of the institution—the condition that there be a dense web, of multiple kinds of attitudes of that institution, that provides a holistic background against which so intending makes rational sense.

An analogous point concerns Davidson's condition (i)—the condition that there be a dense web of associated beliefs on the part of the subject of the purported intention. A purported institutional intention to send aid does require a minimal level of agreement among the participants about what it is to send such aid.[10] But there can nevertheless be significant disagreement among the participants about what the institutionally intended action would in fact involve.[11] Some think sending the aid would substantially relieve human suffering; others are skeptical. Some think aid would help the local government retain control; others are skeptical. And so on. And in many cases the institution need not settle these disagreements, by way of some sort of institutional acceptance, for it to have its (as I am understanding it) institutional intention to send the aid.

In these ways, what I have characterized as social-procedural-rule-based institutional intentions are compatible with significant disagreement among participants both with respect to intention, desire, and evaluation, as in (ii), and with respect to belief, as in (i). And these disagreements can induce significant partiality/incompleteness in the institutional framework. Social rules of procedure are a social technology that can issue in coordinated guidance of temporally extended, socially embedded thought and action even given such disagreement and resulting partiality/incompleteness within the institution. But if Davidson is right that the attribution of intention needs to be embedded within a dense holistic interpretation of the subject of that intention, then we are making a mistake in characterizing these crystallized outputs of social rules of procedure as *intentions of the institution*.

These reflections indicate that, given common forms of disagreement, institutional outputs of the sort under discussion will not in general be embedded in a Davidsonian dense holistic web of attitudes of that institution. So, if we accept this Davidsonian model of the densely holistic mental infrastructure, we should reject the claim that these institutional outputs are in general *intentions* of the institution.

We can cast this challenge roughly as follows:

(1) Dense holism about an *individual's* intentions, grounded in a theory of interpretation.
(2) Extension of this dense holism condition to *any* system that has intentions.

(3) Normal failure of institutions to satisfy these constraints of dense holism, given common forms of pluralistic disagreement.

So:

(4) The institutional crystallized outputs of an institution's social procedural rules are normally not intentions of that institution.

If we want to continue to see institutional action-focused crystallized outputs of the social rules of procedure central to organized institutions as normally intentions of those institutions, we need to block this argument. But the argument—or anyway, a more regimented version—is valid. So, we need to challenge one of the premises. But rejecting premise (1) would be a high price to pay: Davidson's insights about the holistic constraints on interpretation of *individual* subjects, though they are subject to qualification, need to be adjusted to incorporate roles of intentions and plans, and do not solve all the problems in this neighborhood, are broadly compelling. So, we are faced with the prospect of challenging either (2) or (3).

8.4 Ludwig, List and Pettit, Rovane, and dense holism

A first step is to reflect on several discussions that in effect focus on (3) and its connection to (4). On the one hand, Kirk Ludwig comments (citing Davidson) that "the usual holistic constraints on attitude attributions are absent in the case of attributions to organizations"—thereby evidencing his acceptance of versions of (1), (2), and (3)—and indicates that this supports his conclusion that "we find behind the curtains only individual agents" and that talk of the intentions of an institution should be understood only in an "analogical" sense (2017, 237–38).[12] So we should, as Ludwig would see it, accept a version of (4).

On the other hand, Philip Pettit also indicates his acceptance of versions of (1) and (2) when he writes:

What sort of rationality do we expect in an intentional subject? By a line of argument that has been widely endorsed in recent philosophical thought, a system will count as an intentional subject only if . . . it displays a certain rational unity. (Pettit 2003, 180)

And Pettit argues that in important cases, especially those that involve "discursive dilemmas," institutions are under practical pressure to achieve some such rational unity—to achieve, as List and Pettit later put it, "a single, robustly rational body of attitudes."[13] This idea of rational unity includes what List and Pettit call "attitude-to-attitude standards of rationality," standards that apply to all intentional agents and include "consistency and completeness" (List and Pettit 2011, 67). In particular, this rational unity will satisfy what they call the "collective rationality" requirement, understood as the condition that there is a web of "consistent and complete group attitudes towards the propositions on the agenda" (49). List and Pettit indicate that the rational unity they have in mind is in the spirit of Rovane's appeal to "a single system of belief and desire . . . a single vision."[14] And such a Rovane-type system will be, more or less, a dense holistic subject.

So, I think that a natural reading of Pettit, and of List and Pettit, is that they endorse versions of (1) and (2) in the cited Davidsonian argument. They then go on to argue that in important cases institutions are under practical pressure to achieve "rational unity," where this involves satisfying a constraint of "completeness" (as well as consistency), and in that way a constraint of holistic density with respect to "propositions on the agenda." And they think that in many important cases institutions succeed in their responses to this pressure.[15] In such cases institutions are "plural centers of intentional life: minds of their own," and so (3) is false about such cases (Pettit and Schweikard 2006, 36; see also List and Pettit 2011, 77–78). Groups that in this way "collectivize reason deserve ontological recognition as intentional and personal subjects" (Pettit 2003, 175). So, we should reject the skepticism about institutional intention in (4).

Pettit does note Sunstein's point that there can be groups that "reach collective decisions on an incompletely theorized basis" (2003, 172). Nevertheless, Pettit insists that "even social groups that differ from the courts in routinely securing only incompletely theorized agreements will have to confront diachronic examples of" discursive dilemmas. So, there will be, in many cases, significant diachronic practical pressures in the direction of "collectivizing reason" in a way that induces a dense holism of group attitude (2003, 173, 175). So, again, we should reject the skepticism about institutional intention at the heart of (4).[16]

So, Ludwig and Pettit, List, and Rovane evidence similar views about (1) and (2) but divergent views about (3), and thereby divergent views about (4). What to say?

Well, on the one hand, given Sunstein-like considerations, I do think that many organized institutions will not satisfy dense holistic demands of a Davidsonian subject. In many cases there will be a violation of the completeness part of the List-Pettit "collective rationality" condition, since there will not be, and need not be, an institutional view about all "propositions on the agenda." On the other hand, we can grant Pettit's point that there may be important cases in which institutions, in response to practical pressures, to some extent do satisfy this holistic density demand with respect to "propositions on the agenda." In light of this dialectical situation, I propose to bypass these disagreements about (3) and instead challenge (2)—the extension of the dense holism condition to any system that has intentions. We steer a path between Ludwig, on the one hand,[17] and List, Pettit, and Rovane, on the other hand, by blocking the overextension of Davidsonian conditions of dense holism. We thereby arrive at a more nuanced approach both to the relation between individual and institutional agency and to the interrelated contributions of interpretation and plan-theoretic construction to our understanding of organized institutions.

8.5 Rejecting the primacy of individual intention: Interpretation and construction

Premise (2) involves a *primacy of individual intention and intentional agency*: we derive essential features of intention and intentional agency quite generally from essential features of *individual* intention and intentional agency. This idea is initially plausible. How else spell out why institutional intention and intentional agency, if such there be, are indeed a kind of intention and intentional agency? How else spell out why institutional intentions, if such there be, have the contents they have? And it is initially plausible to suppose, with Deborah Tollefsen (2015, 104), that "our practice of interpreting the actions of groups is just an extension of our practice of making sense of individuals, and it is governed by the same constitutive rules."[18]

Nevertheless, an alternative idea is available, namely, that intention and intentional agency are generic phenomena one important species of which is individual intentional agency.[19] About that species of individual intentional agency it is plausible, given the role of interpretation, to endorse a version of Davidson's idea that the intentional agent is a more or less holistic subject, one with a dense coherent web of interrelated attitudes (allowing for breakdowns). But perhaps there are other species of intention and intentional agency, species that stand in a more complex relation to Davidsonian interpretation and do not necessarily involve a dense holistic subject.

Indeed, the planning theory can support this last thought. The planning theory understands intention by appeal to interrelated roles in the cross-temporal organization of thought and action. These roles involve temporally extended, cognitively sensitive framing and guidance of thought and action. This framing and guidance involve norms of plan rationality and thereby structure downstream practical thinking. They thereby unify and make sense of activity in ways that track the target of the intention. Attitudes that systematically play these roles are intentions, intentions whose contents are associated with these roles. In the case of *individual* intentional agents, we can accommodate Davidsonian pressures of interpretation for understanding that individual as a more or less coherent, dense holistic subject. But in the institutional case it seems that these forms of thought-infused cross-temporal organization do not require that the institutional states at the center of the organization be embedded within a dense holistic subject. It seems that such institutional states can rationally function to induce relevant temporally extended unity of socially embedded thought and action in ways that are characteristic of intention, even though this need not involve the unity of a dense holistic Davidsonian subject. Granted, given partiality of institutional view, questions of how to respond to certain counterfactual circumstances may remain unsettled. But intentions need not solve all such counterfactual challenges.

The idea, then, is that we can have a broadly functionalist model of institutional intention, one that involves appeal to a rational plan dynamics within that institution, without seeing dense holism as essential at the level of that institution. We can separate these two ideas—rational plan functionalism and dense holism—even while allowing that, given the nature of interpretation, there is, plus or minus a bit, a dense holism requirement on *individual* intentional agents. To do that, however, we need to challenge (2).[20] Once pressures for a dense holistic subject play their role in the interpretation of individual participants and their content-involving attitudes, interpersonal structures of intentions of the sort highlighted by our plan-theoretic constructions can build on these attitudes of individual subjects in a way that can realize plan-theoretic conditions for an intention of the institution. This does require that relevant crystallized outputs be *institutional* outputs. So, it precludes unresolved inconsistency of outputs and functionally undermining, non-compensated cognitive divergence. But these limited constraints allow for disagreements about underlying rationales and about significant factual matters, and thereby for incompleteness of institutional view—they allow for "incompletely theorized agreements." So, they do not ensure a densely holistic web of attitudes—they do not ensure a dense holistic institutional subject.

In understanding the intentions of an institution, we are not simply extending Davidsonian interpretation from individuals to those groups. We are instead adding to the resources of Davidsonian interpretation of individuals the further, plan-theoretic, constructive resources developed here. And I have tried to explain how these two theoretical resources—holistic interpretation of individual subjects, together with our plan-theoretic constructions—can combine in our efforts to model organized institutions. We combine these two philosophical resources to model organized institutions and their web of social rules and institutional intentions, and to specify contents of their social rules and institutional intentions. We thereby model institutional intentions without institutional densely holistic subjects.

In this way we reject the primacy of individual intention in articulating the functional roles essential to intention. We do this even though our construction of institutional intention is broadly individualistic. We seek to bring together broadly individualistic construction with function, but we do not thereby assume that the specification of that function derives simply and directly from the case of individual intention. Instead, we allow that the background theory that underlies the relevant functional specification can be to some extent different in the individual and institutional cases.

Indeed, a potential divergence of underlying, function-specifying theory was already noted in Chapter 7. In the individual case, the cognitive background for the functioning of intentions of the individual will be beliefs and acceptances of that individual. In contrast, in the institutional case the cognitive background for the functioning of an institutional intention can involve a mix of acceptance-focused outputs/institutional acceptances and a distributed web of beliefs/acceptances of multiple individuals. In this way the function-specifying theory for the institutional case differs from that for the individual case. But we retain the general functional connection between institutional intention and cognitive correlates while allowing for complexity about those cognitive correlates in the institutional case. And we are now allowing for yet a further potential difference in function-specifying theory, a difference with respect to a condition of dense holism. In each case, however, the basic functioning at the institutional level supports the idea that the cited institutional action-focused crystallized outputs are institutional intentions, functionally speaking.

John Rawls (1971) criticized classical utilitarianism for "extending to society the principle of choice for one man" (27). Premise (2)—the extension of the dense holism condition to any system that has intentions—involves an analogous extension from individual to institutional. I think an analogue of Rawls's skepticism is apt in our reflections on premise (2). We need to avoid an overly simple extension from the individual case to the institutional case; and I have been arguing that we can thereby avoid skepticism about institutional intention.

9 INSTITUTIONAL INTENTION WITHOUT A DENSE HOLISTIC SUBJECT

The key is the role of intention in the cross-temporal organization of thought and action. I proceed to discuss how this supports the idea of institutional intention in the absence of a dense holistic subject. I then address, in Sections 9.3–9.5, a series of related issues.

9.1 Cross-temporal, mind-shaped, rational organization

Intentions are plan states, and the characteristic roles of plan states involve temporally extended, cognitively sensitive framing and guidance of thought and action. In the case of individual intentional agency, the guiding intentions will be intentions of that individual, and Davidsonian interpretation induces pressures for understanding that individual as a holistic subject. But in the institutional case, the states that support organization in ways constitutive of intention need not be embedded in a dense holistic institutional subject.

Granted, for there to be relevant forms of coordination-supporting framing and guidance, these structures of institutional intention are under pressure to be consistent, since inconsistencies of intention will tend to undermine coordination. To be effective these structures of institutional intention will need to tend to involve, over time, sufficiently detailed specifications of means and the like. For there to be relevant, minimal forms of shared thinking there will need to be, in the background, minimal agreement on central aspects of what is involved in the intended activity. These conditions cohere with the conditions on institutionalization of output highlighted in

Section 6.2. But these constraints do not entail the presence of a single coherent, dense rationalizing framework of institutional attitudes.

The web of intentions and related attitudes of the institution can be, in part in response to substantial disagreements, thin and partial. Though there is not inconsistency in the intentions of the institution, or failures to adequately specify relevant means, there may nevertheless be no single, overall, unified, institutional view of the substantive grounds in support of the institutional intention, or of the context in which the intention is to be carried out, or of what is involved in carrying out that intention. So, there may be no overall institutional view of a fully detailed specification of the option favored by the institutional intention. There does need to be limited functionally relevant, non-compensated cognitive divergence concerning what is involved in the intended activity. However, such limited cognitive divergence still allows for significant disagreement—and resulting partiality/incompleteness—about aspects of, and the rationale for, that activity.

Suppose that Medic Supply arrives at an institutional crystallized output that is an institutional intention to send medical aid to C. The proper functioning of this intention will involve a dispersed but in relevant respects unified web of coordinated temporally extended individual and shared intentions and activities, including those of managers concerning the overall activity of sending the supplies and of employees concerning truck driving. This will normally involve a more or less consistent web of intentions, adequate specifications of means, and minimal agreement about what it is to send such aid. But it need not involve a holistic, Davidson-friendly institutional subject. It need not be settled within the attitudes of Medic Supply whether the aim is simply relief from suffering, or supporting the local government or the local economy, or respecting promises made to donors, or satisfying certain religious obligations. There may here be substantive disagreements among participants and good reasons for Medic Supply not to take a stand. There can also remain significant disagreement in beliefs about the context of sending the aid (e.g., about features of the target country) and what is involved in sending the aid. In many cases the institution itself need not take a stand on these matters of disagreement and may be well advised not to. Nevertheless, despite this multifaceted, disagreement-driven partiality/incompleteness in institutional framework, this crystallized output of the social rules of procedure of Medic Supply can be an institutional intention of Medic Supply, functionally speaking.

A familiar complication is that this partiality can sometimes be mitigated by way of induced further teleology. Perhaps the social-procedural-rule output is to send the supplies *in order to support the local government*. So, even if different participating individuals have different views about the value of this end, this end is an aspect of an institutional intention. But it is one thing for this one end to be built into an institutional intention, another for that intention to be embedded in a dense holistic framework that takes a stand on a wide range of potential considerations—for example, the importance of implicit promises to donors, or of religious demands. And it is one thing for this one end to be built into an institutional intention, another for there to be a rich web of views of the institution concerning a wide range of relevant matters—for example, the impact of the shipment on local markets. The phenomenon of induced further teleology, while it may to some extent mitigate the impacts of disagreements and partiality, does not ensure that institutional intentions will be embedded in a dense holistic institutional subject.

Once interpretation-based pressures for a holistic subject play their role in the interpretation of individual participants, interpersonal structures highlighted by our plan-theoretic constructions can build on these content-involving attitudes of individuals to realize functionalist conditions for an intention of the institution. Such institutional intentions will induce standards of success of institutional activity as well as criteria of inclusion of subactivities within the overall intentional activities of the institution.[1] They will help to make sense of those activities. But, given common forms of disagreement and incompleteness, such institutional intentions will not in general require a dense holistic institutional subject.

It follows that the epistemology of our knowledge of the intentions of institutions is not a direct extension of the epistemology of our knowledge of the minds of individual participants: we reject Tollefsen's maxim that "our practice of interpreting the actions of groups is just an extension of our practice of making sense of individuals, and it is governed by the same constitutive rules" (2015, 104). In understanding the intentions of an institution, we are not simply extending Davidsonian interpretation from individuals to those groups. We are instead adding to the resources of Davidsonian interpretation, as applied to individuals, the plan-theoretic, sequential constructive resources developed here. What is missing in Tollefsen's maxim, and in the direct application of Davidsonian interpretation at the level of the institution, is a focus on the *constructions* that underlie the functioning that is the target of interpretation.² Here our efforts at sequential, shared-policy-infused construction (in contrast with simply a parallel appeal to plans and planning at the institutional level) bear fruit.

This makes room for an interpretation-based holistic-subject constraint on individual intention, while rejecting this as a general constraint on all intention. The conditions on institutionalization of output, the means-end coherence involved in institutional intentions, and the partial unity of temporally extended social agency they support need not ensure holistic, Davidsonian unity of subjecthood at the level of the institution. This is so even if some such unity of subjecthood is presupposed in our practice of interpreting individual agents. The relevant crystallized, institutional outputs of an institution's social-rule-supported procedures can play cross-temporal roles characteristic of intentions: stably pose problems, filter solutions, and thereby frame, coordinate, organize, and make sense of temporally extended, individual, and social thought and action. So, these crystallized outputs can be intentions of the institution, functionally speaking. And this is so even given partiality/incompleteness in background institutional view that baffles a dense holistic institutional subject.

Here again we bring together construction and function, and we retain the idea that the keys to whether there is intention at a given level (individual, shared, institutional) are the intention-defining cross-temporal organizing functional roles at that level. But we resist the idea that our access to the presence of these institutional constructions is by way of a simple and direct extension of Davidsonian interpretation from the individual to the institution.

9.2 Giving "substance" to institutional intention

Return to Davidson's (2001a, 200) guiding thought about the content of attitudes:

> Beliefs are identified and described only within a dense pattern of beliefs. I can believe a cloud is passing before the sun, but only because I believe there is a sun, that clouds are made of water vapor, that water can exist in liquid or gaseous form; and so on, without end. No particular list of further beliefs is required to give substance to my belief that a cloud is passing before the sun; but some appropriate set of related beliefs must be there.

How does our model of institutional intention "give substance" to that intention without embedding it in such a "dense pattern"? How can institutional intentions have the content they have without being embedded in such a holistic web?

The answer is that one determinant of the contents of institutional intentions is provided by the contents of the attitudes of relevant individuals, attitudes that are, we are supposing, embedded in that individual's "dense pattern." We then add to these content-involving attitudes of the individuals the resources of our plan-theoretic, sequential constructions—including especially social rules of procedure and their crystallized outputs. By putting together these twin theoretical resources we can give "substance" to the contents of output institutional intentions.

So, we construct social rules of procedure; and then we use them to construct outputs that are candidates for institutional intentions. In each case our constructions put us in a position to give "substance" to relevant contents—of the social rule, and of the output intention.

Our account of the content of the social rule is broadly in the spirit of Hart's implicit solution to the problem of social rule content. As Hart saw it, individual participants in a social rule have attitudes with a content that sees a certain pattern of action as a common standard. A social rule is a construction that builds on such content-involving attitudes of individuals. The content of the social rule is grounded in the content of these attitudes of the individuals when these attitudes are put together in the relevant way. To determine the content of the social rule we do not seek an overarching, coherent interpretation of the overall sociality—though one may be available. Instead, we build up the social rule from interrelated attitudes of relevant individuals with relevant contents. Insofar as we apply Davidsonian pressures for dense holism we apply them at the level of those individuals, not directly at an overarching social level. But we still see how those content-bearing attitudes of those individuals can help "give substance" to the content of the social rule given the way that social rule involves a construction that builds on those attitudes of individuals.

In our next step we go beyond Hart's explicit views and see certain crystallized outputs of social rules of procedure as constructions that are institutional intentions. And we can see the contents of those crystallized outputs as shaped in part by the contents of the social rules that are shaped in part by the contents of the involved individual attitudes. We "give substance" to the contents of these institutional intentions without depending on a direct application of holism-requiring interpretation at the institutional level. We thereby reject Tollefsen's maxim. And we reject premise (2)—the extension of the dense holism condition to any system that has intentions—in the Davidson-inspired argument for skepticism about institutional intention.

Recall now that even in the case of small-scale shared intention, the fully specified intentions of each might not completely match. Perhaps you intend that we paint as a way of reducing the mildew, whereas I intend that we paint as a way of changing the color. To get at the joint-act type with respect to which there is shared intention we need to find the relevant overlap of these different contents—in this case, the more generic act of painting the house—where each intends that as well.

And now we note an analogous complexity concerning the shared policies that underlie the social rules of procedure whose crystallized outputs are, in certain cases, institutional intentions. Here too there may be commonality in more generic contents of relevant attitudes of each but divergence in more specific contents. Perhaps, for example, each intends that the procedures involve consultation with a certain subgroup, but different participants have different understandings of what is involved in such consultation. This may lead to disagreements that block the successful functioning of the procedures. It might instead provide an occasion for the operation of yet further social rules of procedure that aim at resolving such problems. And in a third case, it may be that there is, despite the disagreement, sufficient overlap in understandings of the nature of relevant consultation for the "incompletely theorized" procedures to work their way through to an institutional intention.

My conjecture is that we can recognize these different possibilities, including potential threats to institutional functioning, but still bring together our two different theoretical resources—more or less holistic interpretation of individuals together with our plan-theoretic, sequential constructions—in the indicated way. We thereby provide for content-involving social rules of procedure that can issue in crystallized outputs that constitute content-involving institutional intentions in the absence of a holistic institutional subject.

9.3 Discursive dilemmas and incompleteness

One of the contributions of List and Pettit is to focus on the implications of "discursive dilemmas" for our understanding of group attitudes. In this section I explain how my approach to institutional intention can accommodate their insights.

In a central example, a group of three workers needs to decide whether to install a new safety system, where this would involve a pay cut to each (Pettit 2003). They see each of a trio of relevant considerations ("premises") as an answer to a different question: Is the danger serious? Would the system be effective? Is the loss bearable? Each person answers exactly one of these questions (though a different one in each case) in the negative. So, each thinks they should not go ahead with the system.

The views of each can be represented as follows (Pettit 2003):

	Serious danger?	Effective measure?	Bearable loss?	Pay sacrifice to install safety system?
A	Yes	no	yes	no
B	No	yes	yes	no
C	Yes	yes	no	no

If the group were to reach a decision that simply responded directly to the views of each concerning whether to endorse the pay cut and install the system, its decision would be no. This would involve a "conclusion-centered" form of reasoning. Suppose, in contrast, that the group begins with an assessment of attitudes of each toward each premise, privileges the majority view on each premise, and then arrives at a conclusion based on those views of the premises. The group is guided by a rule that says: if a majority favors premise P_i, then use premise P_i in further reasoning concerning whether to install the safety system. This premise-centered reasoning would lead to a conclusion in favor of the safety system even though, bracketing such reasoning, each member of the group individually supports the opposite conclusion. So, for a group that follows such a premise-centered procedure, there would be a discontinuity between that group's premise-driven conclusion and the pre-procedure view of the individual members of the group concerning that conclusion. Yet, as Pettit argues, there are occasions where a group has good practical reason to follow such a premise-centered procedure.[3]

As Pettit understands such a premise-centered procedure, its upshot is that the group has judgments that answer each premise question affirmatively, thereby has a judgment that answers the conclusion question affirmatively, and so intends to install the new system. There is here an *induced rational completeness* within the group: these resulting elements cohere with each other in support of the conclusion and are "complete" with respect to "propositions on the agenda,"[4] where the "agenda" includes both potential premises and potential conclusions. Such completeness is a kind of dense holism with respect to the "propositions on the agenda." And, as Pettit sees it, given such completeness we are on our way to "all the functional marks of an intentional subject."[5]

This view purports to explain how sensible procedures will tend to induce such holistic completeness, without simply assuming that we ascribe the relevant group attitudes by way of directly interpreting the group in Davidsonian fashion. This returns us to Tollefsen's maxim that "our practice of interpreting the actions of groups is just an extension of our practice of making sense of individuals, and it is governed by the same constitutive rules." There are indications that List and Pettit would be sympathetic with this maxim (List and Pettit 2011, chap. 1). But the view we are now discussing concerning the impact of premise-driven procedures is not that we arrive at attributions of intention to an institution directly by way of overall, Davidson-like interpretation of that institution. Instead, the thought is that in the context of discursive dilemmas the combination of interpreted attitudes of individuals *together with pragmatically sensible institutional structures/procedures* will normally issue in a web of institutional attitudes that involves the holistic completeness we would have sought if we were directly to apply Davidson-type interpretation at the level of the institution. We arrive at such holistic completeness without relying on Tollefsen's maxim about the uniformity of the epistemology of individual and group minds.[6] But the view continues to respect the general claim that "if a group is to perform robustly as an agent, it must generally avoid attitudinal incompleteness" (List and Pettit 2011, 53)

Indeed, List and Pettit's procedure here for arriving at group-level attitudes is in this respect in the spirit of (and of course pre-dates) my proposal that in arriving at attributions of institutional intention we add to Davidsonian interpretation of individuals the further constructive resources of our theory of rule-guided institutional procedures. List and Pettit's thought is that in the context of discursive dilemmas the combination of interpreted attitudes of individuals together with pragmatically sensible institutional procedures will normally issue in a web of institutional attitudes that involves a kind of holistic completeness. But the way we arrive at these attributions of attitude to the institution is not directly to apply Davidson-type interpretation at the level of the institution. We instead add to the interpreted attitudes of individuals a relevant "organizational structure."

However, despite this agreement on the role of group-level procedures in taking us from attitudes of individuals to attitudes of the group/institution, I worry about the tight connection List and Pettit draw between the outputs of relevant institutional structures/procedures and dense holistic completeness. Once we tie the pressure to satisfy the completeness condition not to overarching Davidsonian interpretative pressures but to outputs of pragmatically sensible procedures, we need to see whether such procedures quite generally have outputs that satisfy this completeness condition. And I think they do not.

To see this, distinguish the premise-centered procedure List and Pettit have in mind—whose upshot induces group judgments on *both* premises and conclusions—from a premise-centered procedure along the lines of:

> (P) See which individual premises are supported by a majority, treat those premises as privileged for the procedure in the present case, and then arrive at a group conclusion in a premise-driven way. However, there need not be a *group judgment on the premises,* and perhaps there are reasons for the group *not* to arrive at a group judgment concerning each of the premises.

The idea is that a group can use a majority-supported premise in the functioning of its "organizational structure" in a given case without there being a *group judgment* that the premise is true. This use of the premise may only be a step along the way within a procedure whose output will be a group judgment. The group can use a majority-supported but nevertheless controversial premise as a step along the way in reaching a group conclusion in favor of a certain policy, but still not have a group view/ group judgment that that premise is true. A minority might be willing for the premise to be used in this way in this specific context, but not be willing for the group to be committed to this premise more generally. And the group's procedure may respect this view of the minority and eschew treating this use as an expression of the group's judgment of the truth of the premise.

(P) privileges individual premises that are supported by a majority but does not insist that there be a corresponding group judgment in favor of those premises. It says only to use majority-supported premises as part of a procedure aimed at a concluding group intention. This contrasts with the output commitment, in Pettit's example, to endorse the pay cut and install the system, a commitment that is set to shape a wide range of downstream thought and action. So, there can be a premise-centered procedure for resolving discursive dilemmas where that procedure supports the cited conclusion but where it need not induce an overall web of group judgments that would satisfy the List-Pettit completeness condition.

This is where Pettit (2003) appeals to diachronic cases where earlier conclusions (and so, group judgments) are themselves potential downstream premises. But even granting that there may be such diachronic cases (especially in the courts), there can sometimes be a sensible premise-centered procedure for resolving discursive dilemmas where that procedure need not induce a complete, unified web of group judgments concerning premises and conclusions, but only a group conclusion. Such a procedure would privilege certain premises without requiring a group judgment in favor of those premises.

In a case of this latter sort of premise-centered procedure, there is no longer the argument that, by way of its operation, the group satisfies the completeness condition. Nevertheless, the output of the procedure (e.g., the group endorses a new safety system) seems potentially to count as the group's *intention*. And we could develop this idea by way of our shared policy model of a social rule of procedure and its institutional crystallized outputs. In such cases there can be group/institutional intentions that are the issue of a group's "organizational structure" despite the absence of group completeness with respect to all "propositions on the agenda," and so despite the absence of a group/institutional holistic subject.

List and Pettit connect

(i) the condition that the group's "organizational structure" resolve a practical problem by issuing in a group conclusion by way of a premise-driven procedure

with

(ii) the condition of induced rational completeness.

Condition (i) outlines a kind of construction of institutional intention: institutional intention is a state that is the problem-resolving output of the proper functioning of relevant organizational structures. And their further idea is that this output will in general involve the satisfaction of the holistic constraint in (ii). But we have seen reason to take seriously cases of (i) in the absence of (ii), and these can be cases of group/institutional intention in the absence of group/institutional dense holism. And even in cases in which there is such a dense holism at the level of the institution, what constitutes the group/institutional intention is not, at bottom, that dense holism but the conclusion-focused output of the premise-driven procedure, and the intention-like functioning of that output. Granted, such procedures, as understood here, would be grounded in social rules that involve Lockean cross-temporal ties, and so forms of diachronic constancy.[7] But constant procedures need not induce a complete, unified web of group judgments concerning premises and conclusions.

9.4 Social extendedness and content

Our theory sees institutional intention and its execution as potentially involving a socially extended network of minds even while the content of the intention is anchored in narrower social rule kernels. Suppose that an organized institution intends to A. This institutional intention involves interrelated minds of different individuals. Some of these individuals are in the kernel whose shared policies are central to the social rule of procedure whose issue is the institutional intention. In a case in which relevant social procedural rules are hybrid, some of these individuals will be in a penumbra. Among those in that penumbra, some will have intentions that are associated with the specific institutional intention. This will include individuals who, in response to (perhaps intentionally induced) extending reasons, intend to act in ways that support A. For example: an "outside" lawyer.

So, there is potentially an extended web of individuals who are involved in the institutional intention and its execution. Nevertheless, our theory highlights a privileged group of individuals (one that can change over time) who participate in the kernel of the relevant social rules of procedure. And we have highlighted the role of that kernel in giving "substance" to the content of hybrid social rules. It is, for example, because the kernel shared policy favors procedure X that the overall social rule, one that also involves a relevant penumbra, has the rule content: follow procedure X.[8] These kernels then play a basic role in constituting the content of institutional intentions that emerge from relevant social rules of procedure.

Since penumbral participants will not be in such a kernel, their minds do not play the cited role in constituting the *content* of the institutional intention. But when such penumbral participants—such as our outside lawyer—are involved in the intended activity, their minds are involved in the *cross-temporally organized thought and action* by virtue of which the institution has, functionally speaking, certain *intentions*. This is a way in which relevant institutional functioning, and so the institutional intention, can involve a socially extended network of minds even while it is anchored in narrower, content-shaping kernels.[9]

9.5 Further aspects of intention?

When the outputs of social rules of procedure play the cited organizing roles without being embedded in a dense holistic subject they are not playing the role of being embedded in such a holistic subject.[10] A Davidson-inspired objection might be to insist that the defining roles of intention include not only the cited cross-temporal coordinating/organizing roles but also the role of being embedded in a dense holistic subject. So, we should throughout use a concept of intention—*D-intention*, we might say—that brings the role of being embedded in such a subject explicitly within the essential roles of the attitude.

We are, then, faced with a choice between a framework that includes the role of being embedded in a dense holistic subject within the essential functional roles of the relevant attitude (D-intention) and one that rejects that idea but instead treats the cited cross-temporal organizing roles as sufficient. How wide a net should we cast for social-psychological functions that are essential to intention?

My answer returns to the fundamental reason for introducing intentions and plans into the basic psychology. This is their role in helping to support and to explain a central feature of our resource-limited human agency: cross-temporal mind-shaped practical organization and coordination. My aim has been to work through the implications of that basic idea, including implications for our understanding of shared agency and institutional organization. The conjecture is that this is a fruitful framework within which to develop a theory of human practical organization. Within this framework we do not yet have reason to insist that being embedded in a dense holistic subject is an essential feature of intention quite generally. And we can reject this insistence even while seeing dense holism as an aspect of individual minds, an aspect grounded—if Davidson is right—in the interpretation of those individual minds.

In light of these reflections, I propose to reject the primacy of individual intention in articulating the functional roles that are central to intention.[11] But I do not propose that we put in its place a primacy of group/institutional intention. My proposal, instead, involves a primacy of mind-shaped cross-temporal organization and coordination. Individual intention plays basic roles in the cross-temporal organization of individual agency. If Davidson is right, individual intention is also subject to interpretation-based holistic constraints. But in our overall approach to intention and intentional agency we should give primacy not to those interpretation-based holistic constraints on individual intention but rather to the basic phenomenon of mind-shaped cross-temporal, practical organization.

In rejecting the primacy of individual intention in articulating the roles essential to intention we nevertheless retain our broadly individualistic construction of institutional intention. We bring together individualistic construction with characteristic function; but we reject the assumption that the specification of that function simply and directly derives from that of individual intention. This book constitutes an argument in favor of the theoretical fecundity of this approach.

But do we not need holistic constraints at the level of institutional attitudes to "give substance" to the contents of purported institutional intentions? After all, we have followed Davidson in supposing that such constraints do help constitutively to shape the contents of attitudes of individual subjects.

My response, as anticipated, is that once we have available interpreted attitudes of relevant individual holistic subjects, we can draw on those attitudes, as they are embedded in relevant plan-theoretic constructions, to fix the contents of relevant institutional intentions. We do not need directly to impose dense holism constraints at the institutional level. The institutional intention *to send medical resources to a certain city* has this content primarily because of the interpreted contents of individual attitudes that help constitute the relevant social rule of procedure and the interpreted contents of attitudes of those individuals who participate in those procedures. These interpreted contents induce, by way of our plan-theoretic construction, relevant contents of relevant social rules. And this, together with the processes involved in the functioning of these social rules, allows us to assign contents to relevant institutional intentions without requiring that the institution is itself a dense holistic subject.

The idea, then, is that there is a structure of more or less holistically interpreted individuals, and that their attitudes help constitute robust social rules of procedure with rule contents. These social rules of procedure can then interact with interpreted individuals to issue in institutional intentions whose contents are induced by the cited social web. In this way the content of those institutional intentions is grounded in the contents of attitudes of interpreted individuals as they are incorporated within our plan-theoretic sequential construction of institutional functioning.

In both the individual and institutional cases there can be hard problems in trying to get the contents right, and we may encounter indeterminacy and/or vagueness and/or disagreement. But different epistemologies are at work. In interpreting individual agents/subjects, Davidsonian holistic constraints of interpretation come directly to bear. In contrast, in determining the contents of relevant social rules and institutional intentions the primary issue is not how to construct an overall, dense holistic, social subject. The primary issue concerns, rather, what emerges from the interactions between the individual, interpreted psychologies and our plan-theoretic sequential constructions.

Return to Liao's (2018) comments about Facebook. What could make it true that Facebook intends to assist the dissemination of hate speech on its platform is a social-procedural-rule-induced institutional intention that favors assisting the dissemination of this kind of speech.[12] Though this would involve satisfying constraints of being an institutional output, we would still not need to suppose that Facebook is itself a dense holistic subject.

Now, one central motivation for focusing on institutional intention is a concern about whether institutions are morally accountable in ways that go beyond the individual accountability of their individual participants (Ortis and Smith 2017; Tollefsen 2015, chap. 6; Sepinwall 2016). How does my treatment of institutional intention bear on this concern?

My proposal can incorporate the thought that if an institution were morally accountable for its activity, then it would need to have associated institutional intentions.[13] This does not entail, however, that institutional intention is sufficient for such accountability. After all, we know from reflection on children that, even given intention, other incapacities can baffle moral accountability. So, there are further questions about a move from institutional intention to institutional moral accountability. My strategy is to develop a model of institutional intention that does not presuppose complete answers to these further, difficult questions about institutional moral accountability. It aims to provide a philosophical foundation for one plausibly essential element of institutional moral accountability—institutional intention—while leaving open for further research what further elements are needed and whether they might be expected to be realized.

Does an institution that has such institutional intentions thereby have a *mind*? Well, it does not follow that the institution has a *phenomenally conscious* mind (Tollefsen 2015, sec. 3.1; List 2018). Nor does it follow that the institution has a Davidsonian, *densely holistic* mind. Given institutional intentions, we can, if we want, talk of a limited institutional mind. However, given the normal association of talk of mind with ideas of phenomenal consciousness and/or of dense holism, this runs the risk of being misunderstood. What is central is that we are legitimizing our talk of institutional *intention*.

10 INSTITUTIONAL INTENTIONAL AGENTS

The next step is to use our account of institutional intention to understand institutional intentional *agency*. I provide a basic account in Sections 10.1 and 10.2 and explore related ideas in sections 10.3 and 10.4. I pull some pieces together in section 10.5, and in 10.6 explore different aspects of social unity.

10.1 Guidance by institutional intention, guidance by institutional intentional agent: Robustness

I have highlighted the organizational roles of intention, a central aspect of which is the guidance of action. Talk of guidance of action by intention is, so far, talk of guidance by an *attitude*. But in the individual case guidance by intention is normally partly constitutive of intentional guidance by an *agent*—of intentional *agency*. In the individual case it is normally true that *I* guide those activities that my *intentions* guide. Should we then say that, analogously, guidance by institutional intention is normally partly constitutive of intentional guidance by the *institutional agent*? Can we move from our model of institutional *intention* to a model of institutional intentional *agency*?

Now, even in the individual case it is a deep problem to explain when and why guidance by *intention* helps constitute guidance by an intentional *agent*.[1] This is not the place to try to solve this problem, though I will return to it in Section 10.2. Here I focus on the analogous problem about the relation between guidance by institutional intention and guidance by an institutional intentional agent.

If, as I have argued, organized institutions can be intenders, can we infer that when institutional intentions guide in a characteristic way, the institution itself is an intentional agent who so intends and thereby guides action? Can we reason from

(1) There is guidance by an institutional *intention*

to

(2) There is guidance by an institutional intentional *agent* who so intends?

I take it that we can reason from (1) to

(3) There is guidance by an intentional agent.

But our question is whether we can reason from (1) to an *institutional* intentional agent, as in (2).

Given that the institutional intention in (1) does not require a densely holistic institutional subject, we should reject an inference from (1) to

(4) There is guidance by a densely holistic institutional intentional agent.

But what about an inference from (1) to (2) that does not go by way of appeal to a densely holistic subject?

My answer comes in two parts. I first articulate an initial prima facie case for an inference from (1) to (2), one that draws on the robustness of institutional intention. I then note a challenge and respond by drawing on a Frankfurt-inspired idea about agency.

Suppose that you and I share an intention to paint the house together. If I were to drop out and some third person were to take my place, our shared intention to paint would no longer exist. Our shared intention is *fragile* with respect to changes in participants. In contrast, an institutional intention will be *robust* with respect to certain changes in participants. Suppose that such an institutional intention successfully guides. So, there is guidance by an intentional agent. Who?

Well, this guiding institutional intention is robust in the face of change in individual participants. And an initially plausible principle is

(5) If the intention that guides is robust in the face of change in individual participants, then so is an intentional agent who so intends and thereby guides.

After all, if the guiding intention persists despite changes in participating individual agents, and if this guidance by the persisting intention induces guidance by an intentional agent, then it seems plausible that that intentional agent will also persist despite these changes in participating individual agents. So, if the intention that guides is robust then an agent who so intends and thereby intentionally guides is robust. But if, given the guidance by an institutional intention, we are looking for a relevant, robust intentional agent, the obvious candidate is the institution itself. So, we can reason defeasibly from (1), (3), and (5) to (2): a relevant intentional agent who so intends and thereby guides is the institution itself. We thereby arrive at (2) by appeal to robustness, but without appeal to a densely holistic institutional subject.

Consider in contrast

(6) There is guidance by a shared intention.

Since a shared intention is not robust, we cannot reason, in the way just mooted, from (6) to

(2*) There is guidance by a group intentional agent who so intends.

Instead, given our theory of shared intention, what we should say is that if (6) then

(7) There is guidance by participating interrelated individual intentional agents

where the individual agents are those who participate in the shared intention. Granted, (1) will also involve participating individual intentional agents. But we have seen reason to claim that in the case of (1) we can *also* reason to (2), given the robustness both of institutional intention and of institution.

The idea that institutions and institutional intentions are robust fits with our commonsense understanding of organized institutions. List and Pettit (2011) make it a condition of being a group, in the relevant sense, that it "have an identity that can survive changes of membership" (31). And Ludwig (2017, 5) emphasizes that institutions "survive changes in their membership." Institutional structures need to play basic cross-temporal organizing roles. Given the ways in which individual participants come and go, playing these organizing roles will involve persistence of institutional structures despite change in individual participants. So, there is a presumption that institutions and, if such there be, institutional intentions are robust with respect to changes in participants. And this commonsense idea coheres with our overall model of institutional functioning and institutional intention.

But now we need to consider a challenge. Suppose we have a case of guidance by a robust intention that is not embedded in a dense holistic Davidsonian web. A skeptic can ask: Why think this guidance by this robust intention constitutes the guidance *by any agent at all whose intention it is*? Why not say that even though, in such a case, the guiding *intention* is robust, there is, quite simply, no robust intentional *agent* whose intention it is and who thereby guides? After all, the guiding intention is not embedded in a dense holistic web of attitudes.

This is, then, a challenge to our use of (5) in our inference to (2). The challenge grants that if the intention that guides is robust in the face of change in individual participants, and if there is a guiding intentional agent whose intention this is, then that guiding intentional agent will also be robust in this way. But the challenge is to the idea that there is any intentional agent at all whose intention this is and who thereby guides.

One might think—perhaps Davidson did think—that the explanation of why intention guidance constitutes guidance by an intentional *agent* who so intends is that the guiding intentions are embedded in a dense holistic web. But if that is what we think, then we should be skeptical of the idea that guidance by an institutional intention that is not embedded in a dense holistic web constitutes guidance by an institutional intentional agent who so intends.

To answer this challenge, I will return to ideas from Harry Frankfurt concerning an agent's standpoint.

10.2 Guidance by institutional intention, guidance by institutional intentional agent: Institutional standpoint

We have seen that the social rules of procedure of an institution, and the institutional intentions in which they can issue, are robust with respect to changes in participating individuals. We have asked whether this sufficiently supports an inference from guidance by institutional intention to an institutional intentional agent who guides, as in (2). And the objection is that it does not and that this inference requires a further condition of dense holism.

In response, return to Frankfurt's ideas about an agent's standpoint. Frankfurt thought that certain structures of will—in particular, hierarchies of desire—are at the heart of where "the person himself stands" and of acting of one's own free will. And my somewhat analogous thought will be that certain structures of the "will" of an institution are at the heart of an institutional standpoint whose functioning supports the status of that institution as intentional agent. And these structures need not be embedded in a dense holistic institutional subject.

A complication is that Frankfurt's appeal to higher-order desires aims to say when guidance by certain attitudes constitutes acting of one's own free will. It is not offered more broadly as an account of individual intentional agency. After all, the unwilling addict is an intentional agent who does not act of her own free will—hers is a weaker form of intentional agency. In contrast, my appeal here to Frankfurtian ideas aims to help explain when guidance by institutional intentions constitutes institutional intentional agency. This leaves open the question of whether there are weaker forms of institutional intentional agency. But it will suffice for my purposes here—namely, to legitimize, within our planning framework, appeals to institutional intentional agency—if we can articulate sufficient conditions for such agency without overly strong conditions of dense holism.[2]

In earlier work, I appealed to three interrelated ideas in developing this Frankfurtian idea of an agential standpoint whose guidance can constitute a strong form of individual agency (Bratman 2007b, sec. 2, 5; 2014b, 319–22; 2017a). First, the attitudes that constitute the standpoint support a thick web of interconnections over time, interconnections that parallel those highlighted within Lockean approaches to the persistence of a person over time. Second, these attitudes rationally shape and anchor basic forms of practical thinking within the system. Third, these attitudes are appropriately stable. The thought is that guidance by a standpoint that satisfies, in a coordinated way, this trio of conditions can constitute a non-homuncular, strong form of individual agency.

We can now apply these ideas to institutional agency. The thought is that guidance by interlocking social rules of procedure and their institutional crystallized outputs can satisfy an analogous trio of conditions. This guidance will induce and support a thick web of Lockean ties, both over time and across participants.³ It will rationally shape and anchor practical thinking—individual, shared, and institutional.⁴ In many cases these elements will be stable, perhaps in part because of concerns with realizing a kind of institutional agency for which such stability is needed. And while such broadly Lockean interconnections help knit together important temporally extended functioning, they do not ensure a robust, densely coherent institutional subject (Bratman 2014a, 127–28).

So, an institution's robust rule-guided procedures for settling important practical issues, and their institutional crystallized outputs, are a central aspect of that institution's standpoint and thereby, potentially, its intentional guidance. Since these institutional crystallized outputs are intentions of the institution, we arrive at the conclusion that guidance by institutional intention can help constitute guidance by an institutional intentional agent who so intends.

These stance-providing, knitting-together, rationally anchoring, organizing roles of robust social rules of procedure and their institutional crystallized outputs might be embedded in a dense holistic web of institutional attitudes. But even given the conditions imposed by institutionalization of output, they might not. That is a lesson we learned from reflection on the possibility of "incompletely theorized agreements," together with the observation that thin forms of consistency do not ensure dense holistic, completely "theorized" coherence. And the proposal is that this overarching framing and guidance by relevant social rules of procedure and their institutional outputs can constitute the sort of broadly Lockean, temporally extended structure of (what we can call) the institution's "will" that is such that this guidance constitutes the institution's agential guidance. We thereby put together Frankfurt's insight about the potential significance of the structure of a system's "will," and of where the system "stands," with our account of the Lockean organizing structures at work in the rule-guided infrastructure of a human, organized institution. What gets us from robust social rules of procedure and their crystallized outputs to an institutional intentional agent need not be a dense holistic subject but, rather, these roles in constituting where the institution stands.

I conclude that when we turn to organized institutions, we should reject the idea that the basic explanation of why certain kinds of intention guidance constitute guidance by an intentional agent who so intends is that the guiding intentions are embedded in a dense holistic web. So, we have the further support we need for our inference to (2) (in Section

10.1)—support for appeal to an institutional intentional agent whose guidance of action is constituted by the guidance by the institutional intention in a way that does not depend on being embedded in a dense holistic institutional subject.

This involves stepping away from a Davidson-inspired focus on subjecthood and dense holism and stepping toward a Frankfurtian focus on the structure of an institution's "will" and the standpoint of that institution. Important forms of skepticism about institutional intentional agency are grounded in an assumption that it would require a densely holistic subject (Ludwig 2017). But our reflections on the Frankfurt-inspired idea of institutional standpoint argue against this assumption while retaining the idea that an agent's intentional action involves guidance by an intention of that agent.

Further, when we combine the idea that an institutional intention can help constitute the institution's stance with the idea from Section 5.5 that the target of such an intention can be a general rule, we model a kind of depersonalization of such institutional rules.[5] What is key is that the institutional rule is the content of an intention *of the institution*, an intention that helps constitute that institution's relevant stance.

Our proposal retains a distinction between institutional and shared intentional action. And it allows us to continue to reject an inference from

(6) There is guidance by a shared intention.

to

(2*) There is guidance by a group intentional agent who so intends.

Shared intention—in contrast with institutional intention—is not robust with respect to changes in individual participants over time. And guidance by shared intention need not be guidance by a social psychological structure that constitutes an overall group stance and that plays relevant rationally anchoring, Lockean knitting-together and organizing roles. Shared intentions normally are too limited, too partial, too transitory, and too cross-cutting, and involve too much divergence of background projects and reasons, to involve a web of Lockean ties that is sufficiently thick to help constitute a group intentional agent.[6]

This model of institutional intentional agency aims at sufficient conditions for such agency. This allows that there may be other sufficient conditions. In particular, if there were a Davidsonian, densely holistic institutional subject then the densely holistic web of institutional attitudes might be such that its guidance constitutes the institution's intentional guidance. That said, my conjecture is that a standard way this will happen is by way of the kinds of social rules of procedure whose functioning we have been chronicling. And in such cases, it is this functioning, together with its crystallized outputs, that provides the basic elements of institutional agency.

This returns us to a tension in the List-Pettit view. As noted in Section 9.3, their view highlights both (i) the role of "organizational structure" and its outputs, and (ii) the rational unity of completeness and an associated dense holism. I have argued that these phenomena can come apart. So, we need to ask which is the more basic aspect of institutional intention and intentional agency.

Recall Tollefsen's maxim that "our practice of interpreting the actions of groups is just an extension of our practice of making sense of individuals, and it is governed by the same constitutive rules." If this is how we understand institutional intention, and if we have a Davidsonian view of interpretation of individual agents, then it will seem that it is (ii)—the rational unity of completeness and an associated dense holism—that is the key to institutional intention and intentional agency. We would then see the procedures in (i) as just a way of arriving at the needed holism. In contrast, my own proposal about institutional intentional agency answers instead along the lines of (my version of) (i). The key to institutional intention and intentional agency in our pluralistic world is the functioning of social rules of procedure and their crystallized outputs, not a condition of completeness and dense holism.

10.3 Constructive reduction

My proposed construction of institutional intentional agency is reductive in spirit. A basic appeal is to individual planning agents who are at the bottom of shared intentionality and, thereby, social rules. Webs of these social rules—in particular, procedural social rules—help constitute organized institutions. The crystallized outputs of these social rules of procedure can constitute institutional intentions. And these social rules and their output institutional intentions can constitute an institutional standpoint whose guidance can constitute that institution's agential guidance.

Should we interpret this sequence of constructions as implying that there are, in the world, nothing but various individual planning agents thinking and acting in the ways we have highlighted? Should we conclude that, as Kirk Ludwig says, "we find behind the curtains only individual agents" (2017, 237) and so that ours is an *eliminative* reduction? Or should we instead see our theory as providing an explanation of what can constitute institutional intentional agency—as a *constructive*, rather than eliminative, reduction?

Consider the analogous issue about reductive approaches to individual intentional agency. A common causal theory sees individual intentional action as consisting in certain kinds of causal/psychological/rational structures and processes. In specifying such structures and processes, such a theory aims to say, as Velleman (1992) aptly puts it, "what happens when someone acts." The idea is not to eliminate the intentional agent. The idea, rather, is to solve the "Where's the Agent Problem" by articulating agency-constituting structures that are realized by these causal/psychological/rational webs (Yaffe 2000, 121–26). The idea is that there is individual intentional agency; there are individual agents who guide intentional action; and the cited causal/rational structures and processes are, in certain basic cases, that in which these agential phenomena consist. These causal/rational structures involve agency-constituting forms of psychological organization. This idea is not that when we pull back the curtain there are no agents, just causally interacting attitudes; the idea, rather, is that these webs can constitute individual intentional agency. The proposed reduction is understood as a construction, not elimination, of individual intentional agency. Granted, we do not find behind the curtain the irreducible agent-as-cause to which Roderick Chisholm tries to point (Chisholm 1966). But a thought behind such causal theories is that it is a mistake to see our non-eliminated individual intentional agency as requiring such an irreducible agent-as-cause (Bishop 2010). And if we see—as I think we should see—standard causal theories of individual intentional agency as in this way constructive rather than eliminative, then we have analogous reason to see our theory of institutional intentional agency as constructive rather than eliminative.[7]

Granted, causal theories of individual intentional agency do not construct the intentional activities of an individual out of the intentions and intentional activities of subelements that are themselves intentional agents. The basic elements in such reductions—beliefs, intentions, and the like—are not themselves intentional agents. In contrast, the elements in our model of institutional intentional agency include individual intentional agents. But my conjecture is that this difference should not lead us to different understandings of whether the reductions on offer are best seen as constructive.

Support for this conjecture comes from each of the two phases of our defense of the step from

(1) There is guidance by an institutional *intention*.

to

(2) There is guidance by an institutional intentional *agent* who so intends.

We observed in Section 10.1 that the institutional structures and crystallized outputs to which our model of institutional intention appeals are, in contrast with small-scale shared intentions, robust with respect to changes in individual agents. These structures and outputs involve forms of social organization that go beyond the interpersonal sharing of small-scale shared agency and its conditions of unanimity and constancy of participant. We then observed in Section 10.2 that these forms of social organization can constitute an institutional standpoint.

In both respects, then, we understand institutional intentional agency in (2) as involving forms of social organization that go beyond those involved in individual and shared intentional agency. This is a parallel between our understanding of institutional intentional agency and the appeal to agency-constituting forms of psychological organization that is built into common causal theories of individual intentional agency. And this supports the idea that if our construction of individual intentional agency is non-eliminative then so is our construction of institutional intentional agency.

This leaves open the possibility of arguing quite generally that the reductions both of individual intentional agency and of institutional intentional agency are eliminative. And I cannot here provide a conclusive rebuttal to such general nothing-but philosophical thoughts. My proposal is, instead, conditional: if you think—as it is reasonable to think—that standard causal theories of individual intentional agency are best seen as constructive rather than eliminative, then that is what you should think about our theory of institutional intentional agency. What I am rejecting is the thought that standard causal theories provide a constructive reduction of individual intentional agency and yet the model proposed here leads to an eliminative reduction of institutional intentional agency.[8] If you think there are individual intentional agents and that a broadly causal theory of the sort on the table helps us understand in what such agency can consist, then you should be prepared to think that there are institutional intentional agents and that our social rule model of institutional intentional agency helps us understand in what they can consist.[9]

10.4 Acting for a reason, rational guidance

When we put our model of institutional intentional agency together with our reflections on pluralistic disagreement and partiality of institutional view, we arrive at a further conclusion: an institution may A intentionally and yet not A for a reason of its own. An institution might, for example, intentionally send supplies to C even though there is too much divergence within the institution about reasons for doing this, and too much resulting incompleteness/partiality in institutional attitudes, for there to be a reason of the institution for which the institution acts.

This allows that in many cases when an institution intentionally acts, it does act for a reason of its own. In many cases, an institutional intention will be embedded in a web of institutional acceptances of grounds for it, and the associated institutional action will be for reasons associated with those grounds. The institution's acceptance of these grounds may be involved in the procedures that issue in that intention. Perhaps Medic Supply institutionally accepts certain norms of justice in the distribution of medical resources, and this impacts many of its specific decisions.[10] There are also cases—including cases of induced further teleology—in which the procedures that lead to the specific institutional intention also lead to the acceptance of reasons for so acting. Perhaps an institutional output of Medic Supply's procedural rule is to send the supplies to C in order to save lives. In cases of both sorts, the institution's intentional action is performed for reasons of its own. Perhaps there are also cases in which there is a sufficiently homogenous dispersed web of relevant reasons of individual participants, a web that induces a reason for which the institution acts. But my claim is that there can also be cases in which there is neither relevant institutional acceptance nor induced further teleology, and there is too much underlying divergence and resulting partiality for there to be a substantive reason of the institution for which it acts.

Granted, even given such divergence with respect to substantive reasons in support of the institutional activity, there is at work what we might call a procedural reason. We can say that the reason the institution so acted is that this is what was enjoined by an output of relevant social procedural rules. However, such talk of a procedural reason is talk of a certain rational process. So, I think it is clearer just to say that what we are noting is the possibility of such rational guidance within an institution's functioning despite the absence of a substantive reason of that institution for which the institution is acting.

So, in certain cases of institutional intentional activity there is a breakdown in the connection between intentionality of action and acting for a reason.[11] Nevertheless, the guidance by the institutional intention is a kind of rational guidance. This rational guidance makes sense of the institutional activity as in a broad sense directed at a goal provided by the institutional intention. It provides a background framework for relevant, goal-responsive thought and action. This rational guidance provides a description under which the activity is intentional. But in certain cases of significant disagreement within the institution and resulting partiality of institutional view, there is not a substantive reason of the institution for which it acts. So, not all rational guidance by an institutional intention of that institution's intentional activity is a case of the institution acting for a reason of its own.

10.5 Social rule model of institutional intentional agency

Guidance by procedural-social-rule-induced institutional intentions can help ensure that the institution is an intentional agent. This institutional intentional agency need not involve strictly corresponding shared intentional agency; nor need it involve a densely holistic institutional subject; nor need it involve acting for a reason that is that institution's reason. Call this the *social rule model of institutional intentional agency*. This model allows us to take institutional intentional agency seriously without overextending to this case either a Davidsonian model of individual intentional agency and its dense holism or our model of shared intentional agency and its assumptions of constancy of participants and unanimity of intent.

This model of institutional intentional agency is compatible with the insight of List and Pettit that there can in special cases be pragmatic pressures—perhaps tied to conditions of discourse—in the direction of a dense, coherent, complete holistic web of institutional attitudes. But practical pressures in the direction of a context-specific dense holism need not be pressures in the direction of a necessary element of institutional intentional agency. Further, our model is in tension with the idea that the intentional agency of organized institutions is, as Pettit puts it, "of a kind with individual agents" (2018, 257). There is, to be sure, an important commonality across the individual and institutional case: guidance by intention.

However, guidance by an institutional intention, in contrast with guidance by an individual's intention, need not involve a corresponding dense holistic subject.

Such institutional intentional agency involves social procedural rules that anchor relevant practical thinking and that can issue in crystallized institutional outputs that constitute institutional intentions. These structures of social rules and output institutional intentions are such that their guidance can constitute that institution's intentional guidance. While this does involve satisfaction of conditions of consistency/authorization, functional role, and limited functionally relevant non-compensated cognitive divergence, it does not necessitate a dense holistic institutional subject. Nor do we need to appeal to such a dense holistic subject to "give substance" to the contents of the cited institutional intentions. Our plan-theoretic sequential constructions have enabled us to characterize the contents of institutional intentions in ways that do not require the dense holism at the institutional level that would be involved in the direct application of Davidsonian interpretation at that institutional level. So, we have found a path between collapsing institutional intentional agency into shared intentional agency and requiring that institutional intentional agency involve a Davidsonian, dense holistic subject.

We have discussed what in a basic case would make it true that Facebook intends to assist the dissemination of hate speech on its platform. We now see that if this institutional intention appropriately guides relevant downstream activity, we can conclude that Facebook intentionally assists the dissemination of the hate speech. This also gives us resources to characterize an extended—and likely more common—form of intentional activity on the part of an organized institution like Facebook. Suppose there were an institutional intention to garner a large market share of advertising in Myanmar. And suppose that there is a cognitive convergence within Facebook's managerial subgroup on the proposition that garnering this market share would in fact assist the dissemination of hate speech. We would then be able to say that Facebook *intentionally* assisted the dissemination of this hate speech even if it did not *intend* to do so. This would be an extension to the institutional case of the idea that causing an expected but non-intended upshot of what one intends can constitute intentionally causing that upshot.[12]

Consider now a case discussed by Manuel Velasquez:

> On March 6, 1984, the Department of Defense (DoD) charged that between 1978 and 1981 National Semiconductor had sold

them some twenty-six million computer chips that had not been properly tested and then had falsified records to cover up the fraud. . . . Semiconductors manufactured for such military purposes are supposed to undergo lengthy, costly, and highly rigorous tests to guarantee that each works perfectly. Officials at National Semiconductor, however, admitted the company had omitted the tests between 1978 and 1981 when it fell behind its contract deadlines because of worker strikes, technical production problems, and because intense infighting about the company's direction had led to the resignation of several key managers. To cover up the omissions, National Semiconductor managers set up teams in the company's production department to falsify the documents testifying that each chip had been tested. (Velasquez 2003, 534)

Drawing on our theory, a plausible understanding of this case is that National Semiconductor had social procedural rules that accorded authority to certain managers; that these procedural rules issued in an institutional output in favor of covering up its omissions; that this institutional output constituted an institutional intention; and that given the downstream guidance by that institutional intention, it is true that National Semiconductor intentionally covered up those omissions.[13]

This is not yet to say that in cases in which an organized institution like National Semiconductor intends and is an intentional agent, that institution is *morally accountable* for the activities it intentionally guides. In Section 9.5 I noted that my account of institutional intention does not aim to provide sufficient conditions for institutional moral accountability, and a similar point applies here. A step from intentional guidance by an agent to a judgment that that agent is morally accountable is a normatively substantive step that raises difficult further issues. Nevertheless, in basic cases intentional agential guidance would be a main (though not sufficient) element in grounding such accountability. And we have seen a systematic way of making room for such intentional, agential guidance on the part of organized institutions. This is one—but only one—piece of the puzzle of figuring out in what sense, if any, organized institutions can themselves be morally accountable in ways that are compatible with but go beyond the concomitant accountability of individual participants (Pettit 2017; French 2017; Sepinwall 2016).

10.6 Institutional commonalities and social unity

I have emphasized that institutional agency can accommodate disagreement among participants and associated partiality/incompleteness in institutional view. But it is also important to keep track of the forms of commonality that are potentially present within the policy-infused infrastructure of an organized institution. Our social rule theory can model forms of unified institutional infrastructure while allowing for different degrees of commonality and of pluralism. It can thereby articulate multiple ways in which organized institutions can involve, or fail to involve, social unity.

Begin with a trio of contrasts concerning the social rules of procedure underlying institutional functioning. First, these social rules of procedure may or may not specify common weights to be used within relevant social thinking. For example, a simple majority-rule voting procedure sets up a framework for debate and bargaining without specifying relevant weights to be used within that framework. It is *common-weight-non-implicating*. In contrast, a procedure that specifies, for example, that the group decision process must concern itself with certain economic properties (e.g., long-term financial stability) or other fiduciary duties does (at least implicitly) specify certain common weights. It is *common-weight-implicating*.

A specified common weight may itself be subject to disagreement in application. Perhaps a social rule of procedure in Medic Supply's web specifies that substantial weight be given to reduction of human suffering. But perhaps different participants have different understandings of the relative significance of physical and psychological suffering; and perhaps different participants have different understandings of the relevance of a distinction between causing and allowing suffering. These differences may get sorted out in a way that helps shape the background, kernel shared policies and thereby the operant social rule of procedure; but they may not. There may continue to be forms of potential disagreement in the application of the social rule of procedure that are not resolved by that social rule. In the face of such disagreement, there is room for interpersonal argument and influence—including bargaining or moral argument. And there may be sufficient commonality to support the ongoing functioning of the social rule of procedure even though it does not by itself determine a unique output.[14]

Second, the interpersonal sharing in the shared policy kernels of operative social rules of procedure may be more or less extensive. At one extreme, these social rules of procedure involve universally shared policies. These are *universal-kernel* social rules of procedure. At another extreme, the kernel of the social rules of procedure is limited in its participants, but the reason-grounded extension is large enough to support relevant institutional functioning. These are *minimal-kernel* (hybrid) social rules of procedure.

Each of these two contrasts points to a feature that will be present in varying degrees. Focusing on the extremes, we have an initial 2×2 matrix:

	2A. Universal-kernel, non-hybrid social rules of procedure	2B. Minimal-kernel, hybrid social rules of procedure
1A. Common-weight-implicating social rules of procedure		
1B. Common-weight-non-implicating social rules of procedure		

An organized institution will fall somewhere in the spaces between 1A and 1B, and between 2A and 2B. We can say that 1A and 2A involve forms of *strong* commonality, and 1B and 2B involve forms of *weak* commonality. Weak commonality of the 1B type arises from more or less pure procedures that are neutral with respect to different substantive weights. Weak commonality of the 2B type is made possible by extensive reason-grounded extension. So, focusing on the extremes, we can characterize four possibilities of extent of commonality:

	2A. Universal-kernel, non-hybrid social rules of procedure	2B. Minimal-kernel, hybrid social rules of procedure
1A. Common-weight-implicating social rules of procedure	strong-strong	strong-weak
1B. Common-weight-non-implicating social rules of procedure	weak-strong	weak-weak

This brings us to a third contrast, one concerning induced further teleology. Different social rules of procedure can issue in outputs that involve in varying degrees such induced further teleology, and thereby institutional activities with built-in institutional aims. Speaking roughly, let's say that social rules of procedure can be in their normal functioning more or less *induced-further-teleology friendly*. So, focusing again on extremes, we can contrast induced-further-teleology-friendly social rules of procedure (3A) with induced-further-teleology-non-friendly social rules of procedure (3B).

So, focusing on the extremes, we have eight possibilities. With respect to extent of commonality, we can label the 1B-2B-3B case as the *weak-weak-weak* case, and the 1A-2A-3A case as the *strong-strong-strong* case.

Procedural-social-rule-shaped institutional functioning is grounded in a social psychological framework of, inter alia, social rules of procedure and output institutional intentions. This framework is compatible both with significant commonalities within the institution (as in strong-strong-strong cases) and with significant limitations in such commonality (as in weak-weak-weak cases). Throughout, this shared-policy-shaped framework is a key to important forms of institutional functioning and institutional intention and intentional agency. Such shared-policy-shaped forms of institutional sociality are a fundamental strategy for achieving institutional organization in our pluralistic world. But these shared-policy-shaped forms of sociality leave room for multiple forms of commonality, or its absence, within these institutions. Relevant commonalities will vary in different cases, and they will have different advantages and/or disadvantages in different cases.

Recall that our theory of social rules allows us to characterize certain forms of divergence from strong cases of our together organizing how we live with each other: extensive alienation, extensive pretense, and the withering away of kernels. We can now combine this point with our current analysis of multiple forms of institutional commonality. With respect to basic social procedural rules of an institution, each of these forms of divergence would move that institution in the direction of 2B: limited or perhaps entirely non-cotemporaneous kernels of those social procedural rules. And these variants of 2B can combine with different variations along the dimensions of 1A-1B and 3A-3B. We thereby arrive at a multidimensional characterization of ways in which the rule-guided functioning of an organized institution can realize, or fail to realize, social unity.

IV TOWARD A BROADER PHILOSOPHY OF HUMAN AGENCY

11 RETHINKING THE DAVIDSONIAN SYNTHESIS

Let's begin to sum up. A first step is to reflect on the relation between these ideas concerning human practical organization and central threads in the field-shaping work of Donald Davidson.

Our model of institutional intentional agency in the absence of a holistic institutional subject draws from Frankfurt's reflections on agential standpoints. And this diverges from Davidson's idea, tied to his theory of interpretation of mind, that intentional agency and holistic subjecthood are necessarily connected. Further, when we put our model of institutional intentional agency together with our reflections on pluralistic disagreement, we infer that an institution may A intentionally, in ways rationally guided by institutional intention, and yet not A for a substantive reason of its own. And this is in tension with the tight connection between acting intentionally and acting for a reason that Davidson thought he could defend (1980a, 6).

So, when we turn to organized institutions, we see seeds of a pair of adjustments to Davidson's theory. A first adjustment involves turning from a central appeal to the dense holism of subjecthood that derives from Davidson's approach to interpretation of mind to Frankfurt-inspired structures of will and agential standpoints. A second adjustment concerns the relation between acting intentionally and acting for a reason. The social-procedural-rule-shaped process leading to institutional intention, and thereby to institutional intentional action, is a rational process. But in rationally guiding action, institutional intentions can support institutional intentional action even if those intentions, and their institutional substructure, do not ensure that there is a substantive (subjective) reason of that institution for which that institution acts.

Granted, guidance by an institutional intention to, for example, send medical supplies to C involves goal-directedness, where the goal is given by that institutional intention. This goal-directedness involves tracking means and eschewing incompatible actions. But it need not consist in guidance by a substantive reason of the institution. After all, the institution might prescind from endorsing, as an institution, any of the specific substantive reasons on the table.

Both adjustments concern, so far, our model of institutions. But our first adjustment points to the thought that even in the individual case appeal to Frankfurt-inspired structures of will and agential standpoints will be, over and above appeal to interpretation-induced dense holism, central to our understanding of individual agency. And our second adjustment points to the conjecture that even in the individual case, what lies behind the tight (but perhaps not universal) connection between intentional action and action for a substantive reason of one's own goes beyond what is built into rational intention-guidance itself.[1] Our discussion suggests that what lies behind this connection involves, further, the impact of the dense holistic constraints built into Davidsonian interpretation of the individual. These constraints promise sufficient density of attitude to support our confidence that when there is such intention-guidance of an individual's action it will be, at least normally, for a substantive (subjective) reason of the agent's own. But this confidence is grounded in part in the holistic density of attitude induced by interpretation of the individual, not solely in the bare-bones story of rational intention-guidance.

Consider Warren Quinn's (1994) example of a person who goes around turning on radios but, as it seems, for no further reason. We can think of this person as having a general intention to turn on radios. This intention can guide action—for example, by guiding movements when in sight of a radio. This guidance involves various forms of responsiveness: he turns on radios but does not turn on televisions; he presses as hard as need be on the radio on-off button; and he would move appropriately if the radio were to be moved. In this sense, this intention rationalizes his actions (Asarnow 2021). Quinn would rightly emphasize that, nevertheless, such a person is barely intelligible to us: why would he care about this? However, we can still recognize the rational guidance of action by his intention, guidance that tracks means, eschews incompatible actions, and is stable in the absence of reconsideration.[2] We recognize this local, rational guidance but want to understand the larger orientation of the agent within which it makes some sort of sense. A Davidson-inspired thought is that when we arrive at a more holistic account of his mind, we will identify some (subjective) reason for which he is turning on the radios. We might wonder if this is true quite generally; but in any case, it is not a claim about the intrinsic nature of intention-guidance but rather about the implications of holistic interpretation.[3]

The idea that the relevant form of rational guidance in intentional action essentially involves guidance by a substantive (subjective) reason of the agent for the action is in the spirit of Davidson's early work (1980a). The underlying idea—drawn from Anscombe—was that intentional action is, normally, action explainable by appeal to reasons for which the agent acts.[4] Davidson then fills this in (1980b, 1980d) by understanding a reason for which one acts as involving a pro-attitude whose expression is a prima facie evaluative proposition.[5] Davidson also (1980d) went on to introduce attitudes of intending, and he recognized that such intention-attitudes guide and coordinate over time. But it is not clear whether he saw how this potentially introduced a form of rational guidance and of making sense of action that did not necessarily involve guidance by the kind of substantive (subjective) reasons he had modeled in part by appeal to evaluatively expressed pro-attitudes. Davidson may have thought that there is no deep difference here, since, as he thought, the relevant expressions of intending are also evaluative: they are all-out evaluative propositions (1980d, 99). But if we reject this understanding of intending as an evaluative attitude (Bratman 1999b), we do not have available this strategy for seeing guidance by intention as guidance by substantive reasons. And the proposal of the planning theory is to see intentions that guide not as in general providing substantive considerations to be weighed in deliberation but rather as providing a background framework for that deliberation.

In developing his theory of mind and action, Davidson was influenced by both Anscombe's *Intention* (1963) and Quine's *Word and Object* (1960). In light of Quine's work on the indeterminacy of translation, Davidson arrived at the holism of the mental; and in light of Anscombe's work on "why?" questions, he arrived at a tight connection between intentional action, acting for a reason, and the practical syllogism. Much discussion within post-Anscombe-Davidson philosophy of action has focused on differences between them—especially concerning "practical knowledge" (which was fundamental for Anscombe, but which Davidson downplayed)[6] and the role of mental causation in intentional agency (which was at the heart of Davidson's project but not Anscombe's). But it is also important that one of Davidson's major contributions was to articulate a view about mind and intentional agency that synthesized important insights from the different philosophical threads represented by Anscombe and by Quine (as well as from ideas within expected utility theory).[7]

My planning theory (Bratman 1987) begins to diverge from this synthesis, especially with respect to the desire-belief model built into Davidson's early work (and in standard forms of expected utility theory). It does this by highlighting future-directed intentions and plans as central elements in mind and intentional action—elements that involve a distinctive, rational dynamics that is not simply that of guidance by desire-belief "primary" reasons. And these plan-shaped elements are insufficiently theorized within this synthesis.[8]

The planning theory agrees with the Davidsonian idea that the distinction between a merely causal system and intentional agency lies in the role of rational guidance. But the planning theory highlights that the rational guidance at the heart of planning agency involves not just guidance by primary reasons but, further, intention-guidance in accord with norms of plan rationality. And it highlights that a primary aspect of this guidance by prior intentions is providing a rationally sensitive background framework for further weighing of reasons, rather than providing new reasons to be weighed.

And we have now noted a pair of further forms of divergence from this overall Davidsonian synthesis, forms of divergence that emerge when we use these plan-theoretic resources to understand organized institutions. We need, first, a more nuanced understanding of the relation between being an intentional agent and being a dense holistic subject. And we need, second, a more nuanced understanding of the relation between rational intention-guidance and intentional agency, on the one hand, and acting for a reason, on the other. While the former adjustment focuses on the institutional case, the latter adjustment also extends to the individual case.

At the bottom of these adjustments to the Davidsonian synthesis is the phenomenon of diachronic rational guidance by intentions/plans, rational guidance that unifies, organizes, and makes sense of temporally extended intentional activity, and that thereby also supports important forms of social organization. Though Anscombe was alive to the significance of a temporally extended, means-end organizing structure within an individual's intentional activities,[9] her views do not incorporate the idea that this organization is grounded in rational guidance by intention-states in a system of largely future-directed plans. This limits the extent to which we can draw on Anscombe's approach to intentional agency in modeling larger forms of social organization, including the intentional agency of organized institutions. And that feeds back into a challenge to the overall theoretical adequacy of Anscombe's approach to intentional agency. Such an appeal to rational guidance by plan states is also absent in Davidson's early work on the role of reasons as causes in individual intentional agency, and it remains insufficiently theorized even when Davidson does to some extent recognize the significance of intending.[10]

In contrast, the planning theory sees plans and planning as fundamental elements in our human, temporally extended agency, and aims to provide theoretical resources to give these phenomena their due. A theme of this book is that the planning theory thereby puts us in a position to make progress in our understanding of shared agency and, in part thereby, of organized institutions and institutional intention and intentional agency. We can thereby understand more deeply these multiple, interrelated forms of mind-induced practical organization that are fundamental to our lives.

In one way the planning theory of individual intentional agency—in introducing coordination-supporting intentions and plans—enriches a more minimal belief-desire model of our human agency. But it is also true that the planning theory gives us resources to theorize about a generic form of intentional agency, one that consists most fundamentally in rational guidance by such intentions and plans. Appeal to this generic form of intentional agency allows for divergence from overly strong assumptions about a dense holistic subject or about the correspondence between rational guidance by intention and guidance by substantive (subjective) reasons.[11]

This takes us to a contrast with the defining concerns within the Anscombe-Davidson tradition. Anscombe helped us focus on two fundamental features of our human agency:

(i) the explanatory role of reasons and associated answers to "why?" questions; and
(ii) apparently distinctive forms of practical self-knowledge.

Davidson tended to underestimate the significance of (ii)[12] but provided an illuminating treatment of (i), one that departed from Anscombe in highlighting mental causation. I have not tried directly to address these differences between Davidson and Anscombe, though I have worked within a broadly causal view of the relation between mind and action. But one lesson of this book is that we need in any case to look at a further fundamental feature of our human agency, namely:

(iii) its striking forms of mind-shaped practical organization—cross-temporal, small-scale social, and institutional.

These forms of mind-shaped practical organization are interrelated and constitute a deep feature of our human agency. We need to locate reflection on this feature of our human agency directly within the main concerns of our philosophy of human agency. And this is what the planning theory of human practical organization—a theory toward which I am working in this book—aims to do.

The Anscombe-Davidson tradition saw the distinctive explanatory role of reasons and (in the case of Anscombe) the role of apparently distinctive forms of self-knowledge as the features of our human agency that provide the fundamental target for our theorizing in the philosophy of action. A lesson of this book is that this limitation of focus to these dual elements is a mistake. We need directly to address, at the least, an interrelated trio of basic features, where that includes, in addition to the explanatory role of reasons and our relevant self-knowledge (however understood), the deeply impactful forms of mind-shaped practical organization highlighted here: diachronic, modestly social, and institutional.

And a basic conjecture is that our planning capacities are at the bottom of these multiple, interrelated forms of mind-shaped human practical organization. Our planning capacities are what Rawls called primary goods, ones whose diminution would have significant impacts on our human lives.[13] These capacities are a keystone that supports interrelated forms of organization that are central to our lives.

12 CONCLUSION

OUR CORE CAPACITY FOR PLANNING AGENCY

Beginning with the planning theory of individual human action, our theory articulates a series of models of increasingly larger-scale organization, models that sequentially build on each other. It develops, in sequence, a plan-theoretic model of shared intention, a shared policy model of social rules, a procedural social rule model of organized institutions, a social rule model of institutional intention, and an associated model of institutional intentional agency. It aims thereby to understand human organized institutions in a way that highlights, without overstating, basic roles of our capacity for shared intention—of our capacity for thinking and acting together. And it highlights the Hartian insight that to understand rule-guided, organized institutions we need to understand the social realization of rules.

We have then a sequence of constructions of shared intention, social rules, rule-guided organized institutions, and institutional intention and intentional agency. The basic building blocks for these constructions are the interconnected thinking and acting of individual, human planning agents. This involves a plan-infused practical psychology with a distinctive, rational dynamics. The basic states in this psychology include functionally specified plan states. These functional specifications are implicitly given by a background psychological theory, one that begins with our commonsense psychology but allows for adjustment in ways that support our understanding of our human lives.

Beginning with this psychology of individual human planning agency, we build up our constructions sequentially. In each case, we aim to ground functioning in construction, but we do not claim that our construction is the unique construction that would function in relevant ways.

At each stage, to ground functioning in construction we draw on (i) a specification of relevant functioning and (ii) an argument that the proposed construction normally functions in this way. The idea is that the construction at each step is such that, when functioning in accord with plan rationality, it plays the roles characteristic of the target phenomenon. This was our approach to shared intention in Chapter 1. Chapter 2 treats Hart's schema as giving us a dual design specification for social rules and setting the problem of what construction realizes that dual design specification. Chapters 3 and 4 articulate a shared-policy-infused candidate for a construction of Hart-type social rules—where this involves an adjustment in Hart's schema. Given the underlying rational dynamics and its interplay with the interrelatedness of sharing, this construction normally functions in ways specified in a suitably adjusted version of Hart's basic social rule design specification.

We then turn to the institutional role design specification for social rules. Chapters 5 and 6 articulate constructions of social rules of procedure and of institutional webs of such social rules. We ground rule-guided institutional functioning in our construction of social rules together with aspects distinctive of the institutional case—including authority-according social rules of procedure, an institutional web of social procedural rules, and institutional outputs. We then argue, in Chapter 7, that action-focused institutional outputs realize the functional specification of intentions and so are institutional intentions—though we allow that the characteristic functioning of institutional intention can to some extent diverge from that of individual intention.[1] In Chapters 8 and 9 we respond to a challenge from Davidsonian dense holism by resisting its direct extension from individual to institutional intention. We then, in Chapter 10, use our construction of institutional intention in a construction of institutional intentional agency, one that draws on a Frankfurt-inspired idea of institutional standpoint. We thereby arrive at a model of institutional intentional agency that avoids skepticism about such phenomena of a sort found in the work of Searle and Ludwig, without overextending Davidsonian conditions of dense holism along lines of List, Pettit, and Rovane.

We thereby have:

(1) A planning theory of *individual temporally extended human action* (Section 1.1)
(2) A planning theory of *shared intention*, shared policies, and SIA (Section 1.2)

(3) A shared policy model of Hart-type, criticism/demand/acknowledgment-involving *social rules*, including hybrid social rules with a kernel-penumbra structure (Chapters 2–4)
(4) A shared policy model of *(authority-according) social rules of procedure* (Chapter 5)
(5) A procedural social rule model of the *rule-guided infrastructure of an organized institution* as involving an institutional web of social rules of procedure and their institutional outputs (Chapter 6)
(6) A model of *institutional intentions* as institutional crystallized action-focused outputs of social rules of procedure, a model that requires neither strictly corresponding shared intention nor a dense holistic institutional subject, and a model that makes room for interpersonal disagreement and incompleteness in institutional views (Chapters 7–9)
(7) A broadly Frankfurtian and Lockean model of *institutional intentional agency*, one that highlights guidance by institutional intention (Chapter 10)

The steps from (1) to (7) explain how our capacity for planning agency can underlie our diachronic, shared, and institutional practical organization. So, we have an argument for the interim conclusion:

(8) Our capacity for planning agency is poised to play a core role in support of this interrelated trio of forms of mind-shaped human practical organization.

This argument in favor of (8) is guided by a strategy of sequential construction, one that aims at each stage at sufficient conditions for the target phenomenon. Concerning shared intention and shared intentional activity, our model draws primarily on the resources—conceptual, psychological, metaphysical, and normative—of our planning model of individual temporally extended human agency. In the next move from shared intention to social rules, we highlighted the role of shared intentionality as modeled within our planning theory. In our next move to the social rules central to human organized institutions, we appealed to authority-according social procedural rules that can authorize institutional roles and statuses. We then drew on ideas of an institutional web of social rules of procedure and of the institutionalization of outputs to develop constructions of institutional rule-guided infrastructure and intentions. And we then constructed institutional intentional agency. In place of a simple extension of Davidsonian interpretation from the individual to the institutional, we developed a more complex epistemology of psychological and agential attribution to organized institutions.

We are throughout guided by a model of our planning agency that sees prior plans as framing further reasoning in ways guided by norms of plan rationality. And when the elements in our plan-theoretic construction of shared intention function in accordance with these norms of individual plan rationality, there will normally be satisfaction of analogous norms of social rationality. We contrasted these non-separable norms of plan rationality with other norms—including norms of interpersonal moral obligation and of accountability—that, while central to our human lives, are not in the same way built into the basic structure of our planning agency.

So, we have a series of *realization theses*:

(a) A plan-theoretic realization of forms of cross-temporal organization of individual intentional human agency.
(b) A plan-theoretic realization of shared intentions, shared policies, and SIA.
(c) A shared policy realization of Hart-type social rules (including hybrid social rules with a kernel-penumbra structure).
(d) A shared policy realization of authority-according social rules of procedure.
(e) A social rule realization of the procedural, rule-guided infrastructure of organized institutions, their institutional social-rule webs, and their institutional outputs.
(f) A realization of intentions of organized institutions as institutional outputs of social rules of procedure—where such institutional intentions need be neither shared intentions nor embedded in a densely holistic subject.
(g) A Frankfurtian/Lockean social rule realization of institutional intentional agency that involves guidance by institutional intentions.

Throughout we draw on an argument of the form: if the elements articulated in the underlying construction function in accord with norms of plan rationality, what emerges are the forms of functioning characteristic of the realized phenomenon. And at the bottom of these realization theses, and the argument in favor of (8), is our capacity for planning agency.

Given our strategy of sufficiency, we are not in a position simply to deduce from this argument for (8) that these forms of temporally extended, small-scale social and institutional organization *must* be built on top of our capacity for planning agency. Nevertheless, we have seen how our capacity for planning agency *can* provide basic elements in sequential support of this trio of interrelated forms of human practical organization. And this helps support a defeasible inference to the conclusion that this is how it is with us—adult human agents in our social, institutional world.

This is a defeasible inference to a purportedly best explanation. The conjecture is that the best explanation of the highlighted trio of forms of human practical organization involves, at bottom, our capacity for planning agency and, sequentially, our capacity for shared intentionality. We thereby defeasibly conclude that our capacity for planning agency is a *core capacity* that underlies these forms of human practical organization.[2] We thereby arrive (defeasibly) at *the core capacity thesis*:

(9) Our capacity for planning agency plays a *core role* in this trio of interrelated forms of human practical organization.

And this sets the stage for further examination of the explanatory fecundity of this theoretical framework.[3]

The core capacity thesis points to an overarching planning theory of human practical organization. It thereby points to deep costs that would be threatened were these planning capacities to be undermined. And this has a range of implications for our assessments of our social order, including our educational practices and other social contributions to the development of such planning capacities.

We conclude (defeasibly) that the deeply impactful, mind-shaped organization of much of our human practical lives is to a significant extent grounded sequentially in our capacity for planning agency. We thereby shed light not only on our individual temporally extended projects, our small-scale shared activities, and our informal social rules, but also on the rule-guided structures of myriad organized institutions that frame our living together.

NOTES

OVERVIEW: INTENTION, PLANS, AND PRACTICAL ORGANIZATION

1. In Bratman 2007 I argue that our capacity for planning also supports our self-governance. I extend this to self-governance over time in Bratman 2018a. In the present book, however, I focus primarily on diachronic, small-scale social, and institutional organization.
2. I call this the continuity thesis in Bratman 2014a. (But see Pacherie 2015, and my reply in Bratman 2015a.) I will be reflecting on further forms of continuity and discontinuity as we move from individual temporally extended agency to organized institutions.
3. Which is not to say that the capacity for planning agency suffices for our capacity for SIA. On my account of SIA our planning capacity needs to be supplemented by other elements (e.g., the capacity for complex contents concerning *our* activities). Nevertheless, the capacity for planning agency is, on the model, a central element in our capacity for SIA. And these further elements are broadly continuous with the resources—conceptual, psychological, metaphysical, and normative—at work in the theory of individual planning agency. In contrast, when we turn to organized institutions, we will need to draw on theoretical resources that are not needed in our models of individual and shared intentional agency.

   Let me also note that the targets of the planning theory—and associated theories of SIA and of organized institutions—are distinctive forms of practical organization that, while of fundamental importance in our human lives and subject to moral assessment, do not by themselves ensure moral acceptability.
4. My talk of *organized* institutions is in the spirit of Miller 2019, sec. 1. Miller follows work in sociology that highlights systems of interrelated, occupied, and sometimes hierarchically ordered roles, rules, and practices. In this sense, human language itself is not an organized institution, though relevant rules will be at work,

and there may be an organized institution (e.g., the Académie française) whose function is to regulate the practice. Similarly, informal practices of bartering, or property, or marriage will involve rules but need not be organized institutions—though, again, there may well also be organized institutions whose function is to regulate those practices. And many groups are not organized institutions.

5. Concerning the nature of normative judgment, one proposal is Allan Gibbard's 2003 plan-expressivist theory that our planning capacities underly normative thinking. My strategy of seeing plans and planning as foundational for our human practical organization does not, however, depend on this specific meta-normative theory, and I intend my proposals to be available to a wide range of meta-normative theories.

6. This is in the spirit of the model of a coordination convention developed in Lewis 1969 and Lewis 1983, though Lewis works within a belief-preference framework, not a plan-theoretic framework.

7. This is in the spirit of Deborah Tollefsen's thought (2015, 104) that "our practice of interpreting the actions of groups is just an extension of our practice of making sense of individuals, and it is governed by the same constitutive rules"—an idea to which I return in Chapter 8.

8. Jules Coleman (2001, 95–100) claims, drawing on ideas from Scott Shapiro, that the legal activity of legal officials is a shared cooperative activity (SCA). In his review, Ronald Dworkin (2002, 1663) responds that "it is an empirical question whether the legal officials of any community meet [the] more exacting conditions" of an SCA. And he avers that "American judges are more divided than united by [their] ambitions. They take their walks and build their houses alone or in parties, not all together." Dworkin is here responding to a non-modest proposal that all the legal officials are engaged together in an SCA. In contrast, my view of organized institutions seeks a more modest and modular role for shared intention.

9. So, we need to be cautious about Elizabeth Anderson's image of "the firm as a joint enterprise" (Anderson 2015, 187). However, as Axelle Marcantetti has emphasized, Anderson's focus on a "nexus of cooperative relationships" among "stake holders" (191) coheres with the approach I will be taking.

10. The idea of bringing together my work on individual and shared intention with Hart's theory of law owes to Scott Shapiro, whose ideas have significantly influenced my thinking in this book.

11. The parenthetical qualification signals that one of my questions is in what sense Medic Supply—and not just certain individual agents—decides, and thereby intends, to send the aid. I answer this question in Chapter 7.

12. Liao also makes a similar comment about a second example concerning Facebook. I assume that, in the context of the present example, this talk of an intention "for those things to occur on its platform" is talk of an intention to "assist . . . the dissemination of hate speech." Let me note that on my view the relation between "intend" and "intentionally" is more complex than that

presupposed in this passage (Bratman 1987, chap. 8). I return to this point in Section 10.5.
13. Hart emphasized that our understanding of a legal institution needs to include an understanding of how participants have an internal point of view on relevant social rules. But he also emphasized that this leaves room for an external understanding, on the part of a non-participant, of the internal point of view of participants (Hart 2012, 241–44).
14. Hart's appeal at this stage of his theory of law is to secondary social rules of recognition, change, and adjudication. While I will follow Hart in appealing to actual social rules of a distinctive sort, I will instead appeal to what I will be calling authority-according social rules of procedure.
15. Blomberg adds: "Regardless of whether we *could* explain these cases without these elements" (2015, 346–48). But if we *could* adequately model SIA without these elements, that would suffice for my purposes.

    Katherine Ritchie articulates similar concerns. She argues that given the importance of roles within organized institutions, "the methodological assumption of starting with small group one-off interactions and scaling up to large group long-term interaction should be abandoned" (2020, 100). She considers whether the importance of roles within an institution should be projected back to our understanding of small-scale shared intentionality. On such a "view, cooperation would always involve playing roles in some structure or other—whether it is the structure of a legislative body, that of a family unit, or that involved when two people attempt to move a piano together" (2020, 107).
16. For somewhat related thoughts about *homo prospectus*, see Seligman et al. 2016.

CHAPTER 1

1. Bratman 1987. Some of the inspiration for this idea came from Gilbert Harman's groundbreaking 1976 essay. See also Harman 1986 and Ferrero 2009.
2. My initial formulation of these norms (1987, 32) described them as "defeasible." Later, I appealed to "pro tanto" or "local" rationality (2009, sec. 1; 2012) and then to defeasible pro tanto irrationality (2018a, 211–14). Here I will simply see these as norms of "pro tanto" or "local" rationality. For a proposed reformulation of the intention-consistency norm, see Núñez 2020b. For a challenge to a belief-intention consistency norm, see Núñez 2019, n.d. In Section 3.2, I note complexities about intention agglomerativity.
3. This contrasts with the approach to "plans and the structure of behavior" in Miller, Galanter, and Pribram 1960, who understand intent by appeal "to the uncompleted parts of a Plan whose execution has already begun" (61).
4. So, it is plausible to see their contents as "practitions" in the sense developed in Castañeda 1975. (And see Bratman 1999a.) While Castañeda limits talk of prescriptions to second- and third-personal practitions, I am here extending talk of prescribing directly to intending.

5. For an overview of research on the role of natural language in human thinking, see Carruthers 2012.
6. This is only part of the story. For the rest of the story see Bratman 2018b. An idea there is that one's self-governance over time involves a kind of "acting together with oneself over time" that typically involves forms of continuity of plan-states over time. (See also Bratman 2018c, 2019a, forthcoming a.) And a concern with one's self-governance over time, while not strictly necessary for intentional agency, is a keystone within a human planning agent's psychology.
7. We can say that intentions provide "framework reasons" (Bratman 1987, 34). But the crucial point is that such framework reasons do not provide considerations to be weighed in deliberation but provide rather a background framework for that deliberation.
8. See also Velleman 2021, 915–16.
9. Though my hope is that a version of the main ideas explored here would also be available to a theory along the lines of (a). (For this contrast, see Levin 2018, sec. 3.4.)
10. Godfrey-Smith 2005, 14. A way to put this point is to say that the relevant Ramsey sentence is associated with such a potentially adjusted theory (Lewis 1972).
11. These last two points do not preclude the possibility of developing a plan-expressivist meta-normative theory of the nature of normative judgment along lines of Gibbard 2003, but they do highlight ways in which such a theory cannot simply identify the intention to X with a judgment that one ought to X (Bratman 2006).
12. As indicated earlier, it is also a mistake to identify intentions with ordinary beliefs (Bratman 2018a, essays 2 and 3).
13. Douglas Lavin, in discussing Anscombe's *Intention*, focuses on "the temporality of movement" and highlights that "where a process unfolds over time, there is some principle in virtue of which the phases of the process constitute a whole" (2016, 619). And Lavin sees Anscombe as proposing that the "distinctive type of unity that belongs specifically to intentional actions . . . takes a teleological form" (619–20). The planning theory agrees with the importance of focusing on temporally extended activity and relevant "temporal unity." Its proposal is that the unifying "principle" is an interrelated structure of plans and norms. This includes a norm of means-end coherence, one characteristic of teleology. It also highlights norms of consistency and stability, and associated forms of practical thinking. This multifaceted rational plan dynamics—rather than a simple appeal to "teleological form"—is central to its account of the relevant cross-temporal organization and unity.
14. Though this leaves room for improvisation (Beisbart 2022).
15. Indeed, we are faced with a general question concerning the extent to which shared agency infuses various domains of our lives. A conjecture of this book is that such sharing is central to a wide range of organized human institutions.

Luigino Bruni and Robert Sugden (2008) defend a somewhat analogous conjecture concerning market transactions, a conjecture that departs from Adam Smith's classic model. As they see it, it "is possible and compatible with market efficiency" (36) for participants to see market transactions as a kind of shared agency (though their model of such sharing differs from the one I go on to articulate).

16. Related parallels between an individual life over time and interpersonal social relations are in Sidgwick 1962 and Nagel 1970. This parallel between organization over time and social organization is a central theme of this book. For reasons to be cautious about this parallel, see Asarnow 2020.
17. This qualification coheres with what I will be calling my strategy of sufficiency.
18. As this example indicates, neutrality with respect to shared intentionality does not preclude drawing on the idea of individual intentional activity.
19. For challenges, see Tenenbaum 2015 and my reply in Bratman 2015b.
20. Though these intentions have these distinctive contents, they are the same type of attitude as the intentions modeled by the planning theory of individual agency. That is why they are subject to the same rational dynamics. Contrast with Searle 1990.
21. This allows that if you were to cease intending that we J but were to replace that intention with a personal intention to do what is your part in our J-ing I might still retain my intention that we J (though we would then not have a shared intention to J) (Bratman 2014a, 69).
22. Bratman 2014a, chap. 3. I address complexities about this interdependence in Sections 1.2.3 and 4.1.2.
23. Though in the social case this is not a Lockean tie that should lead us to talk literally of a single supra-person (Bratman 2014a, 97).
24. Bratman 2014, 91, 127; and see Westlund 2015. Contrast with Korsgaard 2009, 192 and Tuomela 2007, 13, 47, 98. (In Section 10.4 I arrive at a related idea of institutional intentional action in the absence of a reason *of the institution* for so acting.) And see Roth's (2020) discussion of the tension between this partiality within our sociality and team reasoning models of shared agency.
25. A complexity, as Mikayla Kelley notes, is that J might involve distinctions in role, as when J is "men wear suits and women wear dresses to a wedding." Here my intention to act accordingly will involve my intention to dress in accord with my gender, as well as my intention to act in ways mandated by the pressures of consistency and means-end coherence on my intention that *we* J (which includes the actions of those in other roles).
26. See also Bratman 2007a.
27. This is in the spirit of what Philip Pettit (2019, 3) calls a "genealogical method" that is concerned with how relevant phenomena "could in principle have emerged" (Pettit 2018, 251). See also Pettit and Hoekstra 2018.

28. This contrasts with Margaret Gilbert's appeals to irreducible phenomena of "joint commitment" or a "plural subject" (1999, 2009). In drawing primarily on ordinary intentions, as understood within the planning theory—though with distinctive contents—it also contrasts with John Searle's (1990) appeal to a distinctive attitude of we-intending. In the background, assuming the success of my approach, is an Ockham's Razor argument against such appeals to further, irreducible phenomena (Bratman 2014a, 36–37).
29. Concerning different ways of understanding models, see Frigg and Hartmann 2020.
30. This use of quotes indicates that each would express their intention using the first-person plural.
31. For a challenge, see Roth 2014b. My brief reply is in Bratman 2014a, 176 n. 23.
32. A nuanced version of this worry is in Velleman 1997. My previous responses are in Bratman 1999c and 2014a, chap. 3). A helpful discussion is in Núñez 2019.
33. Appeal to these social interrelations in the model of shared intention is another difference from Searle's focus on we-intentions in the minds of each. Indeed, as Searle sees it, each may be a brain-in-a-vat (Searle 1990, 406–7). In appealing to these social interrelations, I am agreeing with an aspect of Margaret Gilbert's focus on the interpersonal interrelations central to shared intention. But my understanding of these interrelations appeals to ideas of interlocking, intended mesh, and interdependence rather than Gilbert's idea of obligation-involving joint commitment. See Section 1.2.5.
34. For discussion of complexities, and appeal to "pooled knowledge," see Roy and Schwenkenbecher 2021.
35. Here I put aside the possibility of institutional acceptances, as discussed in Parts II and III.
36. Bratman 2014a, 34. And in Bratman 2014a, 150 I note the further possibility that the individuals might come to share a policy in favor of these norms of social rationality.
37. So, we need to understand the characteristic interdependence of each participant's intentions-that-we in a way that allows for such differences in reasons for which each participates. See White 2016.
38. See Cohen 1993; John Rawls's appeal to "the fact of reasonable pluralism" (2005, 36–37); and Cass Sunstein's (1995) appeal (to be discussed in Section 8.3) to "incompletely theorized" agreements.
39. I borrow this terminology, but not his skepticism about the strategy, from Ronald Dworkin (2002, 1659–62). My formulation of this strategy benefitted from comments from Olle Blomberg.
40. We will be considering in Chapter 4 social rules in a group some of whose participants do not buy into the relevant activity of the group. In this way, social rules impose a weaker constraint on the buy-in of each than do shared intentions.

41. So, I do not aim to articulate structures that uniquely provide what Mark Greenberg (2004, 158) would call "sole determinants" of (2), social rules, or (3).
42. A query from, among others, Stephen White.
43. See Scott Shapiro's discussion (2014, sec. 2) of "shared intentional activity with authority"—though my treatment differs from Shapiro's. Taylor Madigan has been investigating the role of related phenomena within our practices of accountability.
44. In each case, according authority creates what Shapiro (2014, 269) calls a "mesh-creating mechanism."
45. Hohfeld 1919; Feinberg 1973, chap. 4; Wenar 2020. Shapiro, in contrast, tries to characterize "shared intentional activity with authority" without appeal to such Hofeldian structures: "A has J-authority over S if and only if (a) A intends that the other adopt the content of her directives as subplans and revise S's subplans so that they mesh with the directive. (b) S intends to adopt the content of A's directives as subplans and to revise his subplans so that they mesh with the directives. (c) (a) and (b) are common knowledge" (2014, 267).
46. Darwall (2006, 3) distinguishes *de facto* and *de jure* authority. I am extending this to a distinction between *de facto* and *de jure* rights and duties. My comments here are in this respect also in the spirit of David Copp's 2009 distinction between the "internal 'quasi normativity'" characteristic of, for example, games (30) and "a more robust notion of normativity" (33). My comments are also broadly in the spirit of other observations of Shapiro's. Shapiro sees certain "vertically interlocking" intentions as constituting an authority relation. However, "the mere vertically interlocking of intentions is insufficient to create reasonable authority. This is so because many shared activities are morally noxious, and there can be no obligation to participate in morally noxious enterprises" (2014, 267–68). Note, though, that (like Copp) I do not assume that all relevant substantive normative reasons in support of *de jure* rights and duties must be moral reasons.
47. For an overview, see Levin 2018—though standard theories do not emphasize, as I do, the role in the functional organization of implicitly accepted rationality norms. Classic formulations of these functionalist ideas are in Lewis 1972; Putnam 1967.
48. Davidson 2001b—though in highlighting distinctive norms of plan rationality we go beyond Davidson. A further idea built into Davidson's development of this view about the "constitutive" role of rationality in—to put it more generally—mind is that these rationality norms induce a dense holism of the web of attitudes assigned by an adequate interpretation. This further idea will come under pressure in Chapters 8–9.
49. A main idea is that, over and above the constitutive role of these norms in our planning agency, it is also true both that, given our human limits, there is a two-tier pragmatic rationale for the acceptance of these norms, and that conformity

to these norms is partly constitutive of relevant forms of our self-governance, both at a time and over time. Further, though intentional agency does not require an end of self-governance, our temporally extended planning agency contingently involves an entrenched end of diachronic self-governance. And this end supports norms of synchronic and diachronic plan rationality. Since both the two-tier rationale and the appeal to this entrenched end draw on contingent but deep features of our human practical thinking, this proposal involves a kind of psychologism about plan rationality (Millgram 2019).

50. To simplify, I am assuming that intentions in favor of the effectiveness of the intentions of each and the meshing of subplans across those intentions bring with them intentions in favor of mutual responsiveness. For complexities, see Ludwig 2015 and my reply in Bratman 2015a. David Gauthier discusses a somewhat different "interplay of intention and reason" (1994, 721).
51. Bratman 2014a, 89. For complexities, see Roth 2015 and my reply in Bratman 2015a.
52. Versions of a positive answer are in groundbreaking work by Margaret Gilbert (2014). Her view, as I understand it, is that some such mutual obligations (and not just beliefs that there are such obligations) both are necessary for and can suffice for shared intention. These obligations are partly constitutive of what she sees as the central, non-reducible phenomenon of "joint commitment."
53. I argue against the sufficiency claim in Bratman 2014a, 113–18. See also Bratman 2014b, 329–32.
54. So, we are in the territory of Copp's "more robust notion of normativity" (2009, 33).
55. A worry expressed by Christine Korsgaard in conversation and correspondence. And see Bratman 2014a, 100–101.
56. For a challenge, see Smith 2015 and my reply in Bratman 2015a.
57. Can these theoretical resources also illuminate large-scale, decentralized social organization that is not directly embedded within organized institutions? Consider, for example, protest movements organized by way of the internet in a "bottom-up" way involving a range of interconnected individuals rather than by top-down leadership or other forms of organized institutional structure (Tufekci 2017). While my focus in this book is not on such cases, in Bratman 2014a, 98–100 I note that our model of shared intention supports an idea of a social network that may be useful here.

CHAPTER 2

1. One of Hart's advances over the nineteenth-century Austin was to highlight the role in law of rule-guidance, in contrast with mere habit. In recognizing this insight, however, we still leave room for inchoately organized groups that are not rule-guided organized institutions.

2. "To say that a given rule is valid is to recognize it as passing all the tests provided by the rule of recognition and so as a rule of the system" (Hart 2012, 103). Note that there can be valid primary rules that are not actual social rules.
3. Emphasized in Shapiro 2011, 103. Shapiro thinks Hart was not sufficiently sensitive to this point. As I read Hart, he would acknowledge the idea of rules as abstract objects but insist that we need a theory of how rules are socially realized; and this leads to his distinctive focus on *social* rules. As I proceed to explain, we can see relevant abstract objects as rule *contents* of certain social-psychological social rules. A full theory would need to say more about these abstract object contents. While I do not try to do that, I would be sympathetic to seeing them as, roughly, "practitions" in the sense developed in Castañeda 1975. And see Bratman 1999a.
4. Gideon Rosen noted that this distinction between actual social regularities in the social, causal order and an abstract object rule to some extent parallels David Lewis's distinction between language as a social activity and languages as functions that assign meanings (Lewis 1983).
5. Hart 2012, 57. Compare Michael Tomasello (2019, 249): "Humans have evolved a unique form of social control in which the group as a whole expresses its collective expectations for individual behavior. These collective expectations are known as social norms."
6. This is highlighted in Gilbert 1999. Gilbert thinks that to understand such criticisms and demands we need to go beyond Hart's theory and appeal to "joint commitment." This is because she thinks that a social rule "immediately grounds claims for performance" (156–57) and joint commitments do that. As I will explain, I agree with Gilbert in focusing on distinctive interrelations across participants. But I understand those interrelations by way of my model of shared intention rather than by way of Gilbertian joint commitments. This will lead to an alternative understanding of involved criticisms and demands in Section 3.4, one that is to some extent in tension with Gilbert's talk here of immediacy.
7. This formulation of the problem and its purported solution is mine, not explicitly Hart's; but I think it is reasonable to see these ideas as implicit.
8. So, Hart points to a theory that says, roughly: given individuals with interrelated attitudes with relevant contents—where those interrelated attitudes lie behind social patterns of action of those individuals—here is how to construct social rule contents. This leaves it open how to understand the contents of the attitudes of those individuals.
9. I make a similar point about my approach to shared intention in Bratman 2014a, 12.
10. This will get more complicated when we discuss what I call hybrid social rules.

11. Hart 2012, 255. These remarks have been seen by some (e.g., Postema 1982) as supporting an interpretation of Hart-type social rules as the kind of coordination convention described in Lewis 1969. But the acceptance to which Hart is here appealing involves taking "such patterns of conduct . . . as standards of criticism which may legitimate demands and various forms of pressure for conformity" (255). And it is not clear how this feature of Hart-type social rules is captured within Lewis's framework (which is not to deny that Lewis's framework captures important phenomena). Lewis's 1969 model of a coordination convention does include the condition not only that each prefers to conform given that others do, but also that each prefers that "any one more conform to R, on condition that almost everyone conform to R" (1969, 78). Lewis sees this latter as capturing a condition that a "coincidence of interests predominates" (1969, 69). Lewis says that "this condition serves to distinguish cases of convention, in which there is a predominant coincidence of interest, from cases of deadlocked conflict" (1983, 165). But given that the explanation of the regularity of action is grounded in the preferences of each to conform given that others do, it seems that this further preference for general conformity is, as it were, an add-on to the basic social psychology. So, we can ask whether this is merely a verbal point about the word "convention." Further, even given this "coincidence of interests" it is not clear how the cited further preference serves as a basis for criticisms of/demands on others.

    As noted, Margaret Gilbert (2008) highlights this need to explain the basis within a social rule for such criticisms/demands, and this leads her to turn from Lewis-type coordination conventions to "joint commitments" that essentially involve obligations. I am here agreeing with Gilbert that there is this explanatory need; but I instead turn, in Chapter 3, to shared intentions that need not constitutively involve such obligations but do bring to bear norms of plan rationality that are sensitive to the interpersonal interrelations involved in sharing an intention.

12. Southwood 2019, 30. And see Green 1999, sec. 2.
13. My approach to this issue is in Section 4.1.3.
14. As indicated in Section 1.1, a distinction between rationality and substantive reasons also emerges from reflection on means-end reasoning. Here we do best not to see an intention in favor of an end as quite generally providing a new normative reason for means, since that would raise worries about unacceptable bootstrapping, but instead by appealing to a rational demand for means-end coherence (while allowing that in certain cases intentions can induce new normative reasons for means) (Bratman 1987, 24–27).
15. Such general conformity need only be sufficiently general conformity. And we will need to adjust condition (b) in Section 4.1.4.
16. Perhaps many believe there is the general pattern of action, and these beliefs help support their relevant endorsements, and yet it is false that there is in fact this general pattern (Brennan et al. 2013, 20–21).

CHAPTER 3

1. Guala and Hindriks (2015) see an institution as involving a "correlated equilibrium" in behavior together with a corresponding "*rule* that dictates [to] each player what to do in the given circumstances" (2015, 185). (And see Guala 2016.) I take it that they are thereby appealing to the acceptance of this rule by each. Does this involve the acceptance of a prescription for "the group as a whole"? Well, they say that this rule is "normative only in the weak sense of instrumental rationality: given what the other players do, it is best to do one's part in the equilibrium" (2015, 185). And elsewhere Hindriks rejects "the necessity thesis" that "institutional actions necessarily depend on collective attitudes" (2018, 354). This suggests that their idea is that each accepts a rule that prescribes that she herself acts in conformity with the equilibrium, given her expectations about what others will do. Guala and Hindriks do appeal (sec. IV) to the potential existence of social sanctions and incentives in support of conformity of each to the rule. But, following Hart, we can ask whether there is a more direct connection between the structure of social rules and a prescription for "the group as a whole."
2. As Brian Flanagan noted, this is in the spirit of John Finnis's observation that "sharing of aim rather than multiplicity of interaction is constitutive of human groups, communities, societies" (Finnis 2011, 152).
3. Hart himself sometimes appeals to the shared acceptance of a rule (2012, 102, 115, 138). However, the relevant kind of sharing is undertheorized by Hart. He thought that shared acceptances are "public" (116). But, to my knowledge, he does not explicitly go beyond this. In contrast, my conjecture concerns the sharing involved in shared intention.

    The idea of a connection between Hart-type social rules and shared intention derives from ideas from Scott Shapiro, both in conversation and as reported in Coleman 2001, lecture 7, n. 31. Coleman reports Shapiro's idea that "it might be illuminating to think of the [social] rule of recognition as a shared cooperative activity in Bratman's sense." I am here extending this to an idea about social rules more generally, appealing to shared intention rather than shared activity, and highlighting the implicit contrast with a mere social regularity.

    That said, in developing his own views Shapiro himself is skeptical that our strategy for bringing together Hart's ideas with the planning theory should involve appeal to the shared intentions highlighted within my planning theory. He thinks that the conditions for such shared intentions are too demanding for a model of either "massively shared agency" or law. As he expresses this point (using a term from Shelly Kagan), my conditions for shared intention involve an overly strong "hyper-commitment" (Shapiro 2014, 276–77). In contrast, my conjecture appeals to the kind of shared intention highlighted within my planning theory.

4. This appeal to shared policies is in some respects in the spirit of appeals to shared intentionality in Searle 1995, 2005, 2010 and Ludwig 2017, though I will be noting important differences.
5. This allows that there are also other forms of criticism and demand normally involved in social rules. I discuss such further forms in Section 3.4.
6. For different perspectives on related issues about the roles of language and shared intention in the "birth of ethics," see the exchange between Philip Pettit and Michael Tomasello in Pettit and Hoekstra 2018, 333–58.
7. This paragraph benefitted from discussion with David Estlund.
8. In contrast, I can rationally judge that you ought to X while being fully confident that you will not X.
9. I point to this briefly in Bratman 2009, n. 7, and Bratman 2018a, 213. For detailed discussions, see Shpall 2016 and Goldstein 2016.
10. For this distinction between intending and aiming, see Bratman 1987, chaps. 8 and 9.
11. I say only "central core" since, on the overall view, the policies of each will to some extent interlock and favor mesh in subplans. I will also be making room, in Section 4.1.4, for penumbral participants in a social rule who do not have such a policy about the overall group.
12. I will sometimes just talk informally about shared policies in favor of general conformity. But throughout I understand the target of this talk to be, more precisely, doubly reflexive shared policies in favor of the conformity of each as elements in our sufficiently general social conformity.
13. I consider complexities about this interdependence and interlocking in Section 4.1.2.
14. What if one intends to conform but somehow fails? (A question from Mikayla Kelley.) There are complex questions here, and we may need to extend our understanding of norms of plan rationality directly to action. See Asarnow 2019.
15. We can identify a further potential stage 4 support by first considering a possible supplement to stage 2, one suggested (in conversation) by Sarah Paul. Return to the stage 2 idea that there is defeasible rational pressure for plan/policy stability. This rational pressure is grounded in part in the way in which sticking with one's intentions over time can be an element in one's self-governance over time. And Paul's question is: might a concern with *our* self-governance over time—where the relevant "we" is specified by our shared policy—support a plan-rationality norm in favor of sticking with one's policy in favor of *our* conformity (where we assume that self-governance of both sorts is pro tanto desirable)? This would involve a norm of rational plan stability that is applicable in particular to intentions in favor of *our* activity.

Now, the social rules, and associated shared policies, that are relevant here involve multiple cross-cutting "we's." So, we should talk of my concern with our_n self-governance, for multiple n's corresponding to multiple social rules/shared policies in which I participate. To see such concerns with our$_n$ self-governance as providing a further ground for a norm of rational stability of policy, we would need to suppose that this concern is quite generally present for all n in a way that parallels the conjectured, general presence of a concern with one's own self-governance. But such a general concern, across multiple "we's," may not be sufficiently entrenched to ground a general requirement of plan rationality. Nevertheless, when, for a given k, such a concern with our$_k$ self-governance is present, it can add further normative support in favor of the stability of the shared policy at work in the associated social rule. This is, however, to appeal to a potentially present normative reason of our self-governance that may appear at stage 4, not to a further, distinctive norm of plan rationality in stage 2. (And see Bratman 2017b, 43–44.)

16. Peter Railton seeks "an account of when and why, the kind of acceptance of rules Hart discusses could have genuinely normative character for the individuals concerned" (Railton 2019, 15 n. 10). I am here sketching such an account, one element of which involves generally applicable norms of plan rationality.
17. Indeed, implicit contents of a shared policy and associated social rule might be the target of criticism—as when we criticize a social rule as implicitly racist.

CHAPTER 4

1. Once we have this explanation of the *diachronic* robustness of a social rule, we will have a corresponding understanding of the *counterfactual* robustness involved in the condition that the social rule would persist even if there were a change of a certain sort in underlying participants.
2. And similarly, a *de dicto* intention in favor of mesh of subplans.
3. I return to this idea in Section 4.1.3.
4. For discussion in a similar spirit, see Neufeld 2019, sec. 5.
5. Shapiro 2011, 109–10. And consider the "sentimental hat tippers" in Burge 1975. Shapiro also emphasizes that his fundamentalist does not see the rule as one of several admissible solutions to a coordination problem: she sees the rule as uniquely apt. This is central to Shapiro's argument against seeing Hart's social rule of recognition as the kind of coordination convention described in Lewis 1969, and as proposed by Postema 1982. But my concern here is not with the idea that these rules are not coordination conventions, but with the idea of dependence of rule acceptance on social behavioral pattern. In articulating—as I go on to do—a way in which there is a version of this dependence even in the case of the fundamentalist, I am not supposing that the fundamentalist sees the rule as one of several admissible solutions to a coordination problem. Instead, I am pointing to a strategy for developing Hart's insight concerning dependence without Postema's coordination-convention interpretation of relevant social rules.
6. This treatment of such a fundamentalist depends on appeal to her *intention* in favor of the general conformity. If we were only to appeal to a preference, we

would not be able to draw on the cited cognitive condition on rational intention. As noted, in his model of coordination convention Lewis includes a condition that each not only prefers to conform given that others do, but also that each has a "preference for general conformity . . . rather than slightly-less-than-general conformity" (Lewis 1983, 165). But one may rationally prefer X even while knowing that not-X.

7. Or a social rule to drive at roughly 65 mph. This issue was first raised by Gideon Yaffe; my discussion here was aided by Barry Maguire and Thomas Slabon.
8. To keep the discussion manageable, I here bracket the condition of intended subplan mesh.
9. Shapiro (2011, 108) draws on a slightly different idea of alienation.
10. Young children who intend to conform because of social pressure from adults but do not yet buy into the overall general conformity will count as alienated, in the sense at work here. So, we might want a more nuanced terminology. I put this worry aside here, though I return to such young children later in this section.
11. Such alienated participants should be distinguished from the fundamentalists discussed earlier. Our fundamentalist did intend the group's general conformity; but her justifying reason for this intention did not involve the fact of that conformity. In contrast, an alienated participant does not intend the group's conformity, though she personally intends to conform.

    We can also contrast the idea of alienation at work here with other ideas of alienation. Recall that there can be sharing of intentions in which the participants have different reasons for participating in the sharing. We can apply this point to the shared policies that are at issue here. Some might participate in the shared policy for reasons that involve what they see as the value of the general pattern of action favored by that shared policy. In contrast, others might participate in the shared policy for reasons that instead derive from the advantages of that participation rather than the value of the pattern of action (Kavka 1983). As Erin Kelly highlighted (in conversation), there is a sense of "alienated" such that the latter kind of participant is alienated from, though they do participate in, the shared policy, and in that way alienated from the social rule. But this is not the kind of alienation on which Kutz and Shapiro focus and which poses the current problem for our shared policy model.

    Again, and as Manuel Vargas noted (in correspondence), talk of alienation sometimes alludes to forms of emotional estrangement. In contrast, the kind of alienation from a social rule at issue here need not involve such estrangement; it need only involve the absence of buy-in concerning the general conformity, coupled with relevant personal intentions to conform.
12. This is one of the concerns that leads Shapiro to a "planning theory of law" that does not build on my more demanding construction of shared intentions/policies. Shapiro in effect replaces Hart's appeal to social rules with what he calls

"shared plans" and offers a construction of "shared plans" that is weaker than my model of shared intentions (Shapiro 2011, 136, 149, 204; 2014, 277–83). In contrast, I propose to use my theory of shared intentions/policies to provide an illuminating construction of the relevant kind of social rules. What we have learned from Kutz and Shapiro, however, is that to do this we need to understand how such social rules can accommodate alienated participants.

13. Searle 1995, 2010. These two literatures—Hart-inspired work in jurisprudence on social rules, and Searle-inspired work in social ontology on collective acceptance—have tended to be somewhat isolated from each other. (Though Shapiro's initial idea of a connection between the planning theory of shared intention and Hartian social rules leapt over this gap; see also Ludwig 2020.) That these literatures each face a problem about alienated participants is the tip of an iceberg.
14. Ludwig and I both part ways from Searle and see such we-intentions as ordinary intentions with special "we" contents.
15. See my 2018d. Ludwig's own view is complicated (in a way I failed to note in my 2018d) in allowing that an agent's acceptance of a role that is specified by background we-intentions may be only a "formal acceptance" (2017, 146–47). I take it, then, that he would say that our alienated judge "formally" accepts her role even if she does not have relevant we-intentions. Ludwig also notes that while "in many groups formal acceptance suffices for [institutional] membership, . . . enough must accept substantively for the status role of even those who accept merely formally to have them" (172). This may point to commonalities between Ludwig's understanding of "formal acceptance" and the proposal I go on to make concerning penumbral participants.
16. Searle notes here the relation between this idea and his different discussion in his 1995 book, one that is closer to Ludwig's 2017 approach.
17. This is in the spirit of Ludwig's (2017, 131–35) criticism of Searle's 2010 proposal.
18. "General acceptance is here a complex phenomenon, in a sense divided between official and ordinary citizens. . . . Both aspects must be kept in view if we are to see this complex social phenomenon for what it actually is" (Hart 2012, 60–61). The proposal I go on to make also is in the spirit of Shapiro's distinction (2011, 135) between designers of a plan for a group and others in the group who go along with the design. (See also Shapiro 2014, 277–83.)
19. In Section 4.3, I consider weakening this knowledge condition.
20. This is like, but not the same as, the "snowball effect" I discuss in Bratman 1987, 82. Facundo Alonso discusses a related idea of a *"virtuous circle of mutual reinforcement* of the participants' intentions and of their relations of mutual reliance" (Alonso 2008, sec. 7.3).
21. Having E as an end engages weaker constraints of consistency with belief than does intending E.

22. In intentional-reason-grounded extension those in the kernel group aim to influence those in the larger group by way of reasons that play normal roles in the psychology of a human agent. This contrasts, for example, with the way a group that shares a policy of walking together each morning might set up rewards that shape behavior of their pet dogs on their walk
23. John Searle would note that participants in a social rule might not have explicit representations of the rule but instead have "a set of abilities that are sensitive to specific structures of intentionality without actually being constituted by that intentionality. One develops skills and abilities that are, so to speak, functionally equivalent to the system of rules, without actually containing any representations or internalizations of those rules" (1995, 142). Searle calls such a web of skills and abilities the "background." In this way he makes room for an extension from a central case of representation of the rule. But this background-constituted extension still involves endorsement (albeit implicit) of the general conformity. In contrast, those in the penumbra need not even implicitly endorse the general conformity.
24. See the description of "human children's developing group-mindedness" in Tomasello 2019, 250–54.
25. In Bratman 2014a, 102, I discuss a related distinction between shared intention and shared cooperation.
26. These thoughts about the relevance to cases of pretense of a snowball of reliance, and of reliance-based obligations, owe to comments from Andrea Westlund.
27. I assume Hart would distinguish between taking a "critical reflective attitude" and merely pretending to do so.
28. And see his discussion of "collective pretense" in Darwall 2018, drawing on Walton 1993.
29. I am here assuming that the relevant kernel and penumbra are cotemporaneous. I return to this assumption in Section 4.1.6.
30. Though there may be complexities here that are analogous to those in H. P. Grice's (1941) Lockean account of personal identity.
31. These cross-temporal interconnections between penumbras may be mediated by connections between penumbras and kernels.
32. In some cases, these cross-temporal ties may be strengthened by concerns of participants in favor of an associated kind of temporally extended community.
33. I was helped here by discussion at the Yale Moral Philosophy Reading Group. The possibility I am considering here contrasts with Searle's appeal (1995, 117) to "continued acceptance."
34. Perhaps this is how to understand the discussion in Moltchanova 2019.
35. A further complexity is that pretense is relativized to a (perhaps very general) context. Shapiro's alienated judge pretends in relevant judicial contexts but may well not pretend in discussions with friends. This seems to contrast with social rules. A social rule will normally concern certain contexts—for example, the

context of grocery shopping. But whether there is in a group a social rule of say, wearing a mask in those contexts is not itself context relative. Instead, it is like a belief that in those contexts there is a risk of transmitting a virus: such a belief concerns that context but is not itself context relative. If we have this belief, we have it whether or not we are grocery shopping. Similarly, a group can have a mask-wearing social rule at t whether or not anyone is grocery shopping at t. So, we face the question—though one I will not try to answer here—of whether a context-relative phenomenon of pretense can fully realize a non-context-relative social rule.

36. This is in the spirit of Philippa Foot's observations about the "non-hypothetical use of 'should' in sentences enunciating rules of etiquette, as, for example, that an invitation in the third person should be answered in the third person, where the rule does not *fail to apply* to someone who has his own good reasons for ignoring this piece of nonsense, or who simply does not care about what, from the point of view of etiquette, he should do" (Foot 1972, 308). Thanks to Tristram McPherson for pointing to this connection to Foot's insight and, more generally, for comments that helped me in this section.
37. That is, sufficiently general conformity.
38. This elaboration of the example owes to Edward Hinchman.
39. Shapiro 2014, 279. Such a commitment to letting others do their parts would directly fall out of an intention that *we* act in accord with the plan. However, Shapiro is focusing on those who do not have such intentions-that-*we*, but only personal intentions to do their own personal parts, and his characterization of a shared plan does not specify what motivates or provides reason for such alienated participants to let others do their parts.
40. As Shapiro says, "someone formulates a plan for the group to follow" (2014, 282).
41. This may be Shapiro's strategy, but I am unsure.
42. And in making room for cases of non-cotemporaneous kernels, we make room for an analogue of "designers" from the past in Shapiro's theory of law (Shapiro 2011, chaps. 11–13).
43. The quotation from Marx with which Shapiro begins his 2014 essay (257) starts by saying that "the cooperation of the wage-laborers is entirely brought about by the capital that employs them." This may seem to point to a non-agential source—"capital"—of the organization. But later in this passage Marx appeals to "a plan drawn up by the capitalist," and here the source of organization is agential. My appeal to a background shared policy kernel fits with this second, agential understanding of the source of "the cooperation of the wage-laborers." (Miikka Jaarte is in the process of exploring a non-agential realization of Shapiro's condition (1).)
44. A complexity is that I have been assuming that output-penumbral personal intentions are to do what counts as one's part in a relevant output (e.g., to produce iPhones) and to do this for extending reasons, while knowing that what one

is doing is one's part in that output. While those in this penumbra are alienated from the overall organizing end, they are nevertheless knowledgeable about that end. In contrast, in Shapiro-type massively shared agency many are both alienated and relevantly ignorant, and so are not strictly speaking in the relevant output penumbra as I have so far described it. But nothing stands in the way of an idea of an *enlarged* output penumbra that relaxes the knowledge condition and so includes such agents. (Though this lack of knowledge may limit what kinds of extending reasons can be at work.) The key issue is not the details about how to enlarge the output penumbra, but what the background source of the social organization is.

45. I have followed Hart in talking of social *rules*, whereas these philosophers talk of social *norms*, but I take it that we are concerned with the same phenomena. For their appeal to practice dependence, see Brennan et al. 2013, 59.
46. The quote is from Southwood 2019, 35, but it also expresses a view of Brennan et al. And see the discussion in Brennan et al. 2013, 23, of the Andorrans who desire X without requiring X.
47. This leaves open the possibility of a meta-normative theory that sees normative judgments as expressions of certain plan states (Gibbard 2003). But Brennan et al. do not see their view of social norms as depending on this plan-expressivist meta-normative project. And, as noted, I seek a theory of social rules that is available to different meta-normative theorists.
48. A similar view is in Hindriks 2019. Hindriks appeals to what he calls normative expectations: "a normative expectation is an expectation that others believe that the normative rule applies. Someone who possesses a normative expectation expects others to believe that everybody ought to behave in the manner specified by that rule." Normative expectations, so understood, are not themselves normative judgments. And Hindriks's proposal is that "a social norm exists in a population exactly if its normative rule features in normative expectations of a substantial number of its members" (137).
49. Indeed, Brennan et al.'s central criticism of Bicchieri's proposal (2013, 36) depends on the thought that if folks desire to comply with a principle but nevertheless think they ought not comply ("they cannot rid themselves of the thought that complying . . . is wrong") then there is not in place a norm that says to comply. This worry seems to me not forceful when addressed to the condition that folks do not merely desire but *share a policy* to comply—though a conflict between such a shared policy and corresponding normative judgments would normally be a rational breakdown.

CHAPTER 5

1. In defending an affirmative answer, I continue with my strategy of sufficiency. So, my answer will be compatible with Hindriks's rejection of "the necessity thesis" that "institutional actions necessarily depend on collective attitudes" (2018, 354).

2. Hart 2012, ch. 5, sec. 3. Hart also highlighted the risk posed by this solution (202).
3. This is broadly in the spirit of Peter A. French's emphasis on a corporation's internal decision (CID) structure. See French 1979, esp. 211–15. (Related ideas are in Tuomela 1995, 176–80; Pettit 2003; List and Pettit 2011, 60; Hindriks 2008, 2014; Ludwig 2017, chap. 14; and Flanagan forthcoming.) For French's development of his views within the planning theory of intention, see French 1996, which describes corporations as "planning entities" (152). And see Arnold 2006.
4. As I understand his views, Hart himself pursued both a just-so story of the emergence of legality and its secondary rules (2012, chap. 5, sec. 3), and a construction of the structures that constitute the social rules—both primary and secondary—to which this just-so story appeals.
5. The classic source of this last idea is Arrow 2012. Even given this contrast between the concerns of Arrow-inspired work in social choice theory and Hart-inspired focus on actual social rules, there remains room for appeal to social choice theory in assessing social rules that are at work in a rule-guided institutional infrastructure.
6. This is compatible with the idea that in certain cases our account of the structure of an institution will in some way incorporate certain evaluations. (I return to this idea in Section 6.1.) And it is, more specifically, compatible with the claim that when we turn to *law*, we discover that there are built-in moral constraints.
7. As we will see, however, this leaves room for roles of certain substantive values of an institution.
8. I was helped here by conversation with David Estlund.
9. The implicitly specified range of such a procedural social rule, bracketed here, will be a relevant group—say, a certain club. A complexity, highlighted by César Valenzuela (in conversation), is that a procedure can have sequential stages at each of which there is an interim output. However, for simplicity I will assume that the procedure has a single-stage output, one that sets the stage for follow-through.
10. Will they include activities/modes of thinking of the institution itself? See Chapter 10.
11. In certain cases—ones involving social rules of procedure that are insufficiently concerned with evidence—such divergence may also support a claim that in its public acceptance of P a group is lying or "bullshitting." Such claims are highlighted in Lackey 2021, chap. 1. (See also French 1996 and Tollefsen 2015, 18.) Lackey thinks that to support such claims we need to say that *the group itself believes* not-P, though it publicly accepts P. My suggestion is instead that it can suffice to note the lack of fit between what the group publicly accepts by way of procedures that are not evidence-tracking and what is broadly believed by individuals in the overall group population. While in the individual case to lie that P involves, roughly, believing not-P, we need to avoid an overly simple extension to the institutional case. That said, there will be room in the theory for institutional belief. See Chapter 7.

12. Concerning the last, see Chapter 10.
13. I note a further reason in Chapter 6.
14. As Copp (2009) would say, there may be "internal 'quasi normativity'" (30) in the absence of "a more robust" normativity. (33)
15. I interpret Searle's talk of desire-independent reasons as talk of normative reasons. And see Searle 1964 and Hindriks 2013.
16. So, we are here in the territory of Copp's "internal 'quasi normativity.'" As Copp says (2009, 33), "even an unjust legal system has this kind of quasi-normativity."

CHAPTER 6

1. This section benefitted from comments from Leif Wenar and Axelle Marcantetti.
2. I proceed to explain the reason for this labeling.
3. There may here be to some extent a similarity with an aspect of Greenberg 2004 despite other differences in approach.
4. My discussion of this example also benefitted from extensive comments from Leif Wenar.
5. For example, we can see the debate between Hart and Dworkin as in part about the nature of the richness of social-rule web that is characteristic of a legal system.
6. These rational pressures are induced by the content of these social rules, content that interlocks with the other rules in the institutional web and supports consistency in output across those rules. These pressures will not only apply to those who participate in the shared policy kernels; they will also apply to penumbral participants who intend to conform to the (interlocking and consistency-supporting) rule in ways that mesh with the behavior of those in the kernel and for reasons that are induced by the kernel.
7. See F. A. Hayek's emphasis on knowledge "that is dispersed among many people" (Hayek 1945, 530).
8. We could make an analogous case for a kernel-penumbra structure within the officials/managers.
9. In Chapter 7 I argue that such institutional action-focused crystallized outputs are institutional intentions. It follows that institutional intentions do not in general involve corresponding shared intentions.
10. As Eric Orts observes: "Firms may adopt different objectives and value orientations" (2017, 213).
11. One aspect of this strategy of sufficiency echoes an exchange between Austin and Hart. Consider the Austin-friendly possibility that the kernel of a hybrid social rule of procedure consists simply of a single individual sovereign. A Hart-inspired response is to emphasize that such a sovereign is better modeled as involving important forms of social organization (Hart 2012, chap. 4, sec. 1). Analogously, my appeal to background kernel *shared* policies underlying hybrid social rules allows for a limit case in which the relevant kernel involves only a

single-person sovereign. But the proposal is that we make theoretical progress in our understanding of organized institutions, and of the role of shared intentionality in our lives, by unpacking forms of shared intentionality involved in the kernel in explanatorily central cases.
12. This issue has been posed to me by Hasan Dindjer, Frank Hindriks, David Plunkett, and Annie Stilz, and it is an issue (motivated by the kind of reduction he seeks of institutional agency) behind Ludwig's (2017) emphasis on membership.
13. Ludwig 2017, esp. sec. 11.2. For discussion, see Bratman 2018d.
14. See my discussion of "collective acceptance" in Section 4.1.4.
15. And see Rawls 1955.
16. We might here draw on a Hart-inspired distinction between a valid constitutive rule and a social constitutive rule: it is likely that many valid rules about what counts as money will not be sufficiently widely known to be social rules.
17. For complexities, see Petersson 2015 and my reply in Bratman 2015a.
18. Searle 1997, 450. While Searle does not here explicitly say what it is for this to be "shared," it seems the idea is just that each in fact has the same collective attitude.
19. Here is the longer passage from which this comes: "So, what amounts to the corporation when we set it up? It is not that there is an X that counts as the corporation, but, rather, that there is a group of people involved in legal relationships, thus so and so counts as the president of the corporation, so and so counts as a stockholder in the corporation, etc., but there is nothing that need count as the corporation itself, because one of the points of setting up the corporation was to create a set of power relationships without having to have the accompanying liabilities that typically go with those power relationships when they are assigned to actual human individuals." (Searle 2005, 17).

As we will see, my proposal is also in tension with Ludwig's eliminative reduction of institutional agency.

CHAPTER 7

1. Minimal cooperativeness is built into our model of an organized institution; conditions of institutionalization of output include consistency/authorization and limited functionally relevant non-compensated cognitive divergence.
2. In Bratman 2017b, I argue that "it is a mistake to suppose that a group intention is either a shared intention or an intention of the group that is embedded in a robust holistic structure of inter-related attitudes of that group" (50). My discussion here in Chapters 7–9 aims to improve and deepen my defense of this claim.

Combining resources from Peter French and from the planning theory, Denis G. Arnold writes: "Corporate intentions are states of affairs consisting of both the intersecting attitudes of the class of agents comprising the corporation and the internal decision structure of the organization" (2006, 291). This is, roughly speaking, broadly in the spirit of my proposal concerning institutional intentions—where I understand such internal decision structures as social rules of procedure, and I try to spell out more explicitly the construction that is, functionally speaking, the intention of the institution. However, though this is not clear to me, Arnold seems to suppose that such a corporate intention will in general be a shared intention of those agents; that is an idea I reject. I seek a construction of institutional (as Arnold says, "corporate") intention that draws substantially from the modest and potentially modular role of shared intention in organized institutions, but also does justice to differences between institutional and shared intentions.

3. See Bratman 1987, esp. 28–35. (In this 1987 treatment I do not explicitly say that these intention structures "make sense" of relevant activity, but that thought is implicit.) The idea is not that the *aim* of all this thinking is to make sense of the activity. The aims will normally be specific aims such as getting medical supplies to a certain city. The idea is only that when these structures and associated forms of practical thinking frame, guide, and coordinate in the cited ways, they thereby *do* help make sense of the activity.

4. Epstein (2015, chaps. 16–17) supposes that insofar as a theory like mine can make room for group (as I say here, institutional) intentions, it will see them as shared intentions. This leads Epstein to several objections to what he takes my view to be. I agree with Epstein that we should not identify group/institutional intentions with shared intentions. In my earlier work (as Epstein notes) I refrained from talking about intentions of an organized institution. In this present work (and in Bratman 2017b) I try to make room for group/institutional intention while rejecting an overly simple connection to shared intention. While my sequential plan-theoretic construction of institutional intentions agrees with Epstein that such intentions are not shared intentions, it is in tension with Epstein's skepticism about individualistic approaches.

5. There is a large literature here. For an overview, see Backes 2021.

6. This anticipates a theme in Chapters 8–9. Indeed, we can here make a similar point concerning institutional acceptances. They may interact with institutional intentions and/or with a distributed web of individual and/or small-scale shared intentions. In this respect our functioning-specifying theory concerning institutional acceptances will differ in detail from that for individual acceptances (whose correlates will be attitudes of the individual herself).

7. See the discussion in List and Pettit 2011, 190, and Roth 2014a.

CHAPTER 8

1. Davidson 1980e. In note 14 Davidson highlights the Quinean roots of his proposal concerning the role of "the constitutive ideal of rationality" in interpretation of mind.

2. And see also Daniel Dennett's work on intentional systems (e.g., Dennett 1971).
3. We can understand this appeal to a web of beliefs as also including acceptances.
4. Rovane sees these ideas as continuous with Davidson's. Hess (2014, 245) draws on Rovane's idea of one's "rational point of view" (RPV) and says that "it is the existence and efficacy of this RPV that makes us agents."
5. Tollefsen 2002 discusses closely related ideas. As Tollefsen says: "The assumption of rationality involves the assumption that the agent shares with us a dense pattern of belief and thought, and the contents of thought are, in our everyday practice, attributed on the basis of these other beliefs and their content" (400).
6. We can endorse some such appeal to the structure of a person's will, but not follow Frankfurt in appealing to hierarchies of desire to articulate that structure. For example, Gary Watson appeals instead to a distinction between an evaluation and a motivation system (2004, ch. 1). And I have appealed instead to policies about weights (2007b).
7. Compare Ludwig 2017: "The usual holistic constraints on attitude attribution are absent in the case of attributions to organizations . . . the mind of the committee . . . can really be quite empty except for a handful of thoughts" (238). (The underlining indicates that Ludwig sees this talk of minds and thoughts as being "analogical.") Ludwig's emphasis here is directly on the partiality/thinness of relevant attitudes; my emphasis will be on common forms of disagreement that tend to induce such partiality.
8. Sunstein 1995, 1735–36. For my purposes, the key here is the idea of incompletely theorized agreements within organized institutions. I do not take a stand on Sunstein's specific use of this idea to understand the structure of distinctively legal reasoning. (Shapiro 1997 criticizes this latter use of Sunstein's idea.)
9. Calhoun (1995, 241) discusses an analogue in the case of a single person who "can have reason to resist resolving conflicting commitments."
10. Or at least a compensating acceptance-focused output. See Section 6.2.
11. See Smith 2006, esp. 279–81. Thanks to Smith for helpful discussion.
12. Ludwig's view about the attribution of attitudes to an institution is that "it characterizes thereby something about the functional organization of the relevant institution, realized in the relevant attitudes of its members and their commitments, which is analogous to the functional organization of an individual agent. . . . We may think of the general import of such attitude attributions as being that the organization will act as if it were an agent" (235). But why only "as if"—why not say that what is thereby realized is institutional agency? This is where, drawing on Davidson, Ludwig avers that "the usual holistic constraints on attitude attribution are absent in the case of attributions to organizations" (238). And that manifests his acceptance of (1)–(3).
13. List and Pettit 2011, 75. I discuss discursive dilemmas in Section 9.3.
14. List and Pettit 2011, 34. Rovane 2014 discusses differences between her view and that of List and Pettit.

15. As they see it, one important way this happens is by way of a "premise centered" procedure in response to discursive dilemmas. I discuss this in Section 9.3.
16. Rovane's view also fits this picture: accept versions of (1) and (2); depart from (3) (Rovane 1998, 164); and so, reject the skepticism in (4).
17. And Searle in commenting that "there is nothing that need count as the corporation itself" (Searle 2005, 17).
18. Tollefsen explores the connection of this idea to Daniel Dennett's work on the "intentional stance." See Tollefsen 2002, 402. Relatedly, List (2018, 297) notes that the approach of List and Pettit 2011 "is to begin with a general definition of an agent, and then to apply it to the case of groups." If we add the primacy of the individual case as the source of the "general definition of an agent" we are close to Tollefsen's maxim. My own view is that a "general definition of an agent" should be quite thin, and that a lot of what matters will emerge as features of specific kinds of agency (Bratman 2018a, 110). We should, as I once said (1999, 54n), resist genus envy.
19. Blomberg 2018 points to a version of this idea. And Blomberg (in correspondence) notes a limited parallel between the idea here of a generic functional specification of intention and Andy Clark's idea of "similarity of coarse-grained functional role" (Clark 2008, 99).
20. We thereby challenge a main basis of Ludwig's skepticism about an institutional intentional agent.

CHAPTER 9

1. Concerning intentional activities *of the institution*, see Chapter 10.
2. Backes 2021 also challenges what I am calling Tollefsen's maxim, though for different reasons.
3. List and Pettit (2011, 60–62) later distinguish between an aggregation function—which is an abstract rule—and an "organizational structure" that implements an aggregation function. (This parallels our distinction between an abstract object rule and a corresponding social rule.) We can understand talk here of a premise-centered procedure as talk of an organizational structure that implements a premise-centered aggregation function. This raises the question of what constitutes such organizational structures. And here I would propose my shared policy model of social procedural rules. See Lackey 2021, 26–27, for discussion of the relation between List and Pettit's appeal to organizational structures and the appeals of Margaret Gilbert (1989) to "joint acceptance" and of Raimo Tuomela (1992) to roles of "operative members." See also Gilbert 2004, Tuomela 2004, and Tollefsen 2015, chap. 1.
4. List and Pettit (2011) suppose that a group should satisfy:

"**Collective rationality.** The aggregation function produces as output consistent and complete group attitudes towards the propositions on the agenda." (49)

And this supposition then gets built into

"**Robust group rationality.** The supervenience relation determines consistent and complete group attitudes on the relevant propositions for any possible profile of consistent and complete member attitudes on those propositions." (67)

5. Pettit 2003, 182. List and Pettit focus on discursive dilemmas *for groups*—where groups "have an identity that can survive changes of membership" (2011, 31). So, it is not an implication of their view that if a small collection of individuals—one that is not robust with respect to changes in membership—uses a premise-centered procedure to resolve a discursive dilemma, it would thereby induce a group mind.

6. A useful comparison here is with Ronald Dworkin's idea that there is moral reason for participants in a legal system to treat it as a "distinct moral agent" (Dworkin 1986, 188). The moral reason Dworkin highlights is the role of such "personification" in an argument for the moral justifiability of legal coercion (Dworkin 1986, chap. 6). List and Pettit appeal to the practical benefits of a kind of group unification in discursive-dilemma cases. In neither case is there simply a direct application of Davidsonian holistic interpretation to the overall group. But in each case the moral/practical pressure is thought to be in the direction of some such holism.

7. Pettit appeals to "the degree of constancy as well as the degree of coherence that we expect in any intentional subject" (2002, 458). What we see is that the constancy involved in underlying social procedural rules need not bring with it a strong form of dense holistic coherence.

8. I am here bracketing issues about the range of the social rule.

9. As discussed in Section 6.3, we might, in response to various concerns, distinguish among different individuals in the extended network. And this talk of extended institutional functioning underlying institutional intention points to a possible parallel with discussions of so-called extended minds. See Clark and Chalmers 1998.

10. I am here thinking of the holistic subject constraint as a role that is a candidate for inclusion in the Ramsey sentence that provides the relevant functional specification. This section benefitted from discussion with David Plunkett.

11. And so, reject premise (2) in Section 8.3.

12. Though this intention is not necessary for Facebook intentionally to assist the dissemination of this kind of speech. See Section 10.5.

13. This allows that moral accountability for A might involve an intention to B, where B is not identical to A. It also allows that there may be kinds of non-moral accountability that are not subject to this intention condition—perhaps forms of pragmatically justified legal accountability, as discussed in Hussain and Sandberg 2017.

CHAPTER 10

1. This is an aspect of what, in the spirit of Gilbert Ryle, Gideon Yaffe (2000, 121–26) calls the "Where's the Agent Problem." Following Yaffe, we might say that ours is the *Where Is the Institutional Agent Problem*.
2. And the strength of the institutional agency hereby modeled might help support the conjecture that it is a partial ground for institutional moral accountability.
3. I argued in Section 4.1.5 that the "glue" characteristic of a temporally persisting social rule is broadly Lockean. Here I am extending the point to the temporally extended functioning characteristically supported by such a social rule.
4. This talk of *institutional* thinking takes out a loan on the account of institutional agency I am hereby developing.
5. As noted by Scott Shapiro and Gideon Yaffe.
6. Bratman 2014, 127. As I discuss there, in cases of shared intentional activity the group may constitute a "causal agent." But that does not entail that the group is an intentional agent in the sense presently at issue.
7. I am responding here to a query from Brian Flanagan.
8. In Bratman 2018d I note how Ludwig defends a reductive-eliminative view about institutional intentional agents but accepts a reductive-constructive approach to individual intentional agency. I seek to resist such a non-parallel treatment, but without overextending the condition of a dense holistic subject to the institutional case.
9. This understanding of constructive reduction of institutional intentional agency depends on our focus not primarily on how these phenomena "could in principle have emerged" (Pettit 2018, 251) but on their actual structure. And our Hart-inspired, bottom-up construction of this structure of institutional agency contrasts with a Dworkinian top-down effort to personify the institution (Dworkin 1986, 171).
10. There might be a public claim on behalf of the institution that this acceptance played a role in its institutional decision, though in fact it did not. This would be a kind of public insincerity. (This responds to a query from Abraham Roth.)
11. Jessica Brown discusses the phenomenon of a group acting for a reason, and considers the possibility of an institution's being responsible for its action even though it is not acting for a reason (2021, 15). Cases of institutional intentional action that is not action for a reason of that institution might realize this possibility.
12. This involves rejecting the "simple view" that intentionally A-ing always involves intending to A (Bratman 1987, chap. 8).
13. In these last two comments, I am disagreeing with Velasquez (2003, 546).
14. This is in the spirit of Hart's argument that the "open texture" of rules need not lead to "rule skepticism" (Hart 2012, chap. 7).

CHAPTER 11

1. Nathan Hauthaler (n.d.) provides a different line of argument against this tight connection in the case of individual agency.
2. This is in the spirit of John Bishop's thought (2010, 73) that once we introduce intentions as "*sui generis*" attitudes within our theory, we are led to the view "that the minimally rational cause of an action may be no more than an intention to perform an action of that kind."
3. I am responding here to comments from Sarah Paul (in conversation) who highlighted Quinn's example. My discussion here has also benefitted from correspondence with Samuel Asarnow.
4. As Anscombe put it, such explanations are answers to a relevant kind of "why question"—though she noted that sometimes an answer to "Why?" can be "No particular reason" (1963, 26).
5. I would not follow Davidson here: I think there can be motivating desires that do not fit this evaluative model. Such desires would still need to be distinguished from intentions in their roles in rational motivation and practical thinking. But here I focus on Davidson's theory.
6. Anscombe thought that individual intentional agency involves non-observational, non-inferential practical self-knowledge of what one is doing. I have not addressed this view here. But even if we agreed with this claim about individual intentional agency (though see Paul 2009), we might still reject the idea that institutional intentional agency must involve non-observational, non-inferential practical self-knowledge on the part of the institution (Blomberg 2018). This would then be another way in which we would allow that a feature of individual intention/intentional agency need not be present in the institutional case. (I benefitted here from discussion with Mikayla Kelley and Thomas Ladendorf.)
7. Concerning expected utility theory, see Davidson 1985a, 199; 1985b, 214.
8. And see especially Harman 1976, 1986. This poses the question of how approaches within expected utility theory can best incorporate the insights of the planning theory. See Murray and Buchak 2019 for a partial response. I touch briefly on this issue in Bratman 1987, 180 n. 12.
9. See Lavin 2016 and my remarks about Lavin's essay in Chapter 1, note 13.
10. Davidson says that a future-directed intention is an "interim report" of what it would be best to do (1980d, 100). This seems to see intending as an epiphenomenal spin-off, rather than as playing basic roles in the downstream rational dynamics (Bratman 1999b).
11. This paragraph benefitted from discussion with Barry Maguire.
12. Paul 2009; but see Hunter 2015.
13. As Thomas Ladendorf has emphasized, given their role in our rational functioning, our planning capacities are even more basic than other primary goods whose role depends on that rational functioning.

CHAPTER 12

1. We thereby reject the primacy of individual intention, and so premise (2) in Sections 8.3 and 8.5. This is primarily in response to the possibility of "incompletely theorized agreements" and to different cognitive correlates in the institutional and the individual cases. But we can also allow for different connections to Anscombian practical knowledge and to phenomenal consciousness.
2. There is reason to think that this core role of our planning capacities extends even more widely. In Bratman 2007 I see our planning capacities as supporting our capacities for agential self-governance. In Bratman 2018c I extend this to a planning agent's self-governance over time. And such plan-infused self-governance may have analogues in cases of institutional self-governance. Shapiro's planning theory of law argues that "we are able to create law because we are able to create and share plans" (Shapiro 2011, 181). And Allan Gibbard's 2003 plan-expressivist meta-normative theory implicitly argues that our planning capacities support normative thinking quite generally.
3. An example of such fecundity may come from the use of related ideas to understand democratic institutions (Stilz 2009, chap. 7; Neufeld 2019; Chapman 2020).

REFERENCES

Alonso, Facundo (2008). "Shared Intention, Reliance, and Interpersonal Obligations: An Inquiry into the Metaphysics and Interpersonal Normativity of Shared Agency." PhD diss., Stanford University.

Alonso, Facundo (2009). "Shared Intention, Reliance, and Interpersonal Obligations." *Ethics* 119: 444–75.

Alonso, Facundo (2014). "What Is Reliance?" *Canadian Journal of Philosophy* 44: 163–83.

Alonso, Facundo (2020). "Planning on a Prior Intention." *Journal of Ethics and Social Philosophy* 18, 3: 229–65.

Anderson, Elizabeth (2015). "The Business Enterprise as an Ethical Agent." In Subramanian Rangan, ed., *Performance and Progress: Essays on Capitalism, Business, and Society*, 185–202. Oxford: Oxford University Press.

Anscombe, G. E. M. (1963). *Intention*, 2nd ed. Oxford: Blackwell.

Arnold, Denis G. (2006). "Corporate Moral Agency." *Midwest Studies in Philosophy* 30: 279–91.

Arrow, Kenneth J. (2012). *Social Choice and Individual Values*, 3rd ed. New Haven: Yale University Press.

Asarnow, Samuel (2019). "On Not Getting Out of Bed." *Philosophical Studies* 176, 6: 1639–66.

Asarnow, Samuel (2020). "Shared Agency Without Shared Intention." *The Philosophical Quarterly* 70, 281: 665–88.

Asarnow, Samuel (2021). "Action and Rationalization." *Australasian Journal of Philosophy*. DOI: 10.1080/00048402.2021.1936093.

Atwood, Margaret (1986). *The Handmaid's Tale*. New York: Penguin Random House.

Austin, J. L. (1975). *How to Do Things with Words*. Cambridge, MA: Harvard University Press.

Austin, John (1995). *The Province of Jurisprudence Determined*, edited by Wilfred E. Rumble. [Lectures originally published in 1832.] Cambridge: Cambridge University Press.

Backes, Marvin (2021). "Can Groups Be Genuine Believers? The Argument from Interpretationism." *Synthese* 199: 10311–29.

Beisbart, Claus (2022). "Improvisation and Action Theory." In Alessadro Bertinetto and Marcello Ruta, eds., *The Routledge Handbook of Philosophy and Improvisation in the Arts*, 100–113. New York: Routledge.

Bicchieri, Cristina (2006). *The Grammar of Society: The Nature and Dynamics of Social Norms*. New York: Cambridge University Press.

Bishop, John (2010). "Skepticism About Natural Agency and the Causal Theory of Action." In J. Aguilar and A. Buckareff, eds., *Causing Human Actions*, 69–83. Cambridge, MA: MIT Press.

Blomberg, Olle (2015). Review of *Shared Agency: A Planning Theory of Acting Together*. *Analysis* 75: 346–48.

Blomberg, Olle (2018). "Practical Knowledge and Acting Together." In J. A. Carter, A. Clark, J. Kallestrup, O. Palermos, and D. Pritchard, eds., *Socially Extended Epistemology*, 87–111. Oxford: Oxford University Press.

Bratman, Michael E. (1987). *Intention, Plans, and Practical Reason*. Cambridge, MA: Harvard University Press. [Re-issued by CSLI Publications, 1999.]

Bratman, Michael E. (1999). *Faces of Intention*. Cambridge: Cambridge University Press.

Bratman, Michael E. (1999a). "Castañeda's Theory of Thought and Action." In *Faces of Intention*, 225–49. Cambridge: Cambridge University Press.

Bratman, Michael E. (1999b). "Davidson's Theory of Intention." In *Faces of Intention*, 209–24. Cambridge: Cambridge University Press.

Bratman, Michael E. (1999c). "I Intend That We J." In *Faces of Intention*, 142–61. Cambridge: Cambridge University Press.

Bratman, Michael E. (1999d). "Practical Reasoning and Acceptance in a Context." In *Faces of Intention*, 15–34. Cambridge: Cambridge University Press.

Bratman, Michael E. (2006). "*Thinking How to Live* and the Restriction Problem." *Philosophy and Phenomenological Research* 72: 708–14.

Bratman, Michael E. (2007). *Structures of Agency*. New York: Oxford University Press.

Bratman, Michael E. (2007a). "Valuing and the Will." In *Structures of Agency*, 47–67. New York: Oxford University Press.

Bratman, Michael E. (2007b). "Three Theories of Self-Governance." In *Structures of Agency*, 222–53. New York: Oxford University Press.

Bratman, Michael E. (2009). "Intention, Practical Rationality and Self-Governance." *Ethics* 119: 411–43. [Reprinted in *Planning, Time, and Self-Governance: Essays in Practical Rationality*, 66–109. New York: Oxford University Press, 2018.]

Bratman, Michael E. (2010). "Agency, Time, and Sociality." *Proceedings and Addresses of the American Philosophical Association* 84: 7–26. [Reprinted in *Planning, Time, and Self-Governance: Essays in Practical Rationality*, 110–31. New York: Oxford University Press, 2018.]

Bratman, Michael E. (2011). "Reflections on Law, Normativity, and Plans." In S. Bertea and G. Pavlakos, eds., *New Essays on the Normativity of Law*, 73–85. Oxford: Hart Publishing.

Bratman, Michael E. (2012). "Time, Rationality, and Self-Governance." *Philosophical Issues* 22: 73–88. [Reprinted in *Planning, Time, and Self-Governance: Essays in Practical Rationality*, 132–48. New York: Oxford University Press, 2018.]

Bratman, Michael E. (2014a). *Shared Agency: A Planning Theory of Acting Together*. New York: Oxford University Press.

Bratman, Michael E. (2014b). "Rational and Social Agency: Reflections and Replies." In M. Vargas and G. Yaffe, eds., *Rational and Social Agency: The Philosophy of Michael Bratman*, 294–343. New York: Oxford University Press.

Bratman, Michael E. (2015a). "Shared Agency: Replies to Ludwig, Pacherie, Peterson, Roth, and Smith." *Journal of Social Ontology* 1: 59–76.

Bratman, Michael E. (2015b). "Shared Agency: Replies to Tenenbaum, Copp, and Schapiro." *Philosophical Studies* 172: 3409–20.

Bratman, Michael E. (2017a). "A Planning Theory of Self-Governance: Reply to Franklin." *Philosophical Explorations* 20: 15–20.

Bratman, Michael E. (2017b). "The Intentions of a Group." In Eric W. Orts and N. Craig Smith, eds., *The Moral Responsibility of Firms*, 36–52. Oxford: Oxford University Press.

Bratman, Michael E. (2018a). *Planning, Time, and Self-Governance: Essays in Practical Rationality*. New York: Oxford University Press.

Bratman, Michael E. (2018b). "Introduction: The Planning Framework." In *Planning, Time, and Self-Governance: Essays in Practical Rationality*, 1–17. New York: Oxford University Press.

Bratman, Michael E. (2018c). "A Planning Agent's Self-Governance Over Time." In *Planning, Time, and Self-Governance: Essays in Practical Rationality*, 224–49. New York: Oxford University Press.

Bratman, Michael E. (2018d). "Review of Kirk Ludwig's *From Plural to Institutional Agency: Collective Agency II*." *Notre Dame Philosophical Reviews*. 1–8.

Bratman, Michael E. (2021a). "Precis of *Planning, Time, and Self-Governance*." *Inquiry: An Interdisciplinary Journal of Philosophy* 64, 9: 883–91.

Bratman, Michael E. (2021b). "Shared Intention, Organized Institutions." In David Shoemaker, ed., *Oxford Studies in Agency and Responsibility*, 7:54–80. Oxford: Oxford University Press.

Bratman, Michael E. (forthcoming a). "Acting Together with Oneself over Time: Appendix to 'A Planning Agent's Self-Governance Over Time.'" In Carla Bagnoli, ed., *Time in Action: The Temporal Structure of Rational Agency and Practical Thought*. New York: Routledge.

Bratman, Michael E. (forthcoming b). "A Planning Theory of Acting Together." *Journal of the American Philosophical Association*.

Bratman, Michael E. (forthcoming c). "Reflections on Flanagan on Intentional Legislation." In Ruth Chang, ed., *New Conversations in Philosophy, Law, and Politics*. Oxford: Oxford University Press.

Brennan, Geoffrey, Lina Eriksson, Robert E. Goodin, and Nicholas Southwood (2013). *Explaining Norms*. Oxford: Oxford University Press.

Broome, John (2013). *Rationality Through Reasoning*. Chichester: Wiley-Blackwell.

Brown, Jessica (2021). "Group Motivation." *Noûs*. 1–17. DOI: 10.1111/nous.12366.

Bruni, Luigino, and Robert Sugden (2008). "Fraternity: Why the Market Need Not Be a Morally Free Zone." *Economics and Philosophy* 24: 35–64.

Buchak, Lara (2013). *Risk and Rationality*. New York: Oxford University Press.

Burge, Tyler (1975). "On Knowledge and Convention." *The Philosophical Review* 84: 249–55.

Burge, Tyler (1979). "Individualism and the Mental." *Midwest Studies in Philosophy* 4: 73–121.

Calhoun, Cheshire (1995). "Standing for Something." *Journal of Philosophy* 92: 235–60.

Carruthers, Peter (2012), "Language in Cognition." In E. Margolis, R. Samuels, and S. Stitch, eds., *The Oxford Handbook of Philosophy of Cognitive Science*, 382–401. Oxford: Oxford University Press.

Castañeda, Hector-Neri (1975). *Thinking and Doing: The Philosophical Foundations of Institutions*. Dordrecht: Reidel.

Chapman, Emilee (2020). "Shared Agency and the Ethics of Democracy." *Georgetown Journal of Law and Public Philosophy* 18, 2: 705–32.

Chisholm, Roderick (1966). "Freedom and Action." In K. Lehrer, ed., *Freedom and Determinism*, 11–44. New York: Random House.

Clark, Andy, and David Chalmers (1998). "The Extended Mind." *Analysis* 58: 7–19.

Clark, Andy (2008). *Supersizing the Mind: Embodiment, Action, and Cognitive Extension*. Oxford: Oxford University Press.

Cohen, Joshua (1993). "Moral Pluralism and Political Consensus." In D. Copp, J. Hampton, and J. E. Roamer, eds., *The Idea of Democracy*, 270–91. Cambridge: Cambridge University Press.

Coleman, Jules (2001). *The Practice of Principle: In Defense of a Pragmatist Approach to Legal Theory*. Oxford: Oxford University Press.

Copp, David (2009). "Toward a Pluralist and Teleological Theory of Normativity." *Philosophical Issues* 19: 21–37.

Copp, David (2019). "Legal Teleology." In D. Plunkett, S. Shapiro, and K. Toh, eds., *Dimensions of Normativity: New Essays on Metaethics and Jurisprudence*, 45–64. New York: Oxford University Press.

Copp, David (2021). "Normative Pluralism and Skepticism About 'Ought *Simpliciter*.'" In R. Chang and K. Sylvan, eds., *The Routledge Handbook of Practical Reason*, 416–37. London: Routledge.

Darwall, Stephen (2006). *The Second-Person Standpoint*. Cambridge, MA: Harvard University Press.

Darwall, Stephen (2018). "Contempt as an Other-Characterizing, 'Hierarchizing' Attitude." In Michelle Mason, ed., *The Moral Psychology of Contempt*, 193–215. Lanham, MD: Rowman & Littlefield

Davidson, Donald (1980). *Essays on Actions and Events*. Oxford: Oxford University Press.

Davidson, Donald (1980a). "Actions, Reasons, and Causes." In *Essays on Actions and Events*, 3–19. Oxford: Oxford University Press.

Davidson, Donald (1980b). "How Is Weakness of the Will Possible?" In *Essays on Actions and Events*, 21–42. Oxford: Oxford University Press.

Davidson, Donald (1980c). "Agency." In *Essays on Actions and Events*, 43–61. Oxford: Oxford University Press.

Davidson, Donald (1980d). "Intending." In *Essays on Actions and Events*, 83–102. Oxford: Oxford University Press.

Davidson, Donald (1980e). "Mental Events." In *Essays on Actions and Events*, 207–27. Oxford: Oxford University Press.

Davidson, Donald (1985a). "Reply to Michael Bratman." In Bruce Vermazen and Merrill B. Hintikka, eds., *Essays on Davidson: Actions and Events*, 195–201. Oxford: Oxford University Press.

Davidson, Donald (1985b). "Reply to David Pears." In Bruce Vermazen and Merrill B. Hintikka, eds., *Essays on Davidson: Actions and Events*, 211–15. Oxford: Oxford University Press.

Davidson, Donald (2001a). "The Method of Truth in Metaphysics." In *Inquiries into Truth and Interpretation*, 2nd ed., 199–214. Oxford: Oxford University Press.

Davidson, Donald (2001b). "Thought and Talk." In *Inquiries into Truth and Interpretation*, 2nd ed., 155–70. Oxford: Oxford University Press.

Davidson, Donald (2004). "Deception and Division." In *Problems of Rationality*, 199–212 Oxford: Oxford University Press.

Dennett, Daniel (1971). "Intentional Systems." *The Journal of Philosophy* 68: 87–106.

Dewey, John (1916). *Democracy and Education*. New York: Macmillan.

Dretske, Fred (1994). "If You Can't Make One, You Don't Know How It Works." *Midwest Studies in Philosophy* 19: 468–82.

Dworkin, Ronald (1986). *Law's Empire*. Cambridge, MA: Harvard University Press.

Dworkin, Ronald (2002). "Review: Thirty Years On." *Harvard Law Review*, 115: 1655–87.

Epstein, Brian (2015). *The Ant Trap: Rebuilding the Foundations of the Social Sciences*. New York: Oxford University Press.

Feinberg, Joel (1973). *Social Philosophy*. Englewood Cliffs, NJ: Prentice-Hall.

Ferrero, Luca (2009). "What Good Is a Diachronic Will?" *Philosophical Studies* 144: 403–30.

Finnis, John (2011). *Natural Law and Natural Rights*. 2nd ed. Oxford: Oxford University Press.

Flanagan, Brian (forthcoming). "Intentional Legislation." In Ruth Chang, ed., *New Conversations in Philosophy, Law, and Politics*. Oxford: Oxford University Press.

Foot, Phillipa (1972). "Morality as a System of Hypothetical Imperatives." *The Philosophical Review* 81: 305–16.

Frankfurt, Harry (1988a). "Freedom of the Will and the Concept of a Person." In *The Importance of What We Care About*, 11–25. Cambridge: Cambridge University Press.

Frankfurt, Harry (1988b). "Identification and Wholeheartedness." In *The Importance of What We Care About*, 158–76. Cambridge: Cambridge University Press.

Frankfurt, Harry (1999). "The Faintest Passion." In *Necessity, Volition, and Love*, 95–107. Cambridge: Cambridge University Press.

French, Peter A. (1979). "The Corporation as a Moral Person." *American Philosophical Quarterly* 16: 207–15.

French, Peter A. (1996). "Integrity, Intentions, and Corporations." *American Business Law Journal* 34: 141–55.

French, Peter A. (2017). "The Diachronic Moral Responsibility of Firms." In Eric W. Orts and N. Craig Smith, eds., *The Moral Responsibility of Firms*, 53–65. Oxford: Oxford University Press.

Frigg, Roman, and Stephan Hartmann (2020). "Models in Science." In Edward N. Zalta, ed., *The Stanford Encyclopedia of Philosophy* (Spring 2020 Edition). https://plato.stanford.edu/archives/spr2020/entries/models-science/.

Fuller, Lon L. (1969). *The Morality of Law*, revised ed. New Haven: Yale University Press.

Gauthier, David (1994). "Assure and Threaten." *Ethics* 104: 690–721.

Gibbard, Allan (2003). *Thinking How to Live*. Cambridge, MA: Harvard University Press.

Gilbert, Margaret (1989). *On Social Facts*. London: Routledge.

Gilbert, Margaret (1990). "Walking Together: A Paradigmatic Social Phenomenon." *Midwest Studies in Philosophy* 15: 1–14.

Gilbert, Margaret (1999). "Social Rules: Some Problems for Hart's Account and an Alternative Proposal." *Law and Philosophy* 18: 141–71.

Gilbert, Margaret (2004). "Collective Epistemology." *Episteme* 1: 95–107.

Gilbert, Margaret (2008). "Social Convention Revisited." *Topoi* 27: 5–16.

Gilbert, Margaret (2009). "Shared Intention and Personal Intentions." *Philosophical Studies* 144: 167–87.

Gilbert, Margaret (2014). *Joint Commitment*. Oxford: Oxford University Press.

Godfrey-Smith, Peter (2005). "Folk Psychology as a Model." *Philosophers' Imprint* 5, 6.

Goldstein, Simon (2016). "A Preface Paradox for Intention." *Philosophers' Imprint* 16: 1–20.

Gorin, Moti (2014). "Do Manipulators Always Threaten Rationality?" *American Philosophical Quarterly* 51: 51–61.

Green, Leslie (1999). "Positivism and Conventionalism." *Canadian Journal of Law and Jurisprudence* 12: 35–52.

Greenberg, Mark (2004). "How Facts Make Law." *Legal Theory* 10: 157–98.
Grice, H. P. (1941). "Personal Identity." *Mind* 50: 200, 330–50.
Grice, Paul (1974–75). "Method in Philosophical Psychology (From the Banal to the Bizarre.)" *Proceedings and Addresses of the American Philosophical Association* 48: 23–53.
Guala, Francesco (2016). *Understanding Institutions: The Science and Philosophy of Living Together.* Princeton: Princeton University Press.
Guala, Francesco, and Frank Hindriks (2015). "A Unified Social Ontology." *The Philosophical Quarterly* 65: 177–201.
Harman, Gilbert (1976). "Practical Reasoning." *Review of Metaphysics* 29: 431–63.
Harman, Gilbert (1986). *Change in View: Principles of Reasoning.* Cambridge, MA: MIT Press.
Hart, H. L. A. (1958). "Positivism and the Separation of Law and Morals." *Harvard Law Review* 71: 593–629.
Hart, H. L. A. (2012). *The Concept of Law*, 3rd ed. Oxford: Oxford University Press.
Haslanger, Sally (2018). "What Is a Social Practice?" *Royal Institute of Philosophy Supplement* 82: 231–47.
Hauthaler, Nathan (n.d.). "For No Particular Reason."
Hayek, F. A. (1945). "The Use of Knowledge in Society." *American Economic Review* 35: 519–30.
Hess, Kendy M. (2014). "The Free Will of Corporations (and Other Collectives)." *Philosophical Studies* 168: 241–60.
Hindriks, Frank (2008). "The Status Account of Corporate Agents." In H. B. Schmid, K. Schulte-Ostermann, and N. Psarros, eds., *Concepts of Sharedness: Essays on Collective Intentionality*, 119–44. Frankfurt: Ontos Verlag.
Hindriks, Frank (2013). "Collective Acceptance and the Is-Ought Problem." *Ethical Theory and Moral Practice* 16: 465–80.
Hindriks, Frank (2014). "How Autonomous Are Collective Agents? Corporate Rights and Normative Individualism." *Erkenntnis* 79: 1565–85.
Hindriks, Frank (2018). "Institutions and Collective Intentionality." In Marija Jankovic and Kirk Ludwig, eds., *Routledge Handbook on Collective Intentionality*, 353–62. New York: Routledge.
Hindriks, Frank (2019). "Norms That Make a Difference: Social Practices and Institutions." *Analyse & Kritik* 41: 125–46.
Hohfeld, Wesley (1919). *Fundamental Legal Conceptions.* Edited by W. Cook. New Haven: Yale University Press.
Hume, David (1896). *A Treatise of Human Nature.* Oxford: Clarendon Press.
Hunter, David (2015). "Davidson on Practical Knowledge." *Journal for the History of Analytic Philosophy* 3, 9: 1–19.
Hussain, Waheed, and Joakim Sandberg (2017). "Pluralistic Functionalism About Corporate Agency." In Eric W. Orts and N. Craig Smith, eds., *The Moral Responsibility of Firms*, 66–86. Oxford: Oxford University Press.

Jackson, Shirley (1948). "The Lottery." *The New Yorker*, June 26.
Kavka, Gregory (1983). "The Toxin Puzzle." *Analysis* 43: 33–36.
Korsgaard, Christine (2009). *Self-Constitution: Agency, Identity, and Integrity*. Oxford: Oxford University Press.
Kripke, Saul (1972). *Naming and Necessity*. Cambridge, MA: Harvard University Press.
Kutz, Christopher (2000). "Acting Together." *Philosophy and Phenomenological Research* 61: 1–31.
Lackey, Jennifer (2021). *The Epistemology of Groups*. Oxford: Oxford University Press.
Lavin, Douglas (2016). "Action as a Form of Temporal Unity: On Anscombe's Intention." *Canadian Journal of Philosophy* 45: 609–29.
Levin, Janet, (2018). "Functionalism." In Edward N. Zalta, ed., *The Stanford Encyclopedia of Philosophy* (Fall 2018 Edition). https://plato.stanford.edu/archives/fall2018/entries/functionalism/.
Lewis, David (1969). *Convention*. Cambridge, MA: Harvard University Press.
Lewis, David (1972). "Psychophysical and Theoretical Identifications." *Australasian Journal of Philosophy* 50: 249–58.
Lewis, David (1983). "Languages and Language." In *Philosophical Papers: Volume 1*, 163–88. Oxford: Oxford University Press.
Liao, S. Matthew (2018). "Opinion: Do You Have a Moral Duty to Leave Facebook?" *The New York Times*, November 24, 2018.
List, Christian, and Philip Pettit (2011). *Group Agency: The Possibility, Design, and Status of Corporate Agents*. Oxford: Oxford University Press.
List, Christian (2018). "What Is It Like to Be a Group Agent?" *Noûs* 52: 295–319.
Locke, John (1975). *An Essay Concerning Human Understanding*, ed. Peter H. Nidditch. Oxford: Oxford University Press.
Ludwig, Kirk (2015). "Shared Agency in Modest Sociality." *Journal of Social Ontology* 1: 7–16.
Ludwig, Kirk (2017). *From Plural to Institutional Agency: Collective Action II*. Oxford: Oxford University Press.
Ludwig, Kirk (2020). "The Social Construction of Legal Norms." In M. Garcia-Godinez, R. Mellin, and R. Tuomela, eds., *Social Ontology, Normativity and Law*, 179–208. Berlin: De Gruyter.
McPherson, Tristram (2011). "Against Quietist Normative Realism." *Philosophical Studies* 154: 223–40.
Murray, Dylan, and Lara Buchak (2019). "Risk and Motivation: When the Will Is Required to Determine What to Do." *Philosophers' Imprint* 19, 16: 1–12.
Miller, George, Eugene Galanter, and Karl Pribram (1960). *Plans and the Structure of Behavior*. New York: Holt, Rinehart and Winston.
Miller, Seumas (2019). "Social Institutions." In Edward N. Zalta, ed., *The Stanford Encyclopedia of Philosophy*. https://plato.stanford.edu/archives/sum2019/entries/social-institutions/.

Millgram, Elijah (2019). "Review of *Planning, Time, and Self-Governance.*" *Notre Dame Philosophical Reviews*, May 15: 1–6.

Moltchanova, Anna (2019). "Social Ontology for All (Kinds of Groups)." *The Monist* 102: 187–203.

Nagel, Thomas (1970). *The Possibility of Altruism*. Oxford: Clarendon Press.

Neufeld, Blain (2019). "Shared Intention, Public Reason, and Political Autonomy." *Canadian Journal of Philosophy* 49: 776–804.

Núñez, Carlos (2019). "Intending Recalcitrant Social Ends." *Erkenntnis*. DOI: 10.1007/s10670-019-00203-5.

Núñez, Carlos (2020a). "Requirements of Intention in Light of Belief." *Philosophical Studies* 177:2471–2492.

Núñez, Carlos (2020b). "An Alternative Norm of Intention Consistency." *Thought: A Journal of Philosophy*. DOI: 10.1002/tht3.453. 9:152–159.

Núñez, Carlos (n.d.). "The Independence of Practical Reason."

Orts, Eric W. (2017). "The Moral Responsibility of Firms: Past, Present, and Future." In Eric W. Orts and N. Craig Smith, eds., *The Moral Responsibility of Firms*, 206–23. Oxford: Oxford University Press.

Orts, Eric W., and N. Craig Smith, eds. (2017). *The Moral Responsibility of Firms*. Oxford: Oxford University Press.

Pacherie, Elisabeth (2015). "Modest Sociality: Continuities and Discontinuities." *Journal of Social Ontology* 1: 17–26.

Parfit, Derek (1984). *Reasons and Persons*. Oxford: Clarendon Press.

Paul, Sarah K. (2009). "How We Know What We Are Doing." *Philosophers' Imprint* 9, 1: 1–24.

Paul, Sarah K. (2021). *Philosophy of Action: A Contemporary Introduction*. New York: Routledge.

Petersson, Björn (2015). "Bratman, Searle, and Simplicity: A Comment on Bratman, *Shared Agency*." *Journal of Social Ontology* 1: 27–38.

Pettit, Philip (2002). "Collective Persons and Powers." *Legal Theory* 8: 443–70.

Pettit, Philip (2003). "Groups with Minds of Their Own." In Frederick Schmitt, ed, *Social Metaphysics*, 167–93. Lanham, MD: Rowman & Littlefield.

Pettit, Philip, and David Schweikard (2006). "Joint Actions and Group Agents." *Philosophy of the Social Sciences* 36: 18–39.

Pettit, Philip (2017). "The Conversable, Responsible Corporation." In Eric W. Orts and N. Craig Smith, eds., *The Moral Responsibility of Firms*, 15–35. Oxford: Oxford University Press.

Pettit, Philip (2018). "Corporate Agency: The Lesson of the Discursive Dilemma." In M. Jankovic and K. Ludwig, eds., *Routledge Handbook on Collective Intentionality*, 249–59. New York: Routledge.

Pettit, Philip, and Kinch Hoekstra (2018). *The Birth of Ethics: Reconstructing the Role and Nature of Morality*. Oxford: Oxford University Press.

Pettit, Philip (2019). "Social Norms and the Internal Point of View: An Elaboration of Hart's Genealogy of Law." *Oxford Journal of Legal Studies* 39: 229–58.

Postema, Gerald J. (1982). "Coordination and Convention at the Foundations of Law." *Journal of Legal Studies* 11: 165–203.

Putnam, Hilary (1967). "Psychological Predicates." In W. H. Capitan and D. D. Merrill, eds., *Art, Mind, and Religion*, 37–48. Pittsburgh: University of Pittsburgh Press.

Putnam, Hilary (1975). "The Meaning of 'Meaning.'" In *Mind, Language and Reality*, vol. 2., 215–71. Cambridge: Cambridge University Press.

Quine, W. V. O. (1960). *Word and Object*. Cambridge, MA: MIT Press.

Quinn, Warren (1994). "Putting Rationality in Its Place." In *Morality and Action*, 228–55. Cambridge: Cambridge University Press.

Railton, Peter (2019). "'We'll See You in Court!' The Rule of Law as an Explanatory and Normative Kind." In D. Plunkett, S. Shapiro, and K. Toh, eds., *Dimensions of Normativity: New Essays on Metaethics and Jurisprudence*, 1–22. New York: Oxford University Press.

Rawls, John (1955). "Two Concepts of Rules." *The Philosophical Review* 64: 3–32.

Rawls, John (1971). *A Theory of Justice*. Cambridge, MA: Harvard University Press.

Rawls, John (2005). *Political Liberalism*, expanded ed. New York: Columbia University Press.

Richardson, Henry (1997). *Practical Reasoning About Final Ends*. Cambridge: Cambridge University Press.

Ritchie, Katherine (2020). "Minimal Cooperation and Group Roles." In Anika Fiebich, ed., *Minimal Cooperation and Shared Agency*, 93–110. Cham: Springer Nature.

Roth, Abraham Sesshu (2004). "Shared Agency and Contralateral Commitments." *The Philosophical Review* 113: 359–410.

Roth, Abraham Sesshu (2014a). "Indispensability, the Discursive Dilemma, and Groups with Minds of Their Own." In S. R. Chant, F. Hindriks, and G. Preyer, eds., *From Individual to Collective Intentionality: New Essays*, 137–62. Oxford: Oxford University Press.

Roth, Abraham Sesshu (2014b). "Prediction, Authority, and Entitlement in Shared Activity." *Noûs* 48: 626–52.

Roth, Abraham Sesshu (2015). "Practical Intersubjectivity and Normative Guidance: Bratman on Shared Agency." *Journal of Social Ontology* 1: 39–48.

Roth, Abraham Sesshu (2020). "Proprietary Reasons and Joint Action." In Anika Fiebich, ed., *Minimal Cooperation and Shared Agency*, 169–80. Cham: Springer Nature.

Roy, Olivier, and Anne Schwenkenbecker (2021). "Shared Intentions, Loose Groups, and Pooled Knowledge." *Synthese* 198: 4523–41.

Rovane, Carol (1998). *The Bounds of Agency: An Essay in Revisionary Metaphysics*. Princeton: Princeton University Press.

Rovane Carol (2014). "Group Agency and Individualism." *Erkenntnis* 79: 1663–84.

Searle, John (1964). "How to Derive an 'Ought' from an 'Is.'" *Philosophical Review* 73: 43–58.

Searle, John (1990). "Collective Intentions and Actions." In P. R. Cohen, J. Morgan, and M. E. Pollack, eds., *Intentions in Communication*, 401–15. Cambridge, MA: MIT Press.

Searle, John (1995). *The Construction of Social Reality*. New York: The Free Press.

Searle, John (1997). "Responses to Critics of *The Construction of Social Reality*." *Philosophy and Phenomenological Research* 57: 449–58.

Searle, John (2005). "What Is an Institution?" *Journal of Institutional Economics* 1: 1–22.

Searle, John (2010). *Making the Social World: The Structure of Human Civilization*. Oxford: Oxford University Press.

Seligman, Martin E. P., Peter Railton, Roy F. Baumeister, and Chandra Sripada (2016). *Homo Prospectus*. Oxford: Oxford University Press.

Sepinwall, Amy J. (2016). "Corporate Moral Responsibility." *Philosophy Compass* 11, 1: 3–13.

Shapiro, Scott J. (1997). "Fear of Theory (Reviewing *Legal Reasoning and Political Conflict* by Cass R. Sunstein)." *University of Chicago Law Review* 64: 389–403.

Shapiro, Scott J. (2011). *Legality*. Cambridge, MA: Harvard University Press.

Shapiro, Scott J. (2014). "Massively Shared Agency." In M. Vargas and G. Yaffe, eds., *Rational and Social Agency: The Philosophy of Michael Bratman*, 257–89. Oxford: Oxford University Press.

Shoemaker, Sydney, and Richard Swinburne (1984). *Personal Identity*. Oxford: Blackwell.

Shpall, Sam (2016). "The Calendar Paradox." *Philosophical Studies* 173: 801–25.

Sidgwick, Henry (1962). *The Methods of Ethics*, 7th ed. Chicago: University of Chicago Press.

Simon, Herbert A. (1955). "A Behavioral Model of Rational Choice." *The Quarterly Journal of Economics* 69, 1: 99–118.

Simon, Herbert A. (1983). *Reason in Human Affairs*. Stanford: Stanford University Press.

Smith, Matthew Noah (2006). "The Law as a Social Practice: Are Shared Activities at the Foundations of Law?" *Legal Theory* 12: 265–92.

Smith, Thomas H. (2015). "*Shared Agency* on Gilbert and Deep Continuity." *Journal of Social Ontology* 1: 49–58.

Southwood, Nicholas (2019). "Law as Conventional Norms." In D. Plunkett, S. Shapiro, and K. Toh, eds., *Dimensions of Normativity: New Essays on Metaethics and Jurisprudence*, 23–44. New York: Oxford University Press.

Stilz, Anna (2009). *Liberal Loyalty: Freedom, Obligation, and the State*. Princeton: Princeton University Press.

Strawson, Peter (1962). "Freedom and Resentment." *Proceedings of the British Academy* 48: 1–25.

Stroud, Sarah (2010). "Partiality and Impartiality: Morality, Special Relationships, and the Wider World." In B. Feltham and J. Cottingham, eds., *Partiality and Impartiality*, 131–49. Oxford: Oxford University Press.

Strudler, Alan (n.d.). "Contours of Corporate Moral Agency."

Sunstein, Cass (1995). "Incompletely Theorized Agreements." *Harvard Law Review* 108: 1735–72.

Tenenbaum, Sergio (2015). "Representing Collective Agency." *Philosophical Studies* 172: 3379–86.

Tollefsen, Deborah Perron (2002). "Organizations as True Believers." *Journal of Social Philosophy* 33: 395–410.

Tollefsen, Deborah Perron (2015). *Groups as Agents*. Cambridge: Polity Press.

Tomasello, Michael (2014). *A Natural History of Human Thinking*. Cambridge, MA: Harvard University Press.

Tomasello, Michael (2019). *Becoming Human: A Theory of Ontogeny*. Cambridge, MA: Harvard University Press.

Tuomela, Raimo (1992). "Group Beliefs." *Synthese* 91: 285–318.

Tuomela, Raimo (1995). *The Importance of Us: A Philosophical Study of Basic Social Notions*. Stanford: Stanford University Press.

Tuomela, Raimo (2004). "Group Knowledge Analyzed." *Episteme* 1: 109–27.

Tuomela, Raimo (2007). *The Philosophy of Sociality: The Shared Point of View*. New York: Oxford University Press.

Tufekci, Zeynep (2017). *Twitter and Tear Gas: The Power and Fragility of Networked Protest*. New Haven: Yale University Press.

Valentini, Laura (2021). "Respect for Persons and the Moral Force of Socially Constructed Norms." *Noûs* 55, 2: 385–408.

Velasquez, Manuel (2003). "Debunking Corporate Moral Responsibility." *Business Ethics Quarterly* 13: 531–62.

Velleman, J. David (1992). "What Happens When Someone Acts?" *Mind* 101: 461–81.

Velleman, J. David (1997). "How to Share an Intention." *Philosophy and Phenomenological Research* 57: 29–50.

Velleman, J. David (2021). "Michael Bratman's *Planning, Time, and Self-Governance*." *Inquiry: An Interdisciplinary Journal of Philosophy* 64, 9: 913–25.

Walton, Kendall L. (1993). *Mimesis as Make-Believe: On the Foundations of the Representative Arts*. Cambridge, MA: Harvard University Press.

Watson, Gary (2004). *Agency and Answerability: Selected Essays*. Oxford: Oxford University Press.

Wenar, Leif (2020). "Rights." In Edward N. Zalta, ed., *The Stanford Encyclopedia of Philosophy* (Spring 2020 Edition). https://plato.stanford.edu/archives/spr2020/entries/rights/.

Westlund, Andrea (2015). "Review of *Shared Agency*." *Australasian Journal of Philosophy* 93: 822–25.

White, Stephen (2016). "Review of *Shared Agency*." *Ethics* 126: 816–21.
Williams, Bernard (1981). "Internal and External Reasons." In *Moral Luck*, 101–13. Cambridge: Cambridge University Press.
Yaffe, Gideon (2000). *Liberty Worth the Name: Locke on Free Agency*. Princeton: Princeton University Press.

INDEX

For the benefit of digital users, indexed terms that span two pages (e.g., 52–53) may, on occasion, appear on only one of those pages.

acceptance of a common standard
    rational dependence of, on general conformity, 38, 62–63 (*see also under* fundamentalists)
    supporting criticism and demand, 42 (*see also* criticism and demand; pretense of endorsement; social rules; *under* shared policies)
accountability, moral, of institutions, 169, 184, 227n.13, 228n.2
agential standpoint (Frankfurt), 146, 175
    contrast with aim of self-understanding (Velleman), 146
    unwilling addict, 146, 175
    See also institutional standpoint
alienated judges (case, Hart and Shapiro), 67, 74–75, 79
    See also under hybrid social rule
alienated participants, 66–75
    contrast with fundamentalists, 216n.11
    criticism/demand of (*see under* extending reasons)
    example of children, 73, 216n.10
    generally, 67, 216n.11
    possibility of universal alienation, 78–80
    strategic interaction, involving, 66–67
    See also alienated judges (case, Hart and Shapiro); pretense of endorsement; kernel-penumbra structure: penumbra
Alonso, Facundo, 6, 217n.20
Anderson, Elizabeth, 204n.9
Anscombe, G.E.M., 194–95
    and Davidson, 193–94, 195–96
    Intention, 206n.13
    practical self-knowledge, 193–94, 195, 229n.6
    "why question," 193–94, 195, 229n.4
Arnold, Denis, 223–24n.2
Arrow, Kenneth, 221n.5
Austin, J.L., 26
Austin, John. *See* Hart vs. Austin
authority-according shared intention, 24–26
    interlocking involved in, 24
    merely shared-intention authority relations, 26
    See also under reasons, substantive normative; rights and duties

authority-according social rules of
    procedure, 106–9
  authority acceptance, 108
  contents, 107
  as defining roles and offices, 115–16, 130
  and deontic powers, 108
  as establishing relativized rights and duties, 106–7
    contrast with normatively substantive rights and duties, 107, 108–9
  institutional centrality of, 107
  See also deontic powers; rights and duties

"background" (Searle), 218n.23
Bicchieri, Cristina, 94–95, 96, 220n.49
  See also under social norms/rules and normativity
Bishop, John, 229n.2
Blomberg, Olle, xxi, 205n.15, 226n.19
bootstrapping of reasons, 4, 6, 212n.14
Brennan, Geoffrey, 92–93, 96, 220n.47, 220n.49
  See also under social norms/rules and normativity
Bruni, Luigino, 206–7n.15
Buchak, Lara, 102

Chisholm, Roderick, 179
Coleman, Jules, 204n.8
"collective acceptance" (Searle), 68, 129, 131
  and deontic power, 129–30
"collective pretense" (Darwall). *See* Darwall's challenge
"collective rationality" (List and Pettit), 151, 152, 226–27n.4
commonalities within
  institutions, 182–84
  common-weight-implicating social rules of procedure, 185

common-weight-non-implicating social rules of procedure, 185
  induced further teleology, as a dimension of, 187
  minimal-kernel social rules of procedure, 185–86
  strong *vs.* weak commonality, 186–87
  universal-kernel social rules of procedure, 185–86
constitutive rules (Searle), 130
continuity, xxii, 111–13
  continuity from individual agency to SIA, xvi, 19, 46, 203n.3
  continuity from shared intention and shared policy/rule, 51, 111
  discontinuity
    in move to "joint commitments" (Gilbert), 111–12
    in move to "we-intentions" (Searle), 111–12
  from shared intention to organized institution, xxi, 111, 112–13
"conventional authority relations" (Darwall), 26, 107
  See also authority-according shared intention; authority-according social rules of procedure
coordination conventions (Lewis), 204n.6
  and social rules, 212n.11, 215n.5, 215–16n.6
Copp, David, 209n.46, 210n.54, 222n.14, 222n.16
core capacity, planning agency as a, xv–xvi, xxii, 195–96, 199–200, 230n.2
  explaining institutions, xvi, 117
  explaining small-scale shared agency, xvi, 9
  See also sequential planning theory
"counts as" rules. *See* constitutive rules (Searle)
"creature construction" (Grice), 11, 141
  See also sequential planning theory; strategy of construction

criticism and demand, 55
    of alienated/penumbral participants (*see under* extending reasons)
    characteristic of social rules, 35, 36, 39
    normative language expressing, 93–94
    and substantive obligations
        as common (but non-essential) in cases of shared policy, 51
        non-essentiality of, to support, 54, 55–56
        as supporting, 53–55, 83
        supported by shared intentions/policies, 43, 50–56, 83
        See also under "joint commitments" (Gilbert)
cross-temporal organization
    as explained by capacity for planning agency, xvi, 3, 6
    of individual agency, 3, 8
    See also Lockean ties; persistence

Darwall's challenge, 75, 80–82
    pretense as simulation, 81–82
Darwall, Stephen. *See* "conventional authority relations" (Darwall); Darwall's challenge; *under* rights and duties
Davidson, Donald, 4, 26–27, 229n.5
    and Anscombe, 193–94, 195–96
    future-directed intention as "interim report," 229n.10
    See also Davidsonian synthesis, adjustments to; Davidson's challenge to institutional intentions; dense holism (Davidson); primary reason (Davidson)
Davidson's challenge to institutional intentions, 149–50
    Bratman's reply, 159
    Ludwig and, 150, 151, 225n.12
    Pettit/List and Pettit and, 150–51 (*see also* "discursive dilemmas" [List and Pettit])
    Rovane and, 151, 226n.16
    See also pluralistic disagreement within institutions; primacy of individual intention and intentional agency, rejection of
Davidsonian synthesis, adjustments to
    acting intentionally without acting for a reason, 181–82, 191, 193, 194
    intentional agency without dense holism, 191, 192–93, 194 (*see also* dense holism [Davidson])
    planning theory as undergirding, 194–95
    relevance to individual case, 192
demandingness objection
    to shared intention, 20–21
    for a model for law, 213n.3
    to shared policies, 48
dense holism (Davidson)
    belief attribution, as a requirement for, 143
    and the "constitutive" role of rationality, 209n.48, 224n.1
    as fixing individual attitudinal content, 142, 143, 145–46, 159 (*see also* institutional intentions: content)
    intention attribution, as a requirement for, 143–44 (*see also under* functioning)
    as key element to Davidson's theory of agency, 142, 146–47, 174
    and "making sense" of attitudes, 144, 145–46
    subjecthood, as requirement for, 142, 144–45
    See also Davidson's challenge to institutional intentions

deontic powers
  as central to organized institutions, 111–12 (*see also* authority-according social rules of procedure)
  in practical thinking, 25
  See also rights and duties; *under* "collective acceptance" (Searle)
decentralized social organization, 210n.57
dependence, explanatorily relevant, 87–88
design specification, dual, 40–41, 64–65, 198
  appeal to shared intention to realize, 42–43, 44
  appeal to shared policies to realize, 47
  basic social rule design specification, 40, 41, 198
  institutional-role design specification, 40–41, 67, 198
  See also under functioning
diachronic fragility/robustness. *See* persistence; Lockean ties
"discursive dilemmas" (List and Pettit), 151, 161–66
  conclusion-centered reasoning, 162
  premise-centered reasoning, 162
  pressure towards completeness, 151, 162–63, 178, 182–83, 226–27n.4, 227n.5, 227n.6
divergence of background reasons for participation
  in institutional activity, 147–48 (*see also* pluralistic disagreement within institutions)
  in shared intentional activity, 10, 18
  in shared policy, 80–81, 216n.11
Dretske, Fred, 11
Dworkin, Ronald, xx, 38, 204n.8, 222n.5, 227n.6, 228n.9

endorsement of a common standard. *See* acceptance of a common standard
Engels, Friedrich, 78
Epstein, Brian, 224n.4
extending reasons, 68, 69–70, 86
  contrast with induced further teleology of social rules of procedure, 110
  examples, 70–71
  as grounding criticism/demand of alienated/penumbral participants, 71, 74–75, 83, 222n.6
  informal inducement of, 70
  intentional-reason-grounded extension, 70–71, 218n.22
  moral extending reasons, 69–70
  related to strategic response, 69–70
  See also snowball of obligation-inducing reliance

Facebook (case), xx, 169, 183
"followed social norm" (Bicchieri), 94
Foot, Philippa, 219n.36
"formal acceptance" (Ludwig), 217n.15
Frankfurt, Harry, 145–47, 225n.6
  See also agential standpoint (Frankfurt); higher-order desires (Frankfurt)
French, Peter, 101, 221n.3, 223–24n.2
functionalism, 7, 26–27, 153–54
  See also functioning; strategy of construction
functioning
  characteristic of intention, 7, 23
  for institutions, 105, 136, 137–39, 158, 159, 178
  as not essentially involving holism, 167–68 (*see also* primacy of individual intention and intentional agency, rejection of)

characteristic of shared intentional
activity, 16–17
characteristic of social rules, 50, 76
grounded in construction, 12,
16, 197–98
realizing dual design specification,
41 (*see also* design
specification, dual)
See also functionalism; mimics
of functioning; strategy of
construction
fundamentalists, 62–66
contrast with alienated participants,
216n.11
generally, 62–63
interdependence, and requirement
of, 65, 66
interlocking, and requirement
of, 65–66
rational dependence on conformity
through cognitive constraints,
63, 215–16n.6

"genealogical method" (Pettit), 207n.27
Gibbard, Alan, 204n.5, 206n.11, 230n.2
Gilbert, Margaret, 8–9, 31, 51, 131,
208n.33, 210n.52
See also "joint commitments" (Gilbert)
"glue" relation
in guidance by institutional
intention, 175–76, 228n.3
in shared intentional activity, 10
in social rules, 76–77
See also Lockean ties
Grice, H.P. *See* "creature
construction" (Grice)
Guala, Francesco, 213n.1

Hart, H.L.A. *See* alienated judges
(case, Hart and Shapiro);
Hart's theory of law; *under*

individualism; social rules;
social rule schema, Hart's;
Hart vs. Austin
Hart vs. Austin
on law as providing rule-
guidance, 210n.1
on sovereignty, 60, 90–91, 222–23n.11
Hart's theory of law, xviii
as possessing modest and modular
structure, 33–34
primary rules, 34
on rule skepticism, 228n.14
secondary rules, 34, 99, 113
rule of recognition, 34, 113
step from pre-legal social rules to
legal system, xix, 34, 99–100,
113, 221n.4
validity of rules, 34, 99, 113–14,
211n.2, 223n.16
See also social rules; *under* social rules
of procedure
hierarchical structure of plans, 5
higher-order desires (Frankfurt), 146, 175
Hindriks, Frank, 213n.1, 220n.48
Hohfeld, Wesley, 25, 108
human agents
as distinctively planning agents,
3–4 (*see also* core capacity,
planning agency as a)
as resource-limited, 5
Hume's rowers (case), 15
hybrid social rules, 73
as an explanation of alienated judge
case, 73
See also kernel-penumbra structure

"incompletely theorized agreements"
(Sunstein), 148, 151, 225n.8
individualism
in account of group/institutional
intention, 168, 224n.4

individualism (*cont.*)
  in account of social rule content determinants, 87
  in Hart's approach to social rules, 36, 60
  regarding shared intention, 12, 17
institutional acceptances, 139, 181
  contrast with individual acceptances, 224n.6
institutional beliefs, 139–40
institutional intentional agency, xix
  and guidance by institutional intention, 171–72, 173
  challenge to connection to agency, 174
  contrast with guidance by shared intention, xviii, 173, 177
  as compatible with, but not requiring, holism, 176–77, 182–83 (*see also* Davidson's challenge to institutional intentions)
  reduction, constructive, of, 178–81
    analogy to case of individual intentional agency, 179–81
    constructive vs. eliminativist, 178–79
    social rule model of institutional intentional agency, 182
    without acting for a reason, 181–82 (*see also under* Davidsonian synthesis, adjustments to)
  See also institutional standpoint; National Semiconductor (case, Velazquez)
institutional intentions, xix
  cascading, 138
  consistency/authorization condition, 137–38
  content, 159–61, 168–69
    in absence of completeness/holism, 165–66, 168–69, 183
    related to kernel-penumbra structure, 166–67 (*see also* Davidson's challenge to institutional intentions: Bratman's reply; "discursive dilemmas" [List and Pettit])
  contrast with shared intention, 136–37, 223–24n.2, 224n.4
  as providing a background framework, 138, 140, 154–55, 182
  See also Davidson's challenge to institutional intentions; *under* functioning: characteristic of intention; institutional acceptances; institutional beliefs
institutional outputs
  consistency/authorization condition, 122, 123
  correlates, 122–23
  functional role condition, 122–23
    as leaving room for disagreement, 124
    limited functionally relevant non-compensated cognitive divergence
    as ensuring functional role condition, 125
    induced by functional role condition, 124
  theory of, 126
  web of, 123–24
institutional procedural positivism, 100
institutional standpoint, 175, 176–77
institutional "will," 176
institutional values, substantive, 127–28
institutional web (of social rules of procedure), 115–21
  individuation of, 116
    preliminary theory, 118–19
    revised theory, 119, 120–21 (*see also under* Lockean ties)
    with a single, overarching rule, as a special case, 116, 117, 119, 122

interlocking, 117
minimal cooperativity, 121
output consistency, 117–18
   as strictly unnecessary, 118
   possibly thin and partial, as, 157–58 (*see also* pluralistic disagreement within institutions)
   sufficient richness, 119–20
     examples, 120
   variation, accounting for, 128
   See also institutional outputs
Intention (Anscombe), 206n.13
intentions
   as distinct from normative/evaluative judgments, 7–8, 206n.11
   as distinct from ordinary beliefs, 206n.12
   as distinct from ordinary desires, 4–5, 7–8
   as plan states, xvi, 4–5, 7, 156
     partiality of plans, 3–4, 5, 6
   as providing a background framework, 6, 8, 193, 194, 206n.7
   as stable over time, 5–6
   See also under functioning
interpretation, Davidsonian. *See* dense holism (Davidson)
iPhone, fabrication (case), 89, 90, 91

Jaarte, Miikka, 219n.43
"joint commitments" (Gilbert)
   as accounting for criticisms and demands, 211n.6, 212n.11
   as essential to shared intention, 208n.28, 210n.52
   See also under continuity; criticisms and demands

Kelley, Mikayla, 207n.25, 217n.14
Kelly, Erin, 216n.11

kernel-penumbra structure, 68
   example, 69
   kernel, 68
     augmenting intentions/ends, 82
     minimal-kernel social rules of procedure, 185–86 (*see also* hybrid social rules)
     universal-kernel social rules of procedure, 185–86
   penumbra, 68, 82
     criticism/demand of penumbral participants (*see under* extending reasons)
     output penumbra, 103, 219–20n.44
     procedural penumbra, 103
   possibility of absent cotemporaneous kernel, 78–80
   as satisfying design specification of shared plan, 91–92
   as time-slice projection of a social rule, 68, 72, 102–3
   See also extending reasons; *under* institutional intentions
Kripke, Saul, 19

Lackey, Jennifer, 221n.11
language-infused planning, 5, 10–11, 44
Lavin, Douglas, 206n.13
Lewis, David, 211n.4
   See also coordination conventions (Lewis)
Liao, Matthew, xx, 169
List, Christian. *See under* Davidson's challenge to institutional intentions; *See also* "discursive dilemmas" (List and Pettit); "organizational structure" (List and Pettit)
Lockean ties
   cross-temporal ties
     and individual intentional agency, 8
     and institutional intention, 138

Lockean ties (*cont.*)
    and shared intentional activity, 10, 207n.23
    and social rules, 75–78, 82, 86, 165–66
    and sameness of persons over time, 8, 76–78, 87
    supporting guidance by institutional intention, 175–76, 228n.3
    in a web of social rules of procedure characteristic of an institution, 116
Locke, John. See *Lockean ties*
"Lottery, The," 25–26, 28–29, 38, 54, 108
Ludwig, Kirk, 68, 217n.14, 217n.15, 225n.7
    See also under Davidson's challenge to institutional intentions

Madigan, Taylor, 209n.43
mafia members (case), 13–14, 27
Maguire, Barry, 44, 119–20
Marcantetti, Axelle, 118, 204n.9
Marx, Karl, 219n.43
"massively shared agency" (Shapiro), 89–92, 213n.3
McPherson, Tristram, 55
Medic Supply (case), xix, 122, 135–36, 147–48, 157, 181, 185
meta-normative theory, neutrality with respect to, 204n.5, 220n.48
Miller, Seumas, 203–4n.4
mimics of social functioning, 20–21, 48, 80, 81–82
    See also functioning
mindedness of institutions, 169–70
"minimal normativity" (Southwood and Brennan et al.), 39, 93
    See also under social norms/rules and normativity
modesty and modularity
    in Hart's theory of law, 33–34
    of shared intention in organized institutions, 33–34
multiple realizability, 19–20, 128
    of shared intention, 18–19
    See also strategy of sufficiency
Murray, Dylan, 102
mutual obligation and shared intention
    no necessary connection, 10, 28–32, 210n.52
    obligations as common (though non-essential), 31

National Semiconductor (case, Velasquez), 183–84
normative expectations (Hindriks), 220n.48
norms of plan rationality. *See* rationality norms of planning

"organizational structure" (List and Pettit), 165–66, 178, 226n.3

painting a house (case), 13, 17, 18, 27, 49, 59, 161
partiality of convergence. *See* divergence of background reasons for participation; "incompletely theorized agreements" (Sunstein); pluralistic disagreement within institutions
Paul, Sarah, 28, 118, 214–15n.15
persistence
    fragility of shared intention, 59
    contrast with robustness of social rules, 60, 78, 215n.1
    robustness of institutional intentions/intentional agents, 172–75, 177
    social rules, of, 75–78
    for hybrid social rules, 77
    See also Lockean ties

Pettit, Philip, 20–21, 53–54, 81–82, 128–29. *See also under* Davidson's challenge to institutional intentions
  See also "discursive dilemmas" (List and Pettit); "genealogical method" (Pettit)
"planning on a prior intention" (Alonso), 6–7
  in large-scale cases, 23
plan states, intentions as. *See under* intentions
pluralistic disagreement within institutions, 148–49, 161, 225n.7
  See also commonalities within institutions; "incompletely theorized agreements" (Sunstein)
policies, 4–5
  See also shared policies
Postema, Gerald, 212n.11, 215n.5
"Postscript" to *Concept of Law* (Dworkin), 38
practice theory (Hart). *See under* social rules
pretense of endorsement
  as issuing in extending reasons, 81
  as issuing in obligations, 74–75
  on the part of all participants (*see* Darwall's challenge)
  relativized to context, 218–19n.35
primacy of individual intention and intentional agency, rejection of, 152–55, 167–68, 226n.18, 230n.1
  See also Tollefsen's maxim
primary reason (Davidson), 4, 194
problems of social organization, 100–1
  See also under social rules of procedure
problem of social rule content, 34–35, 36–37, 160
  See also social rules: content
protest march (case), 22–23

Quine, W.V.O., 193–94, 224n.1
Quinn, Warren, 192–93

radioman (case, Quinn), 192–93
rational guidance
  as distinguishing a causal system from intentional agency, 4, 6, 26
  as fundamental to intentional activity generally, 26–27, 194–95 (*see also* core capacity, planning agency as a)
  of institutional intention, 182 (*see also under* institutional intentional agency)
  of ordinary intention, 4, 6
  of shared intention, 8–9, 12–13, 17–18, 26, 29–30
  supported by institutional crystallized action-focused output, 126, 136
  through social subrules of follow-through, 113–14, 126, 136–37
  See also rationality norms of planning
rationality norms of planning, 3–4
  contrast with substantive normative reasons, 38, 93
  social rationality norms, 12–13, 17–18, 26–27, 49 (*see also under* shared policies)
  supporting criticism and demand, 51–53, 83 (*see also* criticism and demand)
  wide-scope of, 27, 29, 52
  See also rational guidance
"rational point of view" (Rovane), 145, 225n.4
  See also under Davidson's challenge to institutional intentions; dense holism (Davidson)
Rawls, John, 155, 196
realization theses, 200

reason-grounded extension. *See* extending reasons

reasons, substantive normative
contrast with motivating reasons, 38
contrast with norms of rationality, 38, 93
not directly entailed in authority-according shared intention, 25–26
and social rule acceptance, 38–39
See also under criticism and demand; mutual obligation and shared intention; rights and duties

reflexivity
double reflexivity of shared intention, 11, 13
double reflexivity of shared policy, 45
first-person/singular of ordinary intention, 4–5, 11
vagueness as to, in large-scale cases, 21–22, 45

rights and duties
authority-according shared intention, involved in, 24–25
contrast with normatively substantive rights and duties, 25
de facto vs. *de jure* distinction (Darwall), 25–26, 209n.46
See also authority-according shared intention; mutual obligation and shared intention; reasons, substantive normative

Ritchie, Katherine, 205n.15
Rosen, Gideon, 211n.4
Roth, Abraham Sesshu, 112
Rovane, Carol, 145
See also under Davidson's challenge to institutional intentions; "rational point of view" (Rovane)

Searle, John, 129–31
See also "background" (Searle); "collective acceptance" (Searle); "status functions" (Searle); "we-intentions" (Searle)

self-governance, 52, 203n.1, 206n.6, 209–10n.49, 214–15n.15, 230n.2

sequential planning theory, xxi, 11–12, 19, 43, 140–41, 197, 199–200
contrasting with other approaches, xvii
as modest, xvii–xviii
See also strategy of construction

Shapiro, Scott, 209n.45, 209n.46, 211n.3, 213n.3, 215n.5
See also alienated judges (case, Hart and Shapiro); "massively shared agency" (Shapiro); "shared plans" (Shapiro)

shared intention, 9–10
content, 18
as possibly implicit/tacit, 20
interdependence of persistence, of, 10, 16
in large-scale cases, 22, 23
interlocking, of, 13–14, 16, 61
in large-case cases, 22, 61–62
meshing subplans, of, 14, 27–28
mutual responsiveness, characteristic of, 8–9, 30, 210n.50
out-in-the-open condition, 16
providing a background framework, 12–13
settling cognitively, as, 14
in large-case cases, 23
settling practically, as, 14
in large-case cases, 23
substitutes, functional, for, 20–21
See also authority-according shared intention; mutual obligation

and shared intention; shared
policies; *See also under*
criticism and demand; design
specification, dual; reflexivity
"shared plans" (Shapiro), 89–90,
216–17n.12
- as articulating a design
specification, 90
  - realized by kernel-penumbra
structure, 91–92
- without shared intention, 89–90

shared policies, 20
- agglomerativity, relaxation of
requirement of, 46–47
- examples, 57
- interdependence, indirect, 61–62
- interlocking, weak, 61–62
- as partially constituted by shared
intention, 47
- prescriptive force, 45–46
- social rationality, as involving, 49–50
- social rule, as involving, 43, 44, 57
  - by realizing acceptance of a
common standard, 47
- speech acts, supportive of, 56–57
- as stable over time, 51–52 (*see also
under* Lockean ties)
- sufficient general conformity,
requiring, 45, 62
- *See also under* demandingness
objection; reflexivity

slavery (case), 14, 74, 108–9
snowball of obligation-inducing
reliance, 69–70, 74–75, 79, 81,
217n.20
socially realized rules. *See* social rules
social norms/rules and
normativity, 92–96
- Bicchieri and, 94–95
- Bratman and, 93–94, 95
- Brennan et al. and, 92–93, 94–95
- "followed social norm" (Bicchieri), 94

See also "minimal normativity"
(Southwood and Brennan
et al.)
social rationality norms. *See under*
rationality norms of planning
social rule model of institutional
intentional agency, 182
See also institutional
intentional agency
social rules
- abstract object rule, relationship to,
34–35, 88–89, 211n.3
- common standard, supported by,
37 (*see also* acceptance of a
common standard)
- content, 80, 84, 88–89, 160
(*see also* problem of
social rule content;
under strategy of abstraction)
- "critical reflective attitude," 35–36
- criticism and demand (*see* criticism
and demand)
- "internal aspect," 35, 41, 44, 75–
76, 82
  - "collective acceptance" (Searle), as
a way to understand, 68 (*see
also* shared policies)
- internal point of view, 35–36, 80, 85,
205n.13
- normativity (*see* social norms/rules
and normativity)
- persistence over time (*see under*
persistence)
- practice theory of, 37
- range, 35, 36, 84–85
  - participant vs. to whom the rule
applies, 84
- sufficient general conformity,
requiring, 37
  - absence of conformity, 64–65
  - as substantive normative reason
for acceptance, 38–39

social rules (*cont.*)
- time-slice projection, 60–61
  - (*see also under* kernel-penumbra structure)
- vs. mere regularities, 35, 37, 42–43
- *See also* hybrid social rules; shared policies; social rule schema, Hart's; social rules of procedure

social rules, hybrid. *See* hybrid social rules

social rule schema, Hart's
- adjusted version of, 72–73, 86–87
- at first pass, 39, 72, 85–86

social rules of procedure, 99
- analogies to Hart's theory of law and secondary rules, 113–14
- and the step from pre-legal to legal, xix, 99–100, 128
- content, 101–2
- historical thickness, 110–11
- institutional roles and offices, induced by, 102, 115–16 (*see also* authority-according social rules of procedure)
- conveying de facto rights and duties, 130
- outputs of, 103–4
  - acceptance outputs, 103, 104–5
  - action outputs, 103, 105–6
  - crystallized outputs, 103–4 (*see also* institutional intentions)
  - contrast with shared intention, 126–27, 135, 160–61
  - event outputs, 103–4
  - induced further teleology, 109–10, 148, 158, 187 (*see also under* extending reasons)
- population base, 121
  - minimally cooperative individuals, 121
- possibility of absent cotemporaneous kernel, 110–11
- risk function, 102
- as solutions to problems of social organization, 101, 116
- variety of, 102
- *See also* institutional web (of social rules of procedure)

social unity in institutions. *See* commonalities within institutions

Southwood, Nicholas, 39, 92–93

"status functions" (Searle), 129

strategic interaction
- contrasted with Hart-style social rules, 42–43, 85
- contrasted with shared intentional activity, 8–9, 15–16
- involving alienated participants, 66–67

strategy of abstraction
- in case of institutional intention content, 161 (*see also* "incompletely theorized agreements" [Sunstein])
- in case of shared intention content, 18, 161
- in case of social rule content, 88–89

strategy of construction, 9–10, 140–41, 158–59, 228n.9
- contrast with providing a just-so story, 11–12, 58, 100, 221n.4
- functioning grounded in construction, 12, 16, 197–98
- models in a, 12
- *See also* functioning; sequential planning theory; realization theses

strategy of sufficiency, 18–20, 41, 81, 96, 128, 177–78, 197, 199–200, 220n.1

string quartet (case), 8–9, 21, 24–25, 29–30, 57
Sugarman, Elise, 112
Sugden, Robert, 206–7n.15
Sunstein, Cass. *See* "incompletely theorized agreements" (Sunstein)

Tollefsen, Deborah, 225n.5
  See also Tollefsen's maxim
Tollefsen's maxim, 152, 158–59, 160–61, 163, 178, 204n.7, 226n.18

Valentini, Laura, 31
Valenzuela, Cesar, 221n.9
Vargas, Manuel, 216n.11
Velazsquez, Manuel, 183–84
Velleman, J. David, 146

walking together (case), 8–10, 42–43, 218n.22
Watson, Gary, 225n.6
web of social rules of procedure. *See* institutional web (of social rules of procedure)
"we-intentions" (Searle), 68, 111–12, 131, 208n.28, 208n.33, 217n.14, 217n.15
Wenar, Leif, 74
"Where's the Agent Problem" (Yaffe), 179, 228n.1
Williams, Bernard, 38
will, structure of. *See* agential standpoint; institutional standpoint

Yaffe, Gideon, 228n.1